INCA, PONCHO (POST-SPANISH)

CHITIMACHA

CHOCTAW

CHITIMACHA

CHITIMACHA

BASKET
WEAVES

CHOCTAW

CHOCTAW

CHOCTAW

CHEROKEE

CHEROKEE

AMERICAN INDIAN
DESIGN AND DECORATION

(formerly titled: Indian Art of the Americas)

LE ROY H. APPLETON

Dover Publications, Inc.

New York

Published in Canada by General Publishing Company, Ltd.,
30 Lesmill Road, Don Mills, Toronto, Ontario.
Published in the United Kingdom by Constable and Company,
Ltd., 10 Orange Street, London WC 2.

This Dover edition, first published in 1971, is an unabridged
republication of the work orignally published in 1950 by Charles
Scribner's Sons, New York, with the title *Indian Art of the
Americas.* Errors noted on the Errata insert of the original edition have been corrected in the present edition. The plates, originally in color, appear here in black-and-white, except for Plates
16, 28, 39 and 69, which appear both in black-and-white and in
color. Plate 56 is entirely new; the area maps have been redrawn.

International Standard Book Number: 0-486-22704-9
Library of Congress Catalog Card Number: 74-151421

Manufactured in the United States of America
Dover Publications, Inc.
180 Varick Street
New York, N. Y. 10014

TO THE MEMORY OF
CLARK WISSLER

PREFACE

"In order to win the friendship and affection of the people, and because I was convinced that their conversion to our Holy Faith would be better provided through love than force, I presented some of them with red caps and some strings of beads . . ."

THUS DID COLUMBUS describe the opening scene of the planting of the cross and the raising of the sword in America. Columbus, thinking he had reached the East Indies, called the natives Indians—a confusing name but we continue to use it.

By 1492, the Indian had spread over the greater part of the Americas. He was still largely in the hunting-fishing-gathering stage of civilization. This civilization had reached its highest points in Mexico and Peru. By the time the Spaniards had reached the mainland—Mexico, 1502; Central America, 1513; Peru, 1530—the archaic cultures in those regions, out of which the higher civilizations had grown, had left their marks and departed.

In North America, the Mound-builders of the Mississippi Valley and the Pueblo groups of the Southwest were still carrying a weak flame from the torch they had received from Mexico. In Middle America, the civilization of the Mayas had declined; their great city-states were in ruins. The Aztec empire was beginning to break up. In South America, the Incas, who had spread their despotic but benevolent sway over a large area, were weakening. Beyond was darkness, perhaps dawn. But what succeeding groups might have built on these declining cultures (as they in turn had built on others) we shall never know. The European was taking over.

After overpowering the aboriginal civilizations, in due time the white man slowly started picking up, and later digging up, the broken pieces. At first, these mementoes of the past were called "curios." Then specialists took over the digging and called their finds artifacts. Archaeologists who discovered in their work not only pottery sherds (just broken pieces of pots and bowls) but a true appreciation of the Indian as artist and artisan—those who started piecing together, literally and figuratively, the story of his work— received little or no encouragement from the art world. The Indians' work was looked upon as the work of savages, having no claim to art. Fortunately that attitude has changed. Greater knowledge and sympathetic understanding of the Indian has brought wider appreciation of his work, and it is just beginning to take its rightful place in the history of world art.

The art of the American Indian is also a living art. In all the Americas, many groups are still producing things of beauty. Historical tribes have adopted from the whites new materials and tools; not many tools, for the best is still handwork. Glass beads have been substituted for porcupine quills, seeds and shells; wool has replaced fibers and cotton; and paper is used for their paintings in place of skins and bark. The potters continue with their old materials; there is no substitue for clay. Practical support of these groups will encourage the carrying on of their traditional art. It is only through the purchase of, and insistence upon, the best work instead of the cheap curios which too many tourists buy, that the Indian will be able to regain his position as artist and craftsman.

In evaluating Indian art we should keep in mind that each family manufactured only for its own use the things they needed. Naturally, ability varied with the individual. Some were craftsmen; some were artists. The great diversity of the Indian's art corresponds to the different stages of his cultural development. Since this varied greatly, the actual state of cultural development of any specific group must be taken into consideration when viewing the work of that group. Their work was not for sale, although there was extensive trade. Only in the higher civilizations with a developed ritual life, as in Mexico and Peru, do we find professional artists.

This book does not pretend to be an archaeological or ethnological report on the American Indian. It gives few dates. It makes few comparisons. Designations of "historic" and "prehistoric" are too arbitrary for use here, as they draw too sharp a line between work the Indian did before and after seeing a white man. Besides, it must be remembered that many Indian groups were influenced by the white man's civilization long before they had actual contact with specific white men, an outstanding example of this being the Northern Plains Indians of North America. When these tribes were first seen by Americans moving westward, they were accomplished horsemen. Their use of horses, of course, can be dated in historical time, and follows on the arrival of the first Spaniards. Yet even in this short time their knowledge and use of the horse had changed their entire mode of living. It has been assumed in this book that the reader is more interested in *what* the Indian did than just *when* he did it. Time, long or short, cannot change the quality of the work and its value to the artist. But, for those who are interested, here is an abridged timetable.

Man's history in America goes back to the Ice Age. How long he roamed here before that time we do not know. His remains have been found with those of extinct mammals, but we cannot be sure at what time these animals became extinct. He came from Siberia by way of the Bering Strait to Alaska, in a primitive state, and most likely because he was hungry. Primitives usually were; their margin of living was slim. It is safe to assume that the Indian brought very little material culture with him—perhaps a spear. He knew how to build a fire. This migration continued over thousands of years, even up to comparatively recent times. Meanwhile, the people fanned out over the two continents, becoming many tribes with a multitude of languages. These people, slowly changing from hunters to farmers, built a new civilization. Their art is the expression of the ideas and ideals that formed their world.

First, perhaps, to reach what we call a civilized condition were the Maya-speaking people of Guatemala and Yucatan; and the Nahua groups, the Mixtec, the Zapotec and the Toltec (to mention but a few), of the Mexican highlands.

Groups from Central America worked their way down through the Isthmus to South America. There, on the west coast in Peru, the Early Chimu and Nazca built their own civilizations on a corresponding plane to the "Old Empire" of the Mayas, and at about the same time—from 200 B. C. to 800 A. D. Later, in Peru the Incas, and in Mexico the Aztec, picked up the torch and carried it, after a fashion, until it was extinguished by the Spanish.

In the meantime, influence from these two centers of New World civilization reached out both north and south. To the north it spread through the American Southwest; up the Mississippi Valley to the people we call the Mound-builders, and to the East Coast. From the valley it spread to the Plains, where the light is lost except for a weak spark on the North Pacific Coast. To the south it reached down the western and eastern coasts of South America but it was unable to penetrate the jungle. Here too, the light was lost.

After working thousands of years building a New World, the Indian faced strange men and gods from the east just as some of his myths had foretold. They had a magic which the Indian could not understand. It pierced his shields and his heart. He fought back but he lost. He was to be civilized.

The work in this volume has been selected from the collections of many museums. Wherever possible the artist, and of course the interested reader, should go to the originals. No reproduction can possibly do this work full justice. But it can serve as a guide to a special interest, and the selected bibliography will start one off on a lifetime quest.

I am indebted for advice and guidance to many museum directors and curators, and museum photographers, who have at all times stood ready to give unselfishly of their time and their wisdom. To the late Doctor Clark Wissler, Curator of Anthropology at the American Museum of Natural History, I owe a special word of grateful remembrance. From the very inception of this work, under a Carnegie grant some twenty years ago, to the present, I have been deeply obliged to Doctor Alfred V. Kidder, Chairman of the Division of Historical Research, the Carnegie Institution of Washington, for his continuing encouragement and help. I am indebted also to Mr. George G. Heye, Mr. Jesse L. Nusbaum, and the late Philip Ainsworth Means for their assistance.

The following list acknowledges the principal collections from which the materials of this book have been drawn: American Museum of Natural History, New York City; Museum of the American Indian, Heye Foundation, New York City; The Brooklyn Museum, Brooklyn, N. Y.; Laboratory of Anthropology, Santa Fe, New Mexico; Peabody Museum, of Harvard University, Cambridge, Mass.; National Museum of Canada, Ottawa; United States National Museum, Washington, D. C.; The New York State Museum, Albany,

N. Y.; Ohio State Museum, Columbus, Ohio; Carnegie Institution of Washington, Washington, D. C.; The University Museum, Philadelphia, Pa.; The Metropolitan Museum of Art, New York City; Museo Nacional de Mexico, Mexico, D.F.; National Museum of Archaeology, Lima, Peru; British Museum, London.

I am grateful also to Mr. Atkinson Dymock of Charles Scribner's Sons for the care which he has taken in all stages of the production of this volume, and for the worth and tact of his suggestions.

LE ROY H. APPLETON

March 15, 1950

TABLE OF CONTENTS

Note: The reader interested in locating the work of a particular tribe or region, or in consulting the original source of a design or myth, may find this information by reference to the above Indices.

THE LAND AND THE PEOPLE

1 *THE PLAINS AND THE LAKES*

2 *THE FOREST AND THE RIVERS*

3 *THE FOREST AND THE SEA*

4 *MOUNTAIN AND MESA*

5 *THE VALLEY, THE PENINSULA AND THE ISTHMUS*

6 *THE COAST AND THE MOUNTAINS*

7 *PAMPAS, JUNGLES AND ISLANDS*

INTRODUCTION

Oh, our Mother, the Earth; oh, our Father, the Sky,
Your children are we, and with tired backs
We bring you the gifts that you love.

THE AMERICAN INDIAN is a myth-maker, a teller of tales of his tribe. His art is social; it is created largely to enrich his tribal ceremonial. As a rule, it has significance beyond its pictorial or design element.

Reaching out and beyond visible forms, the Indian animates or personifies the forces and phenomena of nature. He suggests in his art-forms whatever force or thing he wishes to propitiate or have. To him all things have life, including his baskets and bowls. The potter of the Southwest leaves a break in an encircling line on her jar, the "exit trail of life." The "being" of the jar must be left free. Vessels and weapons (even wives, in some groups) buried with an Indian were "killed" (broken) so that their spirit could travel with their owner and serve him in the next world.

The dweller in the Southwest desired rain for her corn, so the life-forms associated with water were painted on the jars. The dweller on the Plains wished to protect her child from snakebite so she embroidered a zig-zag snake pattern on the child's moccasin as a protective, magic measure.

Indian symbolism may have had its beginning in the first attempts to make decorative art an instrument of magic. The tadpole, painted on the prayer-meal bowl of the Zuni, is used in this way. The tadpole, through an association of ideas, expressed the desire for rain, which in turn meant good crops. The Indian's totem (a sign of his kinship) had magical purposes. A prayer, if you will, for the strength of the bear, if he was a member of the bear clan, or for the sight of the eagle, if of the eagle clan.

From the crude fetish of the primitive to the haughty Feathered Serpent of the Mayas, the Indian made his designs for magical purposes—either to repel or to attract.

In their earliest forms, when man was recording his desires and deeds on rock, bone, and hide, the representations were realistic. Many of them appear to be records of the hunt with no magic content; but it is a question whether the artist would have spent the

1

time and energy involved unless the work of art had some symbolic value—at least, a prayer for good hunting. As the years went by, the magical quality of many symbols was forgotten. The forms became conventionalized and were regarded simply as decoration—as a Pueblo weaver expressed it, they were "to make pretty."

Because many designs are representations of natural objects—birds, animals, serpents, and man himself—the theory has been advanced that whenever a design (however abstract) bears a natural name, that name was given it at the time the design was realistic. Yet, despite the degeneration of some designs to simple, even crude forms of mere dots and bars, it might well be that the designer was limited by the tools and materials at hand and by his own limitations as an artist; or equally by the dictates of important, tribal tradition. In addition, realistic forms may become conventionalized to the point of abstraction, or a simple, geometric design may be given a name because of some fancied resemblance to a natural form. This explains why different groups have different names for the same design unit. And we must remember, too, that the design units are controlled in many cases by technical requirements—the weaving and basketry techniques, for example—and by the flora and fauna of the environment. As we move from regions of low culture, where there was little or no margin of living, to regions of higher culture, designs take on symbolic significance as a result of tribal tradition and developed ritual. They are no longer purely static and abstract.

There is great diversity of form and expression in Indian art as each group was influenced by its religious and social customs. There is no structural ornament. It is surface decoration, characterized by boldness of design and skill in space filling, with a right relation between form, media, and material. It has been well said that the Indian has "a keen sense of decorative propriety."

Conventional designs include many wherein formalization has been carried so far that it is difficult for anyone, not acquainted with the process whereby the changes were made, to identify the source. The Indian combines what are to his mind the characteristic features of his subject, with little or no regard for true proportions. A feature, such as a beak, an eye or a wing, is to him an attribute or symbol. Therefore, he associates forms in ways that are difficult for men of alien culture to decipher. The Indian belief that magic powers resided in inanimate objects, and in men and animals regarded as deities (ideas whose verbal expression will be found in his stories and legends) led the Indian artist to make representations of grotesque creatures—half-man, half-animal; half-bird, half-serpent. To him, these were not grotesques, but realities, symbolically rendered.

THE BASKET MAKER

When an Indian devised a basket, he did not set out to *design* a basket. He wanted a container—something which would carry more than his hands and stomach could hold. His invention of the basket enabled him to advance from a hand-to-mouth existence, dependent on the kill or on seasonal nuts and fruits, to a position of relative independence.

He was able to store up a reserve of food. But because of the universal desire of man to enrich his possessions, the Indian began to decorate his basket. He became artist as well as craftsman.

Basketry has been called the mother of weaving. Only in our own Southwest, however, has the development from basket-weaving to textile-weaving been traced. Its progress has been charted from a pre-basket group, clad in skins, through several stages of basket-weaving up to what archaeologists call "Pueblo I," where was practiced the oldest loom-weaving in North America.

The Indians of the Southwest, of California and the North Pacific coast were among the world's finest basket weavers. Tlingit baskets from Alaska (Plate 31), overlaid with the stems of grass or of maidenhair ferns, are excellent in design, weave and color. The Thompson and Lillooet Indians of British Columbia are the most prolific producers of coiled basketry. Tradition says that the art was taught them long ago by their culture hero "Coyote." One of the characteristic features of coiled baskets, imbrication, is unique among the basket techniques of the world. This is an overlay decoration, applied as the sewing of the basket proceeds. The basket is built up with coils of cedar roots, while grasses, and thin barks dyed red or black, are used to form the design. The coiled trays of the Hopi (Plate 41) are in their way unique as well, for this form is duplicated only in North Africa. The Atlantic and Gulf areas of North America and the Guiana area in South America were other important basket-making localities. (Plates 16 and 78.)

If we may judge by their carvings, the Maya did elaborate basket work in many techniques. (Plates 57 and 59.) Elsewhere in the Americas, basketry was usually lacking in design other than that provided naturally by the weaving process. The techniques were good enough. Baskets were made in a great variety of shapes and sizes, ranging from storage baskets large enough to hold a man down to small catch-alls for trinkets. Basketry was also employed in making fish-traps, mats, clothing, and that excellent American Indian invention—the hammock.

Designs in basketry were worked out by using rushes, reeds, grass, bark, cane, wood splints and vines of different colors, either natural or dyed; also by the addition of other materials, such as beads, shells and feathers. The technique, however, limited the ambition of the designer—his design had to be built up in square or rectangular units, and, unlike textile-weaving, the units had to be large and produced a "stepped" effect. The finer the materials used, the less angularity there was in the design.

THE WEAVER

We have seen that the beginnings of loom-weaving in North America have been found in our Southwest; but the oldest specimens of fabrics known in all the Americas were the products of the Andean region. The excellence of these fabrics argues for a long period of time between the beginnings of the process there and the objects we have. No such perfected technique is born overnight. There is, however, no evidence of this perfecting process. Cotton textiles have been found recently in northern Peru, however, made by a group whose culture appears to have been a pre-corn raising one.

In Peru there were schools for weavers whose chief function it was to produce garments of state for the Inca and his nobles. Their inventiveness knew no limits. No people in the history of fabric-making have ever achieved such technical skill or excelled these people in either design or color (Plates 65 through 70). Theirs is the most perfect weaving record left by any peoples in the world. Superlatives are dangerous, but in this case they have been well earned.

This work in Peru continued after the Spanish Conquest. The use of new materials such as silk, linen, and sheep's wool (originally the Peruvians used native cotton and wool from the alpaca, llama, and vicuña) and the introduction of European design motives resulted in a fascinating blend of Old and New World ideas.

The Maya and the Mexicans, on the evidence of representations on stone (Plates 55 and 59), pottery (Plates 51 and 57), tribute rolls and paintings (Plate 50), did excellent weaving. They used many kinds of weaves. They did dyeing, tie-dyeing and batik, as well as printing with clay stamps. Owing to the moist climate of the area most of this work has been lost, in so far as actual specimens are concerned. It is quite likely that Mayan weaving was as fine as the Peruvian work.

The Spaniards recognized the skill of the Aztec weavers, and most unfortunately for the natives, organized them into factory workers. Spain at last passed laws forbidding the system. The King of Spain, however, was a bit too far away to insure that laws made for the protection of the Indians were enforced. It is interesting to note that where the native Americans upon occasion revolted and drove out their Spanish masters, they still retained some of the foreign design elements which had crept into their work. Examples of these are the two-headed eagle copied from coins, and other bird and flower forms, Oriental as well as European. It is obvious that the Oriental motifs came from the Spaniards as transmitted from Moorish originals.

In the areas where the Indian compromised with the white man he continued to adapt and reinterpret foreign designs. As time passed, forgetting their source, he looked upon them as his own. The Huichol of Mexico weave a jewsharp design in their work. Some Canadian Iroquois have adopted the Masonic emblem in their silver work. The Navaho silver crescent is an "evil-eye" charm from the old world.

Before the white men came with their sheep and with European cloth (which the Navaho unravelled and rewove to make their famous *bayeta* blankets) the chief materials used were cotton, bark, fibers and hair. The cotton-growing area extended from the Southwest through Mexico, Central America and along the west coast of South America to Peru. We do not know where cotton was first cultivated in the Americas. It may have originated in Peru and spread north, or it may have spread north and south from Central America.

There were two types of weaving in aboriginal America—loom or upward weaving, and finger or downward weaving. In loom weaving the weaver begins at the bottom and builds the fabric upward. In finger weaving the fabric is built from the top downward.

The girdleback, or belt loom was used by all the growers of cotton. The long threads, known as the warp, were strung between two parallel bars. The upper bar was attached to a tree or a post. The lower bar had a belt attached to it which was put around the waist of the weaver, who sat or knelt in front of her work. She regulated the tension on the warp by the movement of her body. No shuttle was used. The cross threads, known as the weft, were woven over and under the warp threads with the fingers, or with the aid of a small stick. This loom was from two to three feet wide, and the cloth was woven in one piece to the desired length. If a wide cloth were needed, two strips were sewn together. Looms of this type are still being used today in remote parts of Central and South America.

In making large pieces of cloth or blankets, a vertical loom was used. It had a rigid frame of four poles leaning against a wall, or else the two upright poles were set in the ground. An ingenious arrangement of cords at the top enabled the weaver to lower her loom and so keep the work within a convenient reach of her hands as she sat or squatted at her work. The Navaho weaver will upon occasion turn her loom upside down and start weaving from the other end of a blanket in progress, but always weaving upward.

Outside the cotton growing area, finger or downward weaving was the method used. In this technique the warp threads were hung loosely from a horizontal bar which rested on two uprights. This type of weaving frame, for it is not a true loom, was used in the eastern United States and on the North Pacific coast. On it were woven blankets, bags, mats and flexible baskets. The well-known Chilkat blanket (Plates 29 and 30) was made on such a frame, out of the wool of the mountain goat, sinew and bark.

Closely associated with weaving are feather work, quill work and bead work. Feather work, a method of laying feathers on a woven base of fiber threads and tieing the stems of the feathers into the fabric during the weaving process, had its greatest development in Mexico and Peru. Only a few specimens have been saved. Spanish accounts and Indian drawings give us some notion of its importance as a part of the Indian's ceremonial costumes: cloaks for really important persons; headdresses, shields and standards for the warriors. The designs were the same as those used in weaving. As the reader will discover for himself, textile design influenced all Indian art.

Turkey-feather mantles (cloaks) were made in the Southwest, the Gulf states and the eastern seaboard. Feathers were also used in basketry, some applied, some interwoven; this was done most effectively by the Pomos of California.

The feather headdress of the Plains Indians is well known. It may have reached them through the Mound-builders who in turn inherited it from Mexico. The Maya carvings (Plates 52, 54, 57 and 59) and Aztec drawings (Plate 50) show many forms of feather work. The style also traveled south where the feather headdress is one of the most characteristic traits of the Amazon area.

Beads, as personal adornment, have been used throughout the world by primitive man. Materials, uses and techniques cover a wide range. Seeds, shell, (the wampum belts of the Iroquois are shell beads; see Plate 18) pearls, bone, clay, metal, semi-precious stones, and, after contact with the white man, glass, were the principal materials. They were used in stringing, weaving, sewing, and embroidery. Stringing, as in necklaces, bracelets, and such, was the most widespread use for beads. The techniques used in bead-making were carving, engraving, inlaying and casting of gold, silver and copper.

In North America, the introduction of glass beads—which was an important factor in trade, along with firearms and whisky—brought about an original application. The Indians of the Eastern Woodlands, the Lakes, and the Plains, had been using porcupine quills, dyed in colors, for applied decoration on their costumes and on small articles such as bags and boxes. (Plates 3, 4, 9, 20 and 21.) Several methods were used in quill work; sewing (*appliqué*) being the principal technique, and embroidery. Most of this work was done on deerskin. Weaving, wrapping, and applied work on bark were other methods employed. Woven work was done by interweaving quills on strands of sinew.

Having such a highly perfected technique (including moosehair embroidery; see Plate 21) it was a simple matter for the Indian to substitute beads for quills. The result was a greater use of beads in design than any other aboriginal group attempted. The Plains peoples, with their love of display, went all out. One hundred and twenty thousand beads have been counted on a single Comanche cradle. Surely a labor of love.

THE POTTER

In the Southwest, to return to the archaeologists' happy hunting grounds, baskets have been found daubed with clay to make them watertight—the birth, at least for these people, of pottery.

For nomad man, continually on the run, pottery was impracticable. Pottery did not develop until man settled down, until he outgrew gathering seeds and roots and became a planter of crops. As long as he was a gatherer of seeds and roots, baskets served his purpose. He was never far ahead of hunger, but crops meant surplus, therefore storage. He invented the baked clay container, as he had invented the basket.

Of the many foods which the Indian has contributed to the world's table, corn is outstanding. Indian corn enabled the Pilgrims to survive. Corn was the foundation on which aboriginal American culture was founded. Only in those American areas where the cultivation of corn was practiced was there developed any higher form of civilization—and pottery.

The Indian did not use the potter's wheel, which is perhaps a blessing. Pottery was usually the work of the women, and they produced a greater variety of forms than the Old World potters did, working with the wheel. Forms include jars, plates, bowls, pitchers, urns, with necks, rims, legs, handles and covers—modeled, incised, stamped, carved, moulded, sculptured, and painted. Pottery perforated before firing, ceremonial and mortuary ware (Plate 47) in the Mexican and Central America areas, was the work of professional potters.

Geometric designs, based on textile patterns, are prevalent in painted and incised ware. They were used as bands running around the sides or necks of the jars and bowls, or as sections of bands in diagonal or quadrant patterns. (See Plates 35, 37, 48, 75.) Gradually, through the use of brush and color, the fret of the woven design became a free flowing curved line. These free forms are also found on incised pottery, drawn with a stylus in the still moist clay, or engraved on the fired vessel. Stamped designs, applied by wooden paddles (Plate 13), either cut in low relief or wrapped with a fabric, retained the weaving patterns. Pottery stamps, both flat and roller (Plate 47), used both the geometric weaving patterns and conventional design units. They were also used for body painting and textile printing, which makes the Indian the first printer in America.

The process of pottery making varied according to locality. Vessels were sometimes shaped in a mould—usually a basket—or modeled free hand, worked out from a block of clay and beaten into shape with a paddle. In Central America a true mould was used by the professional potters. As a rule, however, the potter used the coil method. Ropes of clay were rolled out by hand to convenient lengths; the sides of the vessel were built up spirally and afterwards scraped smooth with a pebble. At times the coil marks were retained as a design element. By smoothing certain areas and leaving the coil marks in other areas, decorative bands were made. Add to that, the pinching of the moist clay with the fingers and impressing with the nail or incising with a tool. The design possibilities were endless. (Plates 11, 13, 17 and 77.)

Such were the first steps in pottery decoration, followed by relief, either modeled or applied, and finally painting, first done on the inside of food bowls which had a smooth surface. With the discovery that different kinds of clay and pigments, when fired, gave different colors, it was but a step to the use of clay washes (slips) and painted decoration.

In Central America the "Lost Color" pottery (Plates 63 and 64) was a highly developed technique. The design is painted with a resistant, such as a wax or gum. The vessel then is immersed in a dye or paint. When the vessel is fired, the paint over the wax is "lost" as the resistant melts or is burned, thus leaving the design uncolored. But the finest painted ware was the work of the Maya.

Trade in pottery was extensive, and this has made things difficult for the archaeologist. He finds right things in the wrong places. The Aztec traders were called by two enlightening names: "Men who exchange one thing for another," and "Men who take more than they give." Actually, they were official diplomats and unofficial spies. Tribute to Montezuma (Plate 50) was determined on the basis of traders' reports.

THE SCULPTOR AND CARVER

As sculptor and carver, the Indian coaxed and formed with stone and copper tools —and even reed drills—work that holds its own with the best craftsmanship of the Old World. Sculpture to us means "fine art," a term the Indian would not have understood. His work was not an expression of his own personality, but the expression of his group's religious ideas. We may be sure, however, judging from the work itself, that the craftsman had his own satisfaction in work well done.

The most impressive carving in the Americas was done by the Maya and the Mexicans. Most Maya carving was worked in low relief and incised line, cut into the flat stone. Although there are outstanding exceptions, it is a safe rule that scarcely any Maya sculpture was executed in the round. Most of the carved work was subordinated to architecture, for it was used mainly on buildings or on the great time markers. The Mexicans worked more in the round. Unfortunately, the Aztec work is so weighted down with a death-complex that it is hard for us to judge it on the basis of either art or craftsmanship. It is repellent in theme, for the Aztec gods demanded blood; and the priesthood, who controlled the work, were degraded to butchers.

The impressive stone *stelae* (time markers) of the Maya have been linked with Old World peoples such as the Egyptians and Cambodians, by the "discovery" of sun disks and elephants, proving (?) that the Indian came from Egypt—or Indo-China. These arts have only one thing in common—each was imprisoned by ritual. The Maya's ability to draw and carve the human figure shames the Egyptian artist. Turn to the carved glyphs on Plate 53 if you want proof. Both Mayan and Mexican carving has been criticized on the score of overcrowding, and apparent fear of blank spaces. It is well to keep in mind, though, that most of this work was painted in bright colors (Plates 52 and 54) which did much to clarify the composition.

When freed from the grotesqueness of the ritual formula, which in the case of the Aztec with their human-sacrifice complex is one of horror for us, the Indian sculptor gives us "laughing heads" or a little roly-poly figure in a high hat (Plate 47). The latter is primitive, the heads far from primitive. In humor, we have a common meeting ground. A parallel is found in Peru. The ritual art is cold and forbidding, but when freed, the sculptor and carver give us work we respond to with pleasure. We have nothing in common with Viracocha (central figure, Plate 72), but we respond to the little warrior and his llama (Plate 74). The Peruvians were past masters in building with stone, cutting the huge blocks with such accuracy that they needed no mortar, but only in a few cases is there any surface decoration. It seems strange that the Peruvians, both pre-Inca and Inca, who did such outstanding work in modeling clay and casting metals, did no sculpture that compares with the work in Mexico.

Ritual art of an entirely different sort was carried on in an outpost of aboriginal American civilization, the North Pacific. These groups were practical people. The rules which determined the totem pole figures (Plates 23, 24 and 25) were just as rigid as any laid down by the Maya priest for Mayan glyphs, although the carver was free to place them according to his fancy. These "capitalists" of aboriginal America had one simple idea: To impress, not a god, but their neighbors. The totem pole was their family tree—a symbol of family pride. The white man has his coat of arms or family tree. The intention is the same—identification with the glory of one's ancestors. These Indian ancestors were somewhat strange as their myths also show. They included a mixture of men, animals, fish and birds, natural and supernatural. Tribes were subdivided into groups called clans, which took their names from animals.

While the design forms used in them are old, the totem poles are a late development. The same is true of the fantastic North Pacific ceremonial masks (Plates 27 and 28). Before the Indian received steel tools from the whites the art was limited to the decoration of interior house posts. Versatile is perhaps the word for their work with wood. They steamed and bent it; even sewed it. Vessels and boxes of all shapes and sizes were carved with animalistic figures (Plate 27). Heads and tails, eyes and feet, were put together in a very orderly fashion. They lived in prefabricated houses which they carried with them on their annual fishing trips.

Sea-going dug-outs, with carved and painted figureheads, carried as many as fifty men. There were rivals in shipbuilding, however. The Chumash of southern California made the only planked canoes, building up the sides by sewing strips of wood together.

North Pacific work in slate and horn (Plate 26) is recent, and is still being carried on. The totem poles are no more—except for museum pieces—for well-meaning missionaries fixed that, just as the Conquistadores did with the Aztec and Maya "idols."

Eskimo masks are most imaginative. Their best design work is very old engraving on ivory. (Plate 22) Modern work is fine realistic work—mostly small carvings, toys for the children, models of kayaks, and so on. The "false face" masks of the Iroquois (carved from a living tree; see Plate 17) are original—and horrible. They were intended to be. The carver told his story well.

North of Mexico, the best stone sculpture and modeling comes from the Mound-building area. The shell and copper work (Plates 11 and 12) shows stylistic influence from Mexico. The stone work, however, reached its greatest development in what is now Ohio. The stone pipe (Plate 11) from the Adena Mound is the finest known example. Here is true sculpture in the round.

Better known are the pipes carved in realistic bird and animal forms, so well conceived and executed that there is no difficulty in identifying the subject. No need, however, to try to identify the stylized bird on the diorite bowl (Plate 11): We can still enjoy its excellent design and workmanship.

Florida and California groups did fine wood carving, with shell inlay. But we must turn to Mexico for the finest wood carving. Precious little has survived time and man. Examples are shown on Plates 46 and 58.

Central and South America, and the West Indies, along with other outlying areas of simple cultures, produced their share of crudely carved wood and stone fetishes. Stone stools, and *metates* for grinding corn (Plate 63); and stone "collars" (Plate 79) from the West Indies, are well designed. The use of these collars is a mystery, as are the "yokes" from Mexico (Plate 46).

THE SMITH

"Cortez and some of his captains went in first into the treasury and they saw such a number of jewels and slabs and plates of gold and chalchihuites *(jade)* and other riches that they were quite carried away . . . When I saw it I marvelled . . . I took it for certain that there could not be another such store of wealth in the whole world." Bernal Diaz in 1520 so described the state of affairs at Tenochtitlan (Mexico City). Only a beginning. Had Diaz been able to visualize the treasure of Peru, he might have qualified his statement.

It took the Aztec goldsmiths, under orders from Cortez, three days to melt down into bars the treasure Diaz refers to (Plate 49). Thirteen years later, in Peru, Pizarro's loot, the ransom for the Inca, took the gold and silversmiths, working day and night, a full month to melt down their precious work. El Dorado indeed! (Plate 71). Millions of dollars worth of the Indians' gold was sent to Spain. It also provided a royal holiday for Queen Elizabeth and Sir Francis Drake; for all the gold did not reach Spain.

Unfortunately, the Spanish did not place any value on the artistry of the Indians' work. Only a very small amount was sent intact to his Spanish Majesty to show him the work of the heathen. But European artists recognized its true value. The goldsmiths of Seville despaired of imitating it. Albrecht Dürer wrote: ". . . I never have seen in all my days what so rejoyced my heart, as these things."

Aztec tribute rolls show that gold from the south was part of the tribute paid by subject tribes to the Aztec rulers. So it went; the native rulers took from the people, the Spaniards took from the Indian rulers to give to their ruler. Montezuma is said to have remarked, "The Christians must have a strange disease which can only be cured by gold."

American Indian metalwork had its origin in Ecuador or Peru, spreading to Colombia and up through the Isthmus to Panama and Costa Rica, with a jump to Mexico. Long before the barbarian hunting tribe we know as the Aztec had grown into an empire, the Mixtec in Mexico (sharing honors with the Quimbaya of Colombia) had reached the highest achievement in American goldwork (Plates 49 and 61). Their goldsmiths had as their patron, the god Xipe-Totec—"Our Lord the Flayed" (see Plate 46—stone mask). Their reason for the association of a god who wore the skin of his victim with their sheets of gold is not a very pleasant one to us. The Aztec called gold "offal of the gods." The Inca called it "tears of the sun." Rather enlightening, as we learn more about the first Americans.

The Maya did very little goldwork. Only a few small fragments have been found in early Maya sites. Most of the goldwork dug up from the Well of Sacrifice at Chichen-Itzá (the New Maya Empire) was made in Costa Rica or Panama. It reached Yucatan through trade, or was carried by pilgrims to that holy city. It should be kept in mind, by the way, that while we use present-day political state names throughout this book, they of course had no meaning in aboriginal America. The Indian did not become an Aztec, or Inca, or an Iroquois, by stepping over the dotted line of a map, although the Aztec and Incas did have maps. The Incas made relief maps of clay, and colored them to indicate altitude.

From Mexico to Peru the goldsmiths' techniques were similar but the designs varied greatly. The Indian worked with gold, silver, and copper. He obtained his gold from river sands by picking out the grains, or by washing. Silver and copper were extracted from surface mines by building fires against the rocks.

Miners in Peru had to be married men. Their work was regarded as a tribute—and it was just that—to the Inca. The miner was exempt from farming his own land; he was supplied with food and clothing. He worshipped the hills that hid the metals but there was an earthly reward for hard work—dancing and drinking were part of the worship. Smelting methods were crude. Melting furnaces were heated by charcoal; the draft was forced by blowing on the embers through cane tubes. The melted metal was worked either by hammering or casting. Stone dies have been found in South America, however, and besides hammering and casting, the smiths did plating, gilding, soldering, and welding, embossing, engraving and inlaying.

Casting was by the "lost wax" process. Over a base of clay the design was formed with a prepared wax. The design was then covered over with clay. When the clay was baked the wax melted and ran out of vents, leaving a mold corresponding to the wax design. Molten metal was then poured into the mold, allowed to cool, and the mold broken open.

The Mound-builders (who, by the way, were Indians who built mounds, no mysterious race)—were the outstanding workers of copper. The source of their metal was the Lake Superior region, worked by groups around the Great Lakes and the Mississippi Valley. There is no evidence of smelting; the work was done by hammering and highly skilled engraving, and by relief work with sheet copper (Plate 11). It is the finest metal work north of Mexico. As mentioned before, the designs show Mexican influence. Copper was used also by the North Pacific groups. Their shield-shaped "coppers" were symbols of wealth.

Silver work by the Navaho and Zuni (Plate 41) is of course well known; it was learned from the Spanish. The Iroquois worked with german-silver introduced by the colonial traders (Plate 17). This work was given up several years ago, whereas the Navaho are still doing excellent work—when not working under a white man's factory system.

THE LAPIDARY

The workers and merchants of precious stones were neighbors to the gold workers in the great market of Tenochtitlan. Montezuma gave ornaments of jade to Cortez, saying: "I will also give you some very valuable stones—chalchihuites—not to be given to anyone else, but only to him, your great Prince."

It is reported that Cortez was disappointed, but our faithful reporter Diaz, who planted the first orange seeds in America, was more practical. According to his own report he did not take any gold, but did take four pieces of the jade: ". . . and later on the price of them served me well in healing my wounds and getting me food."

Among the many stones used other than jade, were turquoise, emerald, obsidian, rock crystal, onyx, and amethyst. All were precious to the Indian.

The most skillful carving of jade (Plate 49) was done in Mexico. Considering the material, one of the hardest of stones, and the tools they used—sawing with rawhide and drilling with bone and reed, employing sand as an abrasive—how did the Indian achieve such excellent work? Patience, skill and time. Think of having to drill out the interior of the alabaster vase shown on Plate 64! In the North Pacific outpost, jade was worked, the only jade north of Mexico, but it was used only as a tool. The Andean region and the Southwest regions of North America worked with turquoise, doing inlay and mosaic work.

THE PAINTER

Painted designs have been touched on in the sections on the Potter, and the Sculptor and Carver. We are concerned now with the painting of pictures, regardless of the surface the painter worked on.

The Indian painted pictures on rock walls and plaster walls, on pottery and on skins, on bark, on his own paper, and finally on white man's paper. On the earth, he made sand paintings. North of Mexico there were (and still are) two groups of Indian painters; those of the Plains, and those of the Southwest.

The Plains paintings are picture-writing on skin robes and rawhide; representations of battle and hunting scenes, and "winter counts" or historical records. The drawing is rather crude, without perspective, but spirited, with a fine feeling for pattern, and a strong story-telling quality. Colors were limited; the paints were made from colored earths. The brushes were made from the porous bones of the buffalo. This traditional style of painting is being carried on today by a small band of water-colorists; but like the work of a contemporary group in the Southwest, their work is tribal art only insofar as their subject matter is drawn from Indian life. The paintings are made for their picture value alone, something the artists' forebears would not have understood. Those earlier artists had a story to tell and painting was but one means; for they told their stories by songs, by dances, and pictures.

In the Southwest, the present-day water-colorists are carrying on an art form that had its first expression in pictures painted on canyon walls; later on the walls of the underground ceremonial rooms called *kivas*. The same masks and costumes shown in those paintings can be seen today, worn by the kachina dancers and in the modern paintings. (Plate 41). The Navaho sand paintings (Plate 42) are representations of gods and goddesses, spirits and sacred places. The designs are formed by sprinkling colored powder made from earths, rocks, and charcoal on a bed of sand spread on the floor of the medicine lodge. The artists are medicine men; the paintings are a part of their ceremonial for healing the sick. Four sacred colors are used for the cardinal points—black for north, blue for south, white for east, and yellow for west. Red and brown complete the palette of six colors. Color symbolism varies with the different groups.

The colors are sifted through the thumb and forefinger. The work starts in the center and expands as the design grows, more painters working as the working area increases. The painting is made without any pattern or drawing to follow—and it is done under the direction of the shaman or priest. During the healing ceremony the patient sits naked on the painting, facing the east. After the ritual the painting is destroyed. Next day another one is made. There are many chants and paintings for healing specific diseases—from snake bite, to the chant "Terrestrial Beauty," which restores the mind to beauty.

From the Maya, and the Aztec and other groups of Central Mexico, come murals and manuscripts (Plate 50). From the Maya we have perhaps the finest painted pottery in aboriginal America (Plates 51, 57 and 64).

Writing in ancient America was in a primitive stage. There was no alphabet. Events and action were expressed by pictures. Names were expressed by a figure, part of a figure, or a combination of figures, as in a rebus. The manuscripts were made on deer-skin, or a paper made from beaten bark. The paper was given a smooth surface with a coating of fine white lime. After the conquest European paper was used. Manuscripts were made in book form by folding a long sheet screen-wise; they were bound in hide or wood covers. The average page size is five by eight inches; the largest books unfold to some twenty or thirty feet.

Great numbers of Maya books were found in Yucatan by the Spanish—but only three have survived. One of the first bishops of Yucatan, Diego de Landa, started a bonfire —but let him tell the story. ". . . We found great numbers of books in these letters, but as they contained nothing that did not savor of superstition and lies of the devil we burnt them all, at which the natives grieved most keenly and were greatly pained."

Small wonder! Those books were sacred to the Maya. They contained their calendar, their ritual, their history, and the prophecies of their future. The three surviving books were "found" in Europe; in Austria, Spain and France, the last one three hundred years after the final conquest of Yucatan. There may be more, resting on some dusty library shelf. Let us hope.

After the conquest many books were written on European paper, in the Maya language but with Spanish script. Myths from the *Popol Vuh,* meaning "Book of the Community" (written in the Quiché language), are one example. (See Chapter 5). Hundreds of books from Central Mexico have been preserved, written both before and after the conquest of Mexico. Those not restricted by ritual formula give us a good picture of the people, what they did and how they did it. Surviving also are maps, annals, administrative records and tribute rolls. The Spanish friars used Aztec artists to illustrate their reports with pictures which show an interesting mixture of native and European drawing, including the Indians' first lessons in perspective.

The mural painters never learned the art of perspective (see Plate 50), or the use of scale in their drawings. Their work was finished before the arrival of the Spanish. During the colonial period, the Indians painted frescoes in the schools and monasteries erected by the Spanish, but these were copies of pictures from European religious books. Like the Egyptian and Persian painters, the Indians indicated distance by placing their figures one above the other. The base of the painting represents the part nearest the spectator. Figures above indicate increasing distance, although all the figures were drawn the same size. Colors were used in flat tones, always outlined.

The Maya paintings show greater freedom in drawing than the highly stylized forms used in Central Mexico. There is an apparent contradiction in all this work. The Mexicans did much freer work in their books than in their murals; whereas the Maya show greater freedom in their murals. However, in the case of the Maya, this might be explained by the fact that the only pre-Conquest Maya books we know about are calendarical records, although even here the drawing is freer than the Mexican work. We of course know nothing of the treatment used in the books the good Bishop Landa sent up in flames. There are no manuscripts from the Peruvian area, as they had no system of writing. Fragments of wall paintings have been found, the subject matter similar to the weaving patterns, but in such poor condition that no reproduction can be given.

The pottery painting of the Maya shows great freedom in both drawing and color. While the color is pretty much confined to outlined areas, the figures themselves, released from ritual dogma, are drawn naturalistically. Composition is free and open, not crowded as in their sculpture. (See Plates 51 and 57). The painter made good use of bands and panels of glyphs as a part of his composition. In the sculpture the glyphs are mostly dates; in the pottery paintings, along with date-glyphs are others which may, in some way, explain the scene—but we do not know. According to the late Dr. Morley, only about one-third of the Maya glyphs have been deciphered.

In Peru, as in Mexico and Central America, painted pottery, such as we have been speaking of, is the exception rather than the rule. The paintings, when realistic and showing scenes of daily life (we can be thankful for that), are so stylized that the design element is as important as the pictorial matter. The Peruvian use of color on pottery compares well with the Mayan. From the point of design it is superior to the Mayan. Most of the Maya pottery painting was done on a flat surface; a dish, or a cylindrical vessel. The Peruvian usually painted on a convex surface, in many cases further complicated by odd shapes and modeling. He did an excellent job, both in design and painting.

THE BUILDER

In Mexico, the priest-architects took full advantage of the work of the sculptors and painters to enrich their buildings and the so-called pyramids. The pyramid was not a tomb, as in Egypt, but a base for an altar, and later for the temple which housed their gods.

Their buildings were a religious and ceremonial architecture of temples, palaces, and castles. These terms, used by the Spanish, are a bit misleading with their Old World connotations, including the title "king." With the exception of Peru, where the first Inca proclaimed himself Son of the Sun and founded a line of "royal blood," the head of the tribe was a war chief, appointed by a council and subject to recall if he did not live up to his position. The Spaniards called Montezuma "king—living in a palace with hundreds of retainers." He was no king, but a war chief. His "palace" was a group of one-story, thatched-roof buildings set around a courtyard. His "nobles" for all their fine feathers were tribal headmen. There was rank but no class. The head of a Maya city-state, called "True Man," was a territorial ruler. The real rulers were the priests. They set the style for temples and monuments, painting and picture-writing. They, like the rulers and priests of the Old World, called upon the best artists and workmen.

In our understanding of the term then, building in the Americas achieved the status of architecture only in the ceremonial structures of Mexico and Peru, and the structure of the Pueblos. The Pueblo style is the only native architecture that has influenced our own domestic buildings. In all other parts of the Americas, and even in Mexico and Peru, the common homes of the people were huts of the simplest construction; huts of stone, skin, bark, or grass, and earth-covered lodges, varying greatly in size. In form, they ran from the snow-house of the Eskimo (a winter house; in summer Eskimos used a skin tent) to the pit-dwellings of the Southwest and the skin lean-to of the Fuegians of South America.

As the simple homes of Europe clustered around the cathedral, so did the homes of the Mexicans and Mayans skirt their ceremonial centers. But here all parallels end. The cathedrals of Europe were built to house congregations. In America the ceremonies took place in the open. The mounds and the temples surmounting them were monuments to the gods. Height was a means of dramatizing the ceremony.

The rooms in the earliest Maya buildings were mere slits in the heavy masonry. Time and experience brought about structural improvements. Rooms became wider, and the temple with inner rooms became a shrine to house the god. The evolution was from a low offering platform to a high mound surmounted by a temple. Paralleling this development were the associated buildings of the religious center in which were housed the priesthood. First, a series of one room buildings were strung together by a common wall; a second and third story of recessed rooms was added later by filling in the inside rooms beneath the upper floors. By increasing the width of the openings in the outer rooms, columns, first square, later round, were developed. Still later, these rooms developed into porticos.

The Maya used the false, or corbel arch, built by overlapping stones bridged by a cap-stone. They never discovered the principle of the key-stone. The great height of the arches resulted in a broad surface of exterior walls which was ideal for decoration. The architect took full advantage of his opportunity, using carving and stucco work. He had several exterior areas to play with: the sub-structure, or mound; the building itself; and the super-structure, called a roof-comb if rising from the center line of the roof; called a flying facade if rising from the front wall.

The buildings were covered with intricate designs (Plate 52), carved and painted with bright colors. Sculptured pieces were set in the walls and held by tenons, or set in recesses. Carved and painted serpents crawled around the base of the mounds and up the stairways and pillars. Panels of serpent masks were repeated to cover large surfaces. Mosaics, of separately carved stones in geometric patterns based on textile designs, were used on both exterior and interior walls. Stone and wood carvings and paintings were used on interior walls. *Stelae* and altars were set up at the base of the great stairways of the mounds.

Our knowledge of Aztec architecture is limited pretty much to the accounts of the early chroniclers. Diaz reported, "beautiful stonework and cedar wood and the wood of other sweet-scented trees; with great rooms and courts, wonderful to behold, covered with awnings of cotton cloth." Scouts sent out by Cortez on his march to Tenochtitlan (not knowing at that time that the houses had been whitewashed and burnished) reported that "the walls were made of silver." But then, any city would have looked good to them, promising food and shelter after their long march from the coast.

Fortunately for us, the Mexican custom of enlarging or rebuilding their temples every fifty-two years (corresponding to our century count) has preserved, relatively speaking, the early temples. Old temples were filled in, the mound raised, and a new temple built. Many of the temples built by pre-Aztec groups were abandoned and in ruins at the time of the Spanish conquest. All we have of these are fragments.

To one who stood at the base of a great mound and witnessed an Aztec sacrificial ceremony with all its pageantry, the scene must have been an awesome experience. These were the people who sang the hymns to Huitzilopochtli in Chapter 5. We have the words of the Conquistadores that it was awesome; so much so that they utterly destroyed Tenochtitlan.

The architects of Peru made little use of applied decoration for their buildings. The emphasis was on structure. Technically, Inca buildings are superior to either Maya or Aztec work. Peruvians were the best stonecutters, fitting huge blocks so perfectly that they had no need for mortar. They knew how to bond their walls, something the Mayans and Mexicans never achieved.

Large-scale building projects were a Peruvian characteristic. Stepped pyramids faced with stone, as in Mexico, mounds and buildings built of adobe bricks, palaces for the rulers and great fortifications, were the work of professionals. Under the Incas, the architect and the master masons were government officials, spending full time on government projects. They used clay and stone models in designing their buildings, and in studying town layouts. Compared to the grandiose structures of the Mayans and Mexicans, Peruvian architecture is severe, even forbidding. Decoration was used sparingly; it was confined mostly to doorjambs and lintels. On occasion, however, as in the Chimu city of Chanchan where the adobe walls were enriched with conventionalized forms of birds and fish (for comparison with weaving designs, see Plate 65; the designs were virtually the same), they made effective use of architectural decoration. Another outstanding example is the sculptured band of figures on the Gateway of the Sun at Tiahuanaco (Plate 72).

The Inca architects, seriously concerned with building, beautifying and protecting a new empire, gave free reign to their imaginations but held their emotions in check. In at least one detail, though, they—or the master masons—made an essay in pure decoration. The beveling of the edges of the great stone blocks they employed, broke up the walls into patterns of light and shade, and served no structural purpose whatever.

THE STORY TELLER

Just as the arts and crafts of the American Indian responded to material or spiritual needs, so did his literature, both prose and poetry. The taciturnity of the Indian is proverbial; and for this there was good reason. To the Indian the word was a sacred thing. Some words were not lightly said. With words he could give expression to the ideas which prompted his actions. With words, he could rouse his fellows to high passions. With words, spoken in ceremonial form, he could influence the powers which had made him what he was. The poem, the chant, the legend of migration, the origin myth were magical utterances in the strictest sense of the term. Indian designs and painting are a graphic expression of these utterances; the music and dances a dramatic expression. As we have seen, the Navaho has a sand painting for each healing chant.

The telling of myths and legends, even children's stories, was rarely for amusement. These stories were integrally a part of tribal life. In many instances, they were kept jealously secret as sacred inheritances from the "first ones," the progenitors. Now made available through the labors of anthropologists and folk-lore specialists, they may be considered, for all that the translations lack the stylistic qualities of the originals, as a body of aboriginal philosophy and religious belief. It is not within the scope of this book to examine the authenticity of these myths and legends; they rest on the authority of the expert scholars who have gathered them. But it can be said that the most adequate interpretation of what the Indian artist really meant by the designs he wrought, their actual symbolic value, must be found in the best surviving oral expression of Indian religious beliefs. The stories must be read if the reader desires to know what the original creators of these designs intended them to mean. This is so because, almost universally, the Indian himself ascribed the origin of his arts, as well as his laws and social institutions, to the operations of the gods. Time and again, as you will find in the stories, the gods instructed the Indians in their ritual. With each gift they were given a formula; how to plant their corn, how to hunt their brother the buffalo, how to carve their masks, how to make their sacred bundles. These instructions were handed down orally.

In the higher civilizations, these instructions were formalized by the priesthood into a complex system. Conquering tribes of course took their gods with them, and then proceeded to incorporate the gods of the conquered tribes into their own pantheon. After the European conquest the Indian did the same with the Christian's God, in subtle ways associating God and His saints with their own gods. Even today you will find in some places altars to the pagan gods set up in the public square—in front of the Christian church. It is well to have many gods on your side, the Indian says.

Since Indian literature was oral, much of it has perished. In many cases, what we offer is an unsympathetic European rendering of what was heard; but something of the original ideas survives. With a few exceptions, the legends and myths are given precisely as they were recorded; a full statement of the sources from which they have been chosen is made in the INDEX TO THE STORIES. The temptation to make annotations and to explain who the characters were, or to dwell on the significance of these apparently artless tales to the modern scholar, has been resisted, in order that the legends, like the designs, may make an immediate appeal to the reader and be enjoyed as the Indians enjoyed them. For even in translation, though much of the poetry escapes us, some of the art of the stories comes through. They are marked by vividness of phrase, for the Indian languages were not equipped to employ abstract terms and so relied on richness of imagery and concrete detail. They are marked also by a strong sense of drama, pathos and mystery. And wherever the ceremonial character of the myths did not require certain formal elements of repetition and the intrusion of apparently incongruous episodes, they possess economy of phrasing and fine, narrative directness. But most of all they have personality—not the intruded personality of the story-teller himself (for Indian literature was not an exercise in romantic egotism), but a true projection of the group-mind—they tell us what it was to be an American Indian; all the characteristic traits of stoic bravery, awe in the face of nature, skill in making use of what was available, tenderness with children and the old.

A pioneer in American folk-lore study has well said that religious ideas of primitive people are a key to their psychology and their ideas of beauty. He goes even a little further: "Hence, when authentic historical records are wanting, the student may by close and sympathetic analysis and interpretation of the myths and the religion of a people acquire a fairly accurate knowledge of the history and culture of such a people."

As the Tewa Indian expressed it:
Oh, our Mother, the Earth; oh, our Father, the Sky,
Your children are we, and with tired backs
We bring you the gifts that you love.

1

THE PLAINS AND THE LAKES

FEW PEOPLE THINK OF THE INDIAN of the Plains as anything but a whooping, half-naked savage on a pony, his head covered with a war-bonnet of eagle feathers, his *coup* stick ready for another triumph over palefaces. But, before moving to the Plains, these horsemen had lived in grass-covered huts and earth houses on the forest fringe of the Plains. They raised corn, tobacco, squash and beans. They fished, hunted small game, and made seasonal trips to the Plains to hunt the buffalo. They used the dog travois for carrying their baggage and small children. The papoose rode on the mother's back. In 1540, Coronado saw some of the southern groups and reported: ". . . they travel like Arabs, with their troops of dogs loaded with poles."

They entered the Plains from the south and the northeastern woodlands. So many groups and languages were represented that they developed the most effective sign language ever devised. Each of these groups, entering on the Plains, had its migration legends and origin tales which explained the tribal beliefs and institutions. These make up a great part of the Indian mythology.

Groups to us most typical of the Plains culture, such as the Cheyenne, Arapaho and Dakotas, did not move to the Plains until after 1700. The coming of the horse, the "big dog" (brought by the Spaniards, the horse did not reach the Plains in any number until the late seventeenth century), left the tribes free to roam far and wide. They abandoned their village life and their farming to become nomads, so building an entirely new culture pattern for themselves.

The buffalo was the source of their food and all the raw materials needed in their new life, and so the buffalo was a sacred thing to them. Buffalo skin was used for tipi covers (it took from ten to twelve skins to cover a typical tipi), for clothing and baggage covers, even for cooking utensils and vessels. The bones were used as tools; the hair for weaving and for ornaments. Their art they brought with them, but the large buffalo hides gave them greater scope for their porcupine quill embroidery and especially for their painting. Later, contact with white traders brought them the glass beads which replaced the quills. Cloth replaced hide for clothing, and canvas became the material for their tipis. With the westward expansion of the whites they lost their lands, their freedom, and the buffalo. The pattern was broken. They were literally starved into submission. But the legend of the buffalo lived on in tribal ceremonial, as the Cheyenne story, "The Coming of Buffalo" and the Osage child-naming ritual (pages 29 and 33) abundantly prove.

Realistic paintings on hide, on the sides of their tipis and on their robes and shields, representations of war and hunting scenes and historical records (time counts) were painted by the men. Although lacking a knowledge of perspective, the painters had a keen sense of observation and were able to express it in graphic form—drawings full of animation. Later they made use of the white man's notebooks and ledgers for their colored drawings.

Magic powers were ascribed to the designs on their painted shirts and shields (Plate 1). Designs on their rawhide shields were intended to *attract* the enemy's arrows. These could not go through the tough hide. But the white man's bullets could—and did, and with the coming of the whites this magic failed. The "bullet proof shirt" used in the famous Ghost Dance was the last attempt to rely on the old magic.

The decoration of ceremonial objects, usually accompanied by ritual, was also the work of the men. The treatment here tended to the realistic. Men also did the only carving done among these people—on pipes made of catlinite, a red stone. This stone is named after George Catlin, the artist who first visited the Plains in 1832, and whose paintings and reports are of historical value. The medicine-pipe, or calumet, however, was, as a rule, of an entirely different type. It was rarely smoked, in fact it was frequently without a bowl, although *Thunder* in the Blackfoot tale on page 22, "The Medicine Pipe," ordered that it be smoked. Its magical qualities resided in the decorated stem.

Pottery was made by some of the border groups—also baskets and bags. The western groups made blankets of woven rabbit skins.

Abstract designs, both painted and in embroidery, were the women's work. These consist mostly of geometrical units, such as squares, triangles, diamonds, and so forth, the natural result of work with quills. Strange as it seems to us, they held to the same designs in their painted work. Parallels to this, however, will be found throughout the Americas, owing no doubt to the conservative attitude of the individual conditioned by tribal customs. Modern man is conditioned in the same way. We hold to tribal (national) styles with the same tenacity.

The beadwork of the Plains is outstanding, mostly in embroidery. Greater use was made of glass beads in applied design than by any other aboriginals, the world over. Beadwork (and quillwork, the original form) was applied to clothing and articles such as pouches and bags. Representations of plant forms are rare in the designs. Animals and insects, highly conventionalized, are numerous. Mountains, trails and stars, especially the morning star, represented by a cross, were favorite units. These were graphic expressions of their beliefs. The people of the Plains and Lakes thought of natural phenomena as deities. The sun was pre-eminent. Under him was the moon, sky, earth, and wind, as well as lesser beings, the buffalo, bear, lightning, thunder, (the Thunder-Bird was wide-spread in North America), and whirlwinds. The story of "Scarface" on page 24 shows the close relationship between the Indian and his environment. The dividing line between man, animal, and phenomena is vague.

Not too much stress should be put on symbolism in the abstract designs of the Plains. A design might be chosen because of its name (possibly a symbolic association), or given a name only as a means to teach beginners in beadwork. The same design, when used by another tribe, might symbolize an entirely different idea. Of the designs on Plates 2 and 3, only one, "Life," is a true symbol. To quote A. L. Kroeber, writing about the Arapaho: "Any interpretation of a figure is personal. Often the interpretation is arbitrary. Much depends upon what might be called symbolic context. In a decoration which symbolizes buffalo-hunting, a stripe naturally represents a bow; on a *parfleche* (a rawhide bag), where decoration represents such parts of the landscape as mountains, rocks, earth, and tents, an identical stripe would naturally have the signification of a river or path; but whether a path or river, would depend on the fancy of the maker of the *parfleche*."

Feathers, fringes, shells, bells, bear and elks teeth, and pendants in general were usually symbolic, particularly those attached to ceremonial objects. Colors too had their symbolism; red for blood, earth, sunset; yellow for sun-light or day; green for vegetation; blue for sky; black for night. The Dakota pipe bag on Plate 7 illustrates the story-telling quality of a design. In a sense, it is a military insignia. One can read on it the war record of the owner.

Porcupine quill weaving and moosehair embroidery reached a high point in the Great Lakes area. Quillwork was more widely spread than beadwork. It was used throughout Canada and the eastern United States and finally carried to the Plains. In contrast to the designs of the Plains, the Lakes groups used floral motives, conventionalized in woven work but highly realistic in embroidery. (See Plates 9 and 10). The floral character of the designs, and the fact that these tribes were in early contact with the whites, has caused some scholars to suspect a European influence, but Wissler points out that their oldest and most characteristic designs on bark and skin could not have been so influenced. "All that can reasonably be conceded is that their trade stimulated the use of beads and their decorative preferences tended to emphasize the old floral character." The same holds true for the silk *appliqué* embroidery (Plate 9), wherein they used silk ribbons obtained from the whites.

Woven bags of buffalo wool or bark fibers (sometimes combined with yarn) show both abstract designs and conventional bird and animal figures (Plate 8). The Thunder-Bird and Panther designs on ceremonial bags had magic significance. The way in which the Menomini received their first bags is recalled in the story on page 36, "The Birth of Manabush." In this, and the following stories, something may be learned of the mind of the Lake tribes and their rationalization of the forces of nature. The intricacies of tribal organization are explained in the Winnebago story, "The Origin of the Thunder-Bird Clan" on page 36.

ORIGIN OF THE MEDICINE PIPE

THUNDER—YOU HAVE HEARD HIM, he is everywhere. He roars in the mountains, he shouts far out on the prairie. He strikes the high rocks, and they fall to pieces. He hits a tree, and it is broken in slivers. He strikes the people, and they die. He is bad. He does not like the towering cliff, the standing tree, or living man. He likes to strike and crush them to the ground. Yes! yes! Of all he is most powerful; he is the one most strong. But I have not told you the worst: he sometimes steals women.

Long ago, almost in the beginning, a man and his wife were sitting in their lodge, when Thunder came and struck them. The man was not killed. At first he was as if dead, but after a while he lived again, and rising looked about him. His wife was not there. "Oh, well," he thought, "she has gone to get some water or wood," and he sat a while; but when the sun had under-disappeared, he went out and inquired about her of the people. No one had seen her. He searched throughout the camp, but did not find her. Then he knew that Thunder had stolen her, and he went out on the hills alone and mourned.

When morning came, he rose and wandered far away, and he asked all the animals he met if they knew where Thunder lived. They laughed, and would not answer. The Wolf said: "Do you think we would seek the home of the only one we fear? He is our only danger. From all others we can run away; but from him there is no running. He strikes, and there we lie. Turn back! go home! Do not look for the dwelling-place of that dreadful one." But the man kept on, and travelled far away. Now he came to a lodge,—a queer lodge, for it was made of stone; just like any other lodge, only it was made of stone. Here lived the Raven chief. The man entered.

"Welcome, my friend," said the chief of Ravens. "Sit down, sit down." And food was placed before him.

Then, when he had finished eating, the Raven said, "Why have you come?"

"Thunder has stolen my wife," replied the man. "I seek his dwelling-place that I may find her."

"Would you dare enter the lodge of that dreadful person?" asked the Raven. "He lives close by here. His lodge is of stone, like this; and hanging there, within, are eyes,—the eyes of those he has killed or stolen. He has taken out their eyes and hung them in his lodge. Now, then, dare you enter there?"

"No," replied the man. "I am afraid. What man could look at such dreadful things and live?"

"No person can," said the Raven. "There is but one old Thunder fears. There is but one he cannot kill. It is I, it is the Ravens. Now I will give you medicine, and he shall not harm you. You shall enter there, and seek among those eyes your wife's; and if you

BONE WITH SHELL INLAY, KITKSAN

HEADDRESS, TSIMSHIAN

HEADDRESS, HAIDA

PAINTED HIDE, HAIDA

WOODEN RATTLE, TLINGIT

MASK, BELLACOOLA

MASK, BELLACOOLA

MASK, KWAKIUTL

MASK, KWAKIUTL

PUEBLO POTTERY

SANTO DOMINGO

ACOMA

SAN ILDEFONSO

SANTO DOMINGO

ACOMA

LAGUNA

SIA

ZUNI

SIA

ACOMA

find them, tell that Thunder why you came, and make him give them to you. Here, now, is a raven's wing. Just point it at him, and he will start back quick; but if that fail, take this. It is an arrow, and the shaft is made of elk-horn. Take this, I say, and shoot it through the lodge."

"Why make a fool of me?" the poor man asked. "My heart is sad. I am crying." And he covered his head with his robe, and wept.

"Oh," said the Raven, "you do not believe me. Come out, come out, and I will make you believe." When they stood outside, the Raven asked, "Is the home of your people far?"

"A great distance," said the man.

"Can you tell how many days you have travelled?"

"No," he replied, "my heart is sad. I did not count the days. The berries have grown and ripened since I left."

"Can you see your camp from here?" asked the Raven.

The man did not speak. Then the Raven rubbed some medicine on his eyes and said, "Look!" The man looked, and saw the camp. It was close. He saw the people. He saw the smoke rising from the lodges.

"Now you will believe," said the Raven. "Take now the arrow and the wing, and go and get your wife."

So the man took these things, and went to the Thunder's lodge. He entered and sat down by the door-way. The Thunder sat within and looked at him with awful eyes. But the man looked above, and saw those many pairs of eyes. Among them were those of his wife.

"Why have you come?" said the Thunder in a fearful voice.

"I seek my wife," the man replied, "whom you have stolen. There hang her eyes."

"No man can enter my lodge and live," said the Thunder; and he rose to strike him. Then the man pointed the raven wing at the Thunder, and he fell back on his couch and shivered. But he soon recovered, and rose again. Then the man fitted the elk-horn arrow to his bow, and shot it through the lodge of rock; right through that lodge of rock it pierced a jagged hole, and let the sunlight in.

"Hold," said the Thunder. "Stop; you are the stronger. Yours the great medicine. You shall have your wife. Take down her eyes." Then the man cut the string that held them, and immediately his wife stood beside him.

"Now," said the Thunder, "you know me. I am of great power. I live here in summer, but when winter comes, I go far south. I go south with the birds. Here is my pipe. It is medicine. Take it, and keep it. Now, when I first come in the spring, you shall fill and light this pipe, and you shall pray to me, you and the people. For I bring the rain which makes the berries large and ripe. I bring the rain which makes all things grow, and for this you shall pray to me, you and all the people."

Thus the people got the first medicine pipe. It was long ago.

Blackfoot

ORIGIN OF THE MEDICINE LODGE

IN THE EARLIEST TIMES there was no war. All the tribes were at peace. In those days there was a man who had a daughter, a very beautiful girl. Many young men wanted to marry her, but every time she was asked, she only shook her head and said she did not want a husband.

"How is this?" asked her father. "Some of these young men are rich, handsome, and brave."

"Why should I marry?" replied the girl. "I have a rich father and mother. Our lodge is good. The *parfleches* are never empty. There are plenty of tanned robes and soft furs for winter. Why worry me, then?"

The Raven Bearers held a dance; they all dressed carefully and wore their ornaments, and each one tried to dance the best. Afterwards some of them asked for this girl, but still she said no. Then the Bulls, the Kit-foxes, and others held their dances, and all those who were rich, many great warriors, asked this man for his daughter, but to every one of them she said no. Then her father was angry, and said: "Why, now, this way? All the best men have asked for you, and still you say no. I believe you have a secret lover."

"Ah!" said her mother. "What shame for us should a child be born and our daughter still unmarried!" "Father! mother!" replied the girl, "pity me. I have no secret lover, but now hear the truth. That Above Person, the Sun, told me, 'Do not marry any of those men, for you are mine; thus you shall be happy, and live to great age;' and again he said, 'Take heed. You must not marry. You are mine.'"

"Ah!" replied her father. "It must always be as he says." And they talked no more about it.

There was a poor young man, very poor. His father, mother, all his relations, had gone to the Sand Hills. He had no lodge, no wife to tan his robes or sew his moccasins. He stopped in one lodge to-day, and to-morrow he ate and slept in another; thus he lived. He was a good-looking young man, except that on his cheek he had a scar, and his clothes were always old and poor.

After those dances some of the young men met this poor Scarface, and they laughed at him, and said: "Why don't you ask that girl to marry you? You are so rich and handsome!" Scarface did not laugh; he replied: "Ah! I will do as you say. I will go and ask her." All the young men thought this was funny. They laughed a great deal. But Scarface went down by the river. He waited by the river, where the women came to get water, and by and by the girl came along. "Girl," he said, "wait. I want to speak with you. Not as a designing person do I ask you, but openly where the Sun looks down, and all may see."

"Speak then," said the girl.

"I have seen the days," continued the young man. "You have refused those who are young, and rich, and brave. Now, to-day, they laughed and said to me, 'Why do you not ask her?' I am poor, very poor. I have no lodge, no food, no clothes, no robes and warm furs. I have no relations; all have gone to the Sand Hills; yet, now, to-day, I ask you, take pity, be my wife."

The girl hid her face in her robe and brushed the ground with the point of her moccasin, back and forth, back and forth; for she was thinking. After a time she said: "True. I have refused all those rich young men, yet now the poor one asks me, and I am glad. I will be your wife, and my people will be happy. You are poor, but it does not matter. My father will give you dogs. My mother will make us a lodge. My people will give us robes and furs. You will be poor no longer."

Then the young man was happy, and he started to kiss her, but she held him back, and said: "Wait! The Sun has spoken to me. He says I may not marry; that I belong to him. He says if I listen to him, I shall live to great age. But now I say: Go to the Sun. Tell him, 'She whom you spoke with heeds your words. She has never done wrong, but now she wants to marry. I want her for my wife.' Ask him to take that scar from your face. That will be his sign. I will know he is pleased. But if he refuses, or if you fail to find his lodge, then do not return to me."

"Oh!" cried the young man, "at first your words were good. I was glad. But now it is dark. My heart is dead. Where is that far-off lodge? Where the trail, which no one yet has travelled?"

"Take courage, take courage!" said the girl; and she went to her lodge.

Scarface was very sad. He sat down and covered his head with his robe and tried to think what to do. After a while he got up, and went to an old woman who had been kind to him. "Pity me," he said. "I am very poor. I am going away now on a long journey. Make me some moccasins."

"Where are you going?" asked the old woman. "There is no war; we are very peaceful here."

"I do not know where I shall go," replied Scarface. "I am in trouble, but I cannot tell you now what it is."

So the old woman made him some moccasins, seven pairs, with *parfleche* soles, and also she gave him a sack of food,—pemmican of berries, pounded meat, and dried back fat; for this old woman had a good heart. She liked the young man.

All alone, and with a sad heart, he climbed the bluffs and stopped to take a last look at the camp. He wondered if he would ever see his sweetheart and the people again. *"Hai'-yu!* Pity me, O Sun," he prayed, and turning, he started to find the trail.

For many days he travelled on, over great prairies, along timbered rivers and among the mountains, and every day his sack of food grew lighter; but he saved it as much as he could, and ate berries, and roots, and sometimes he killed an animal of some kind. One night he stopped by the home of a wolf. *"Hai-yah!"* said that one; "what is my brother doing so far from home?"

"Ah!" replied Scarface, "I seek the place where the Sun lives; I am sent to speak with him."

"I have travelled far," said the wolf. "I know all the prairies, the valleys, and the mountains, but I have never seen the Sun's home. Wait; I know one who is very wise. Ask the bear. He may tell you."

The next day the man travelled on again, stopping now and then to pick a few berries, and when night came he arrived at the bear's lodge.

"Where is your home?" asked the bear. "Why are you travelling alone, my brother?"

"Help me! Pity me!" replied the young man; "because of her words I seek the Sun. I go to ask him for her."

"I know not where he stops," replied the bear. "I have travelled by many rivers, and I know the mountains, yet I have never seen his lodge. There is some one beyond, that striped-face, who is very smart. Go and ask him."

The badger was in his hole. Stooping over, the young man shouted: "Oh, cunning striped-face! Oh, generous animal! I wish to speak with you."

"What do you want?" said the badger, poking his head out of the hole.

"I want to find the Sun's home," replied Scarface. "I want to speak with him."

"I do not know where he lives," replied the badger. "I never travel very far. Over there in the timber is a wolverine. He is always travelling around, and is of much knowledge. Maybe he can tell you."

Then Scarface went to the woods and looked all around for the wolverine, but could not find him. So he sat down to rest. *Hai'-yu! Hai'-yu!* he cried. "Wolverine, take pity on me. My food is gone, my moccasins worn out. Now I must die."

"What is it, my brother?" he heard, and looking around, he saw the animal sitting near.

"She whom I would marry," said Scarface, "belongs to the Sun; I am trying to find where he lives, to ask him for her."

"Ah!" said the wolverine. "I know where he lives. Wait; it is nearly night. To-morrow I will show you the trail to the big water. He lives on the other side of it."

Early in the morning, the wolverine showed him the trail, and Scarface followed it until he came to the water's edge. He looked out over it, and his heart almost stopped. Never before had anyone seen such a big water. The other side could not be seen, and there was no end to it. Scarface sat down on the shore. His food was all gone, his moccasins worn out. His heart was sick. "I cannot cross this big water," he said. "I cannot return to the people. Here, by this water, I shall die."

Not so. His Helpers were there. Two swans came swimming up to the shore. "Why have you come here?" they asked him. "What are you doing? It is very far to the place where your people live."

"I am here," replied Scarface, "to die. Far away, in my country, is a beautiful girl. I want to marry her, but she belongs to the Sun. So I started to find him and ask for her. I have travelled many days. My food is gone. I cannot go back. I cannot cross this big water, so I am going to die."

"No," said the swans; "it shall not be so. Across this water is the home of that Above Person. Get on our backs, and we will take you there."

Scarface quickly arose. He felt strong again. He waded out into the water and lay down on the swans' backs, and they started off. Very deep and black is that fearful water. Strange people live there, mighty animals which often seize and drown a person. The swans carried him safely, and took him to the other side. Here was a broad hard trail leading back from the water's edge.

"*Kyi*," said the swans. "You are now close to the Sun's lodge. Follow that trail, and you will soon see it."

Scarface started up the trail, and pretty soon he came to some beautiful things, lying in it. There was a war shirt, a shield, and a bow and arrows. He had never seen such pretty weapons; but he did not touch them. He walked carefully around them, and travelled on. A little way further on, he met a young man, the handsomest person he had ever seen. His hair was very long, and he wore clothing made of strange skins. His moccasins were sewn with bright colored feathers. The young man said to him, "Did you see some weapons lying on the trail?"

"Yes," replied Scarface; "I saw them."

"But did you not touch them?" asked the young man.

"No; I thought some one had left them there, so I did not take them."

"You are not a thief," said the young man. "What is your name?"

"Scarface."

"Where are you going?"

"To the Sun."

"My name," said the young man, "is Morning Star. The Sun is my father; come, I will take you to our lodge. My father is not now at home, but he will come in at night."

Soon they came to the lodge. It was very large and handsome; strange medicine animals were painted on it. Behind, on a tripod, were strange weapons and beautiful clothes —the Sun's. Scarface was ashamed to go in, but Morning Star said, "Do not be afraid, my friend; we are glad you have come."

They entered. One person was sitting there, Kokomikeis *(the Moon),* the Sun's wife, Morning Star's mother. She spoke to Scarface kindly, and gave him something to eat. "Why have you come so far from your people?" she asked.

Then Scarface told her about the beautiful girl he wanted to marry. "She belongs to the Sun," he said. "I have come to ask him for her."

When it was time for the Sun to come home, the Moon hid Scarface under a pile of robes. As soon as the Sun got to the doorway, he stopped, and said, "I smell a person."

"Yes, father," said Morning Star; "a good young man has come to see you. I know he is good, for he found some of my things on the trail and did not touch them."

Then Scarface came out from under the robes, and the Sun entered and sat down. "I am glad you have come to our lodge," he said. "Stay with us as long as you think best. My son is lonesome sometimes; be his friend."

The next day the Moon called Scarface out of the lodge, and said to him: "Go with Morning Star where you please, but never hunt near that big water; do not let him go there. It is the home of great birds which have long sharp bills; they kill people. I have had many sons, but these birds have killed them all. Morning Star is the only one left."

So Scarface stayed there a long time and hunted with Morning Star. One day they came near the water, and saw the big birds.

"Come," said Morning Star; "let us go and kill those birds."

"No, no!" replied Scarface; "we must not go there. Those are very terrible birds; they will kill us."

Morning Star would not listen. He ran towards the water, and Scarface followed. He knew that he must kill the birds and save the boy. If not, the Sun would be angry and might kill him. He ran ahead and met the birds, which were coming towards him to fight, and killed every one of them with his spear. Not one was left. Then the young men cut off their heads, and carried them home. Morning Star's mother was glad when they told her what they had done, and showed her the birds' heads. She cried, and called Scarface "my son." When the Sun came home at night, she told him about it, and he too was glad. "My son," he said to Scarface, "I will not forget what you have this day done for me. Tell me now, what can I do for you?"

"Haï'-yu," replied Scarface. "Haï'-yu, pity me. I am here to ask you for that girl. I want to marry her. I asked her, and she was glad; but she says you own her, that you told her not to marry."

"What you say is true," said the Sun. "I have watched the days, so I know it. Now, then, I give her to you; she is yours. I am glad she has been wise. I know she has never done wrong. The Sun pities good women. They shall live a long time. So shall their husbands and children. Now you will soon go home. Let me tell you something. Be wise and listen: I am the only chief. Everything is mine. I made the earth, the mountains, prairies, rivers, and forests. I made the people and all the animals. This is why I say I alone am the chief. I can never die. True, the winter makes me old and weak, but every summer I grow young again."

Then said the Sun: "What one of all animals is smartest? The raven is, for he always finds food. He is never hungry. Which one of all the animals is most sacred? The buffalo is. Of all animals, I like him best. He is for the people. He is your food and your shelter. What part of his body is sacred? The tongue is. That is mine. What else is sacred? Berries are. They are mine too. Come with me and see the world." He took Scarface to the edge of the sky, and they looked down and saw it. It is round and flat, and all around the edge is the jumping-off place. Then said the Sun: "When any man is sick or in danger, his wife may promise to build me a lodge, if he recovers. If the woman is pure and true, then I will be pleased and help the man. But if she is bad, if she lies, then I will be angry. You shall build the lodge like the world, round, with walls, but first you must build a sweat house of a hundred sticks. It shall be like the sky [a hemisphere], and half of it shall be painted red. That is me. The other half you will paint black. That is the night."

Further said the Sun: "Which is the best, the heart or the brain? The brain is. The heart often lies, the brain never." Then he told Scarface everything about making the

28

Medicine Lodge, and when he had finished, he rubbed a powerful medicine on his face, and the scar disappeared. Then he gave him two raven feathers, saying: "These are the sign for the girl, that I give her to you. They must always be worn by the husband of the woman who builds a Medicine Lodge."

The young man was now ready to return home. Morning Star and the Sun gave him many beautiful presents. The Moon cried and kissed him, and called him "my son." Then the Sun showed him the short trail. It was the Wolf Road *(Milky Way).* He followed it, and soon reached the ground.

It was a very hot day. All the lodge skins were raised, and the people sat in the shade. There was a chief, a very generous man, and all day long people kept coming to his lodge to feast and smoke with him. Early in the morning this chief saw a person sitting out on a butte near by, close wrapped in his robe. The chief's friends came and went, the sun reached the middle, and passed on, down towards the mountains. Still this person did not move. When it was almost night, the chief said: "Why does that person sit there so long? The heat has been strong, but he has never eaten nor drunk. He may be a stranger; go and ask him in."

So some young men went up to him, and said: "Why do you sit here in the great heat all day? Come to the shade of the lodges. The chief asks you to feast with him."

Then the person arose and threw off his robe, and they were surprised. He wore beautiful clothes. His bow, shield, and other weapons were of strange make. But they knew his face, although the scar was gone, and they ran ahead, shouting, "The scarface poor young man has come. He is poor no longer. The scar on his face is gone."

All the people rushed out to see him. "Where have you been?" they asked. "Where did you get all these pretty things?" He did not answer. There in the crowd stood that young woman; and taking the two raven feathers from his head, he gave them to her, and said: "The trail was very long, and I nearly died, but by those Helpers, I found his lodge. He is glad. He sends these feathers to you. They are the sign."

Great was her gladness then. They were married, and made the first Medicine Lodge, as the Sun had said. The Sun was glad. He gave them great age. They were never sick. When they were very old, one morning, their children said: "Awake! Rise and eat." They did not move. In the night, in sleep, without pain, their shadows had departed for the Sand Hills.

Blackfoot

THE COMING OF BUFFALO

THE PEOPLE WERE having a "medicine" hunt; they knew nothing then about the buffalo. Before making a "medicine" hunt, the medicine-men all came together and pledged themselves to make a hunt; they appointed a man to be leader and also his wife, so that, when they caught animals they would get the females as well as the males. After these had pledged themselves, they sent out runners to see what they could find.

This time they chose two men to go out to look for ducks, geese, and other birds. This was when the Cheyenne were far on the other side of the Missouri River where there are many lakes. The men came back and reported that a certain lake was covered with water-fowl of all kinds; so the whole camp moved over to it, the dogs hauling the travois. The lake was not large, and the men, women, children, and dogs surrounded it, and made a great slaughter of birds, for they had called on the spiritual powers to aid them so that the birds should not fly away.

When they moved again, they sent two more runners ahead to see what they could find. These two went toward a high grassy table-land and climbed up on it. They reached it towards sunset, and, as they stood there, they saw the grass moving and found quantities of skunks all around, so they went back to the camp and told what they had seen. Next morning everybody started for the table-land. They all got around it early in the morning and killed great numbers of skunks; everybody was loaded down with them. The next day they again sent two men to the same place, and many more skunks were seen, so that on this day more were killed than the day before. They sent them again the next day, and when they had finished killing they could hardly carry away the meat. Again a fourth time the two men reported skunks there, and many were caught and killed.

The next day they camped near a little knoll, where a spring came out of the rock. This spring is called "Old Woman's Water" (Ma-ta-ma Hehk-a-it). They camped near this spring with the opening of the camp towards it. There was a fine place for the camp in the plain there. There was a little brush near the spring. Nothing happened that night.

In the morning two sets of hoops and sticks were taken to the centre of the camp, and they rolled them there and gambled on the game. Two games were going on. They selected the head of the hunting party as one of the men to keep the count. While they were gambling, a man came from the right side of the camp to the centre, where they were playing. He was naked except for his breech-cloth, and was painted yellow all over and striped down with the fingers; on his breast was a round circle, in red, and on the back a half moon of the same color. His face under his eyes was painted black, and there was a red stripe around his wrists and ankles; he had a yellow down feather on his scalp-lock and wore his robe hair side out. He stood for a time and watched them playing. While he stood there, a man came from the left side of the camp, whose paint and dress were just the same as his. While they were rolling the wheel, the man who had come from the right said to the players, "My friends, stop for a moment." He walked toward the other and asked him to come towards him, so they met in the centre of the camp and stopped a short distance apart. They stood facing each other, and the first one said to the other, "Why do you imitate me? This is spiritual paint." The second said, "Mine also is spiritual paint." The game had stopped and all the players were listening.

The first man said, "Who gave you your spiritual paint, and where did you get it?" The other replied, "Who gave you yours?" The first man pointed to the spring and said, "My paint came from there" (meaning that at the spring he was instructed to paint himself in that way). The other said, "Mine also came from the spring." Then the first man said,

"Let us do something for the hunters, the old men, old women, young women, girls and boys." And the second said, "Yes, let us do so." By this time every one in the camp was listening. So the first man said again, "Soldiers of all societies, every one of you shall feel happy this day," and the other said, "Yes, you shall all feel happy this very day." The first speaker walked toward the spring, and the other followed close behind him. When he came to the spring, he covered his head with his robe and plunged under the water into the opening out of which the spring came. His friend followed him closely and did the same thing. All the people in the camp watched them and saw them go in.

The first man came up under the spring, and there under the knoll sat a very old woman. As he stepped in, she said to him, "Come in, my grandchild." She took him in her arms; held him for a few minutes and made him sit down at her left side. As the other man came in, she said again, "Come in, my grandchild." She took him in her arms, held him for a minute, and set him on her right side. Then she said to both of them, "Why have you not come sooner? why have you gone hungry so long? now that you have come here, I must do something for your people." She had near her two old-fashioned earthen jars. She brought them out and set them down before her and also brought out two earthen dishes; one was filled with buffalo meat, and one with corn. She said, "Come, my children; eat the meat first." They ate it very fast, for it was very good; but, when they had eaten all they could, the dish was still full; it was the same way with the corn. They could not empty the dishes; they were full when the men stopped. They were both satisfied, but the dishes did not show that they had been touched.

The old woman untied the feathers they had on their heads, and threw them in the fire. She painted each man with red paint; striped him, and repainted his wrists and ankles, and the sun and moon, yellow; then she stretched her hand out over the fire and brought out two down feathers painted red and tied them to their scalp-locks. After that, she pointed to her left and said, "Look that way." They looked and could see the earth covered with buffalo. The dust was flying up in clouds where the bulls were fighting. Then she said, "Look this way" (pointing partly behind her), and they saw immense cornfields. She said, "Look that way" (pointing to the right), and they saw the prairie covered with horses. The stallions were fighting and there was much movement. She said, "Look that way again," and they saw Indians fighting. They looked closely, and among the fighters recognized themselves, painted just as they were then. She said, "You will always be victorious in your fights; you will have good fortune, and make many captives. When you go away from here, go to the centre of your village; call for two big bowls and have them wiped out clean. Say to your people, women and children and all the bands of the societies, 'We have come out to make you happy; we have brought out something wonderful to give you.' Tell your people that when the sun goes down I will send out buffalo." To each of the young men she gave some corn tied up in sacks and told them to divide this seed among the people. She told them to take some of the meat from the dish with one hand and some corn with the other, and sent them away. So they passed out of her lodge and came out of the water of the spring.

All the people of the village were sitting in a circle watching the spring. The two young men walked on together to the centre of the village, where the one who had first appeared said, "Old men, old women, young men, young girls, I have brought out something that is wonderful. Soldiers, I have brought out something wonderful for you. When the sun goes down, the buffalo will come out." The other young man repeated these words. The first man stood ahead, and the other right behind him. The first man said, "I want two wooden bowls, but they must be clean." A young man ran to the right and another to the left to get the bowls. They set one down on each side of him, and with his right hand he put the meat in the right-hand bowl, and with his left hand he put the corn into the left-hand bowl. The bowls became half full. The other man did the same, and the bowls were filled.

Just before leaving the old woman, she had said, "The medicine hunter is to eat first," so the medicine hunter performed the ceremony of *niv-stan-i-vo*—making a sacrifice of a piece of the meat at the four points of the compass—and the first man said to him, "Eat all you can."

The old woman had told them that the oldest men and women were to eat first. They all ate, first of the meat and then of the corn; then the young men, young women, and the children ate, but the pile in each dish remained nearly the same. After that the people in the camp ate all they could, and after all had eaten there was but little left. At the last came two orphans, a boy and a girl; they both ate, and when they had finished the meat was all gone and also the corn. It was just as the young men had said, every one was happy, for now they had plenty to eat.

As the sun went down, all the village began to look toward the spring. After a time, as they watched, they saw a four-year-old bull leap out. He ran a little distance and began to paw the ground, and then turned about and ran back and plunged into the spring. After he had gone back, a great herd of buffalo came pouring out of the spring and all night long they could hear them. No one went to sleep that night, for the buffalo made too much noise. Next morning at sunrise the earth, as far as they could see, was covered with buffalo. That day the medicine hunters went out and brought in all the meat they could eat.

The village camped there all winter and never lacked food. Toward spring they sent out two young men to look for moist ground to plant the seed in, for the old woman had told them that it must be planted in a damp place. They divided the corn seed; every one got some, for there was enough for all. They made big caches in the earth to hold the meat they had dried, and then went to the place the young men had found and planted the seed. They made holes with sticks and put the seed in the ground. Sometimes when they were planting the corn they would go back to get their dried meat, for the buffalo had moved to another place. Once, when they returned with their dried meat, they found that some of the seed had been stolen, and they thought that it was the Pawnees or the Arickarees—and that was the way these tribes got their corn.

Cheyenne

ORIGIN CHANT OF THE THO-XE GENS

The people spake to one another, saying: Lo, the little ones are not a people,

Let search be made by the younger brothers for a place where the little ones may become
    a people.

Even as these words were being spoken, a younger brother

Hastened to the first division of heaven,

Close to which he came and paused,

When, returning to the elder brothers, he spake, saying:

Verily, nothing of importance has come to my notice.

Make further search, O younger brothers, the people said,

The little ones are not a people.

Then, a younger brother,

Even as these words were being spoken,

Hastened to the second division of heaven, where he paused,

When, as the god of darkness cast a shadow upon the heavens,

He returned to the eldest brothers and stood.

They looked up and spake, saying: How has it fared with you? It was not your wont to suffer
    so, O younger brother.

He replied: I have been to the second division of heaven.

It is not possible for the little ones to become a people there.

O Younger brother,

We bid you make further search, the people said.

Even as these words were being spoken,

One hastened to the third division of heaven,

He drew near and paused.

The younger brother,

As the god of darkness cast a shadow upon the heavens,

Returned to the elder brothers and stood.

The elder brothers spake: How has it fared with you? It was not your wont to suffer so.

The younger brother replied: It is impossible!

O younger brother, the people said,

We bid you make further search.

Then a younger brother

Hastened to the

Fourth division of heaven.

Close to it he came and paused.

Then the Man of Mystery, the god of the clouds,

Drew near and stood before him.

The younger brother turned to the elder brothers and said: Here stands a man!
A fear-inspiring man!
His name, I verily believe, is Fear-inspiring.
The people spake to him, saying: O, grandfather!
The Man of Mystery replied: I am a person of whom your little ones may make their bodies.
When they make of me their bodies,
They shall cause themselves to be deathless.
Little-hawk
They shall take for their personal name,
Then shall they always live to see old age.
Hawk-maiden, also,
Is a name that is mine.
That name also
Your little ones shall take to be their name,
Then shall they always live to see old age.

O younger brother! the people said,
And the younger brother went in haste
To the Thó-xe *(the Buffalo-bull)*,
Close to whom he stood and spake, saying:
O grandfather!

Then to the elder brothers he said: Here stands a man!
A fear-inspiring man!
The Thó-xe spake: I am a person of whom the little ones may make their bodies.
Whereupon he threw himself to the ground,
Then up sprang the blazing star,
From the earth where it stood in all its beauty, pleasing to look upon.
Thó-xe spake, saying: Of this plant also the little ones may make their bodies.
The people tasted the root of the plant,
And exclaimed: It is bitter to the taste!
Thó-xe spake, saying: This plant shall be medicine to the little ones.
When they use it as medicine,
Their arms shall lengthen in growth,
And they shall live to see old age.
Again Thó-xe threw himself upon the ground,
And the poppy mallow
Sprang from the earth and stood resplendent in its reddened blossoms.

Of this plant also Thó-xe said,
The little ones shall make their bodies.

When they use it as medicine,
Their arms shall lengthen in growth.
The root is astringent,
And, referring thereto, your little ones shall take the name Astringent.
When the little ones make of this plant their bodies,
They shall always live to see old age.

Thó-xe,
Threw himself to the ground,
And a red ear of maize
He tossed in the air,
As he exclaimed: The little ones shall make of this their bodies!
Then shall they always live to see old age.

Again Thó-xe threw himself to the ground,
And a blue ear of maize,
Together with a blue squash,
He tossed in the air as he said:
These plants, also,
Shall be food for the little ones,
Then shall they live to see old age.

A third time he threw himself to the ground,
And a white ear of maize,
Together with a white squash he tossed in the air,
As he exclaimed: These plants also shall be food for the little ones!
Then shall they be difficult for death to overcome them,
And they shall always live to see old age.

A fourth time he threw himself to the ground,
And a speckled ear of maize,
Together with a speckled squash,
He tossed in the air as he exclaimed:
What creature is there that would be without a mate?
And he wedded together the maize and the squash,
Then exclaimed: These also shall be food for the little ones!
And they shall be difficult for death to overcome them.

Osage

THE BIRTH OF MANABUSH

THERE WAS AN OLD WOMAN, named Nokomis, who had an unmarried daughter. The daughter gave birth to twin boys, one of whom died, as did also the mother.

Nokomis then wrapped the living child in soft, dry grass, laid it on the ground at the extreme end of her wigwam, and placed over it a wooden bowl to protect it. She then took the body of her daughter and the other grandchild and buried them at some distance from her habitation. When she returned to the wigwam, she sat down and mourned for four days; but at the expiration of the fourth day she heard a slight noise within the wigwam, which she soon found to come from the wooden bowl. The bowl moved, when she suddenly remembered that her living grandchild had been put under it. Upon removing the bowl she beheld a little white rabbit, with quivering ears, and on taking it up said: "O, my dear little Rabbit, my Manabush!" She cherished it, and it grew. One day the Rabbit sat up on its haunches and hopped slowly across the floor of the wigwam, which caused the earth to tremble. Then the evil underground beings said to one another: "What has happened? A great spirit is born somewhere," and they immediately began to devise means whereby Manabush might be destroyed.

When Manabush grew to be a young man he thought it time to prepare himself to assist the people to better their condition. He then said to Nokomis, "Grandmother, make me four sticks, that I may be able to sing." She made for him four sticks with which he could beat time when singing. When he received these sticks he went away to an open flat place, where he built a long house or wigwam. He then began to sing: "I am born to create animals for my uncles. I can create my fire that the sparks may reach the sky. My arrow I am going to take out, so that while the earth stands there will be enough to eat."

While thus singing and calling together his uncles (the people) he told them that he would give them the Mitawit, so that they could cure disease. He gave them plants for food so that they should no longer want for anything. He gave them medicine bags, made of the skins of the mink, the weasel, the black rattlesnake, the massasauga rattlesnake, and the panther. Into each of these he put samples of all the medicines, and taught their use. Manabush lived for many years after this, and taught his uncles how to do many useful things.

Menomini

THE ORIGIN OF THE THUNDER-BIRD CLAN

IN THE BEGINNING Earth-Maker was sitting in space, when he came to consciousness; and nothing else was there, anywhere. He began to think of what he should do; and finally he began to cry, and tears began to flow from his eyes and fall down below him. After a while, he looked below him, and saw something bright. The bright objects were his tears, that had flowed below and formed the present waters. When the tears flowed below, they became the seas as they are now. Earth-Maker began to think again. He thought, "It is thus: if I wish anything, it will become as I wish, just as my tears have become seas." Thus he thought. So he wished for light, and it became light. Then he thought, "It is as I supposed, the things that I wished for, came into existence, as I desired."

Then he again thought, and wished for the earth, and this earth came into existence. Earth-Maker looked on the earth, and he liked it; but it was not quiet, it moved about, as do the waves of the seas. Then he made the trees, and he saw that they were good, but they did not make the earth quiet. Then he made the grass to grow, but the earth was not quiet yet. Then he made the rocks and stones, but still the earth was not quiet. However, it was nearly quiet. Then he made the four directions (cardinal points) and the four winds. On the four corners of the earth he placed them as great and powerful people, to act as island-weights. Yet the earth was not quiet. Then he made four large beings and threw them down toward the earth, and they pierced through the earth with their heads eastwards. They were snakes. Then the earth became very still and quiet. Then he looked upon the earth, and he saw that it was good. Then he thought again of how things came into existence just as he desired.

Then he first began to talk. He said, "As things become just as I wish them, I shall make one in my own likeness." So he took a piece of clay (earth) and made it like himself. Then he talked to what he had created, but it did not answer. He looked upon it, and saw that it had no mind or thought; so he made a mind for it. Again he talked to it, but it did not answer; so he looked upon it again, and he saw that it had no tongue. Then he made it a tongue. Then he talked to it again, but it did not answer; and he looked upon it, and he saw that it had no soul; so he made it a soul. He talked to it again, and this time it very nearly said something. But it did not make itself intelligible, so Earth-Maker breathed into its mouth and talked to it, and it answered.

As the newly-created being was in his own likeness, Earth-Maker felt quite proud of him, so he made three more just like him. He made them powerful, so that they might watch over the earth. These first four he made chiefs of the Thunder-Birds; and he thought, "Some will I make to live upon the earth that I have made." So he made four more beings in his own likeness. Just like the others he made them. They were brothers, Kunuga, Henanga, Hakaga and Nangiga. He talked to them, and said, "Look down upon the earth." So saying, he opened the heavens in front of where they sat, and there they saw the earth (spread out below them). He told them that they were to go down there to live. "And this I shall send with you," he added, and he gave them a plant. "I myself shall not have any power to take this from you, as I have given it to you, but when, of your own free will, you make me an offering of some of it, I shall gladly accept it and give you what you ask. This shall you hold foremost in your lives." It was a tobacco-plant that he had given them.

He said also, "All the spirits that I create will not be able to take this from you unless you desire to give it by calling upon them during fasts and offering it to them. Thus only can the spirits get any of it. And this also I send with you, that you may use it in life. When you offer anything, it shall be your mediator. It shall take care of you through life. It shall stand in the centre of your dwellings, and it shall be your grandfather." Thus he spoke to them. What he meant was the fire. And then he gave them the earth to live on. So the four thunder-spirits brought the four brothers down to the earth. The oldest one, Kunu, said while on their way down, "Brother, when we get to the earth and the first child is born to me, I shall call him King (chief) of the Thunders, if it be a boy." On they came down towards the earth. When they got near the earth, it began to get very dark. Then the second brother said, "Brother, when we get to the earth and a child is born to me, if it is a girl, it shall be called Dark." They came to a place called Within-Lake at Red Banks, a lake near Green Bay. On an oak-tree south of the lake is the place where they alighted. The branch they alighted on bent down from their weight. Then said the third brother to his brothers, "The first daughter born to me shall be called She-who-weighs-the-Tree-Down-Woman." Then they alighted on earth, but the thunder-spirits did not touch the earth. Then said the fourth and last brother to his brothers, "Brothers, the first son that is born to me shall be called He-who-alights-on-the-Earth." The first thing they did on earth was to start their fire.

Then Earth-Maker looked down upon them, and saw that he had not prepared any food for them, so he made the animals, that they might have something to eat. The oldest brother said, "What are we going to eat?" Then the youngest two took the bow and arrows that Earth-Maker had given them, and started towards the east. Not long after, the third brother came into view with a young deer on his back; and the youngest brother also came with a young deer about two years old on his back. The deer that were killed were brothers, and those that killed them were also brothers. They were very much delighted that they had obtained food. Then said they, "Let us give our grandfather the first taste." Saying thus, they cut off the ends of the tongues, and the heart, and threw them into the fire with some fat. The first people to call on them were the War-People. They came from the west. Then came four others. They were the Thunders. Thus they were called, the youngest brothers. Then came those of the Earth. Then came those of the Deer Clan. Then came those of the Snake Clan. Then came those of the Elk Clan. Then came those of the Bear Clan. Then came those of the Fish Clan. Then came those of the Water-Spirit Clan, and all the other clans that exist. Then there appeared on the lake a very white bird, Swan they called it; and after that, all the other water-birds that exist came. And they named them in the order of their coming, until the lake was quite full. Then the people began to dress the deer-meat. Suddenly something came and alighted on the deer-meat. "What is that?" they said. Then said Kunuga, the oldest brother, "It is a wasp; and the first dog that I possess, if it is black, Wasp I shall call it." Thus he spoke. "And as the wasp scented and knew of the deer-dressing, so shall the dog be towards other animals; and wherever the dog is, and animals are in the windward, he shall scent them." They made a feast with the deer for Earth-Maker, and threw tobacco into the fire and offered it to him. And to the other clans they showed how fire was to be made, and gave them some. "For," they said, "each of you must now make fire for yourselves, as we shall not always lend you some." There the people made their home. It was just the time of year when the grass comes as far as the knee (summer).

38

One day they reported that something very strange was near the camp; but they said to themselves, "We will leave it alone." In a little while it moved nearer. Thus it moved toward the camp, and soon it began to eat deer-bones. They allowed it to become one of the clans, and took it into their house. It was the dog or wolf. They killed one of them, and made a feast to Earth-Maker, telling him all about what they had done. In the beginning the Thunder clansmen were as powerful as the thunder-spirits themselves. It was the Thunder-People who made the ravines and the valleys. While wandering around the world, the Thunder-People struck the earth with their clubs and made dents in the hills. That is the reason that the upper clans are chiefs of all the others, and that the least of all are the Dog-People. So it was.

One day the oldest of the brothers lay down and did not rise again, and he did not breathe, and he became cold. "What is the matter with our oldest brother?" the three others said. Four days they waited for him, but still he did not arise. So the second brother was asked by his youngest brother what the trouble was. But he did not know anything about it, and told him to ask his third brother; but he did not know, either. Then the two older brothers asked the youngest one; but he did not know, either. Then they began to mourn for him, not knowing what to do or think. They fasted and blackened their faces, as we do now when we are mourning. They made a platform and laid him on it. When the snow fell knee-deep, the three brothers filled their pipe and went towards the place of the coming of the daylight, the east. There they came to the first being that Earth-Maker had placed in the east, the Island-Weight, as he was called. They came to him weeping, and went into his tent, turning the stem of their pipe in his mouth. They said, "Grandfather, our brother has fallen, and is not able to rise again. Earth-Maker made you great, and endowed you with all knowledge, and thus you know all things." He answered, and said, "My dear grandsons, I am sorry, but I do not know anything about it; but as you have started to find out, I would refer you to the one ahead of me *(the north)*. Perhaps he can tell you."

So, weeping, they started for the next one. When they got there, and told him their troubles, he told them he could not help them. "But," he said, "perhaps the one ahead of me knows." So they started for the third one *(the west)*, but from him likewise they could learn nothing. He also referred them to the one ahead *(the south)*. When they reached the fourth and last one, they entered the lodge, and, behold! there sat the three to whom they had gone before. Here they asked the last one for help; and not only he, but the other three also, answered them, "Grandsons, thus Earth-Maker has willed it. Your brother will not rise again. He will be with you no more in this world. And as long as this world lasts, so it will be with human beings. Whenever one reaches the age of death, one shall die, and those that wish to live long will have to attain that age by good actions. Thus they will live long. Into your bodies Earth-Maker has placed part of himself. That will return to him if you do the proper things. This world will come to an end some time. Your brother shall keep a village in the west for all the souls of your clan, and there he shall be in full charge of all of you. And when this world is ended, your brother shall take all the souls back to Earth-

Maker; at least, all those who have acted properly. Thus it was. Now you may go home and bury your brother in the proper manner."

The Thunder-People thanked the four spirits and left their tent. When they got home, they took their brother's body, dressed him in his best clothes, and painted his face. Then they told him where he was to go, and buried him with his head toward the west, and with his war-club. They placed the branch of a tree at his grave, and painted a little stick red and tied it to the tree, so that nothing should cross his path on his journey to the spirit-abode.

Winnebago

2

THE FOREST AND THE RIVERS

FOR MANY YEARS the term Mound-builder signified some mysterious, long-vanished race which preceded the American Indian. Where they came from, where they went, no one knew, but there were many wild theories. We know now that the mounds were built by many different tribes of woodland Indians, some of them the ancestors of present-day Indians. Many of the mounds were built after the coming of the whites. DeSoto saw mound-building groups on his trip through the Gulf States in 1540. The mound-building area stretches from the Great Lakes, down the Mississippi Valley, to the Gulf of Mexico. It is indicated by cross-hatching on the map above.

The building of mounds is a Mexican trait. The art of the Mound-builder of the Southeast shows unmistakable Mexican influence. On the other hand, in the north, with Ohio an outstanding area, the Indian developed a purely regional style. But there, just to confuse the archaeologist, the finest known example of stone carving (Plate 11) is definitely a Mexican figure, both in feature and costume. The how and when of a Mexican invasion may someday be told. In the meantime we can admire the finest work in effigy pottery, stone, shell, and metal to be found north of Mexico.

Traveling other Eastern Woodland trails and rivers, we come to names familiar to us in United States history—Pocahontas, Massasoit—whose people met the first colonists from northern Europe. We meet the legendary Hiawatha. The eastern seaboard was the most densely populated region of North America; the home of many tribes speaking many languages. Caught between the rivalries of the English, Dutch, and French, most of the tribes were either exterminated or, later, moved west to reservations. The work shown on

Plates 14-16 is the work of Southeastern tribes who are still carrying on some of their arts. They are no longer living in their original homes but on Middle-Western reservations.

In the north the Algonquins around the Great Lakes and the Iroquois of New York State and Canada were able to hold their ground; the Iroquois largely because of the strength of their League of the Six Nations. In the south the tribes, with the exception of the Seminole who fled to the Florida swamps, met the same fate as the northern tribes.

The Eastern Woodland tribes were hunters, farmers and fishermen. They raised corn, beans, squash and melons; in the south, tobacco. Their villages, fortified with palisades, were scattered through the forest. The Iroquois lived in long houses, built with gabled frames of poles covered over with bark. The Algonquins lived in wigwams and dome-shaped or conical huts covered with bark, matting or grass. Both groups used birch-bark canoes. Coastal groups used dugouts. The southern tribes lived in rectangular huts with curved roofs, or circular huts either with open sides or plaster walls reinforced with wicker-work. As in the north, the villages were fortified. Until the coming of the whites all the woodland groups wore hides for clothing.

With so many different tribes, scattered from Canada to Florida, there is naturally a great diversity in their crafts. In the north, moosehair embroidery, quill and beadwork on skins, bark and cloth were highly developed. Woodcarving was practiced, the best known work being the Iroquois masks. The famous wampum belts were made of shells strung on bark threads. Wampum beads are small cylindrical beads made from the hard-shell clam and fresh water shells. In trading, they were used either in strings or loose. They were used also in ornaments such as necklaces and arm-bands. The belts were used to record important events or to ratify treaties. White beads used alone conveyed peace; purple beads used alone denoted death, or hostility. White beads dyed red denoted war. "The Origin and Use of Wampum," a story from Maine, on page 55, tells something of wampum symbolism.

Pottery making was widely distributed in this area. Vessels were unpainted, the designs incised. Bark vessels were also used; the designs were formed by the use of bark stencils and by scraping away the dark coating of the outer bark. Silverwork was carried on for a short time; the metal was obtained from the whites. Ribbonwork is still produced.

In the south we find woven fabrics (downward weaving) made of bark fiber; feather cloaks, and baskets of cane and splint. Pottery, stamped, incised, and painted, was more developed than in the north. The characteristic scroll designs of the potter were carried over to the later beadwork.

The life and beliefs of these woodland people are well described (by themselves) in the selection of myths and legends which follows. The reader will note their dependence on corn, their reverence for the powers which gave them fire, and the awe in which they stood before the darker manifestations of nature—snow and ice and cold. The healing significance of the famous Iroquois masks is explained in the myth of the Earth Grasper.

42

THE CREATION OF THE EARTH

IN THE BEGINNING the waters covered everything. It was said "Who will make the land appear?"

Lock-chew, the Crawfish, said: "I will make the land appear."

So he went down to the bottom of the water and began to stir up the mud with his tail and hands. He then brought up the mud to a certain place and piled it up.

The owners of the land at the bottom of the water said:

"Who is disturbing our land?" They kept watch and discovered the Crawfish. Then they came near him, but he suddenly stirred the mud with his tail so that they could not see him.

Lock-chew continued his work. He carried mud and piled it up until at last he held up his hands in the air, and so the land appeared above the water.

The land was soft. It was said: "Who will spread out the land and make it dry and hard?" Some said: "Ah-yok, the Hawk, should spread out the soft land and make it dry." Others said "Yah-tee, the Buzzard, has larger wings; he can spread out the land and make it dry and hard."

Yah-tee undertook to spread out and dry the earth. He flew above the earth and spread out his long wings over it. He sailed over the earth; he spread it out. After a long while he grew tired of holding out his wings. He began to flap them, and thus he caused the hills and valleys because the dirt was still soft.

"Who will make the light?" it was said. It was very dark.

Yohah, the Star, said, "I will make the light."

It was so agreed. The Star shone forth. It was light only near him.

"Who will make more light?" it was said.

Shar-pah, the Moon, said: "I will make more light." Shar-pah made more light, but it was still dark.

T-cho, the Sun, said: "You are my children, I am your mother, I will make the light. I will shine for you."

She went to the east. Suddenly light spread over all the earth. As she passed over the earth a drop of blood fell from her to the ground, and from this blood and earth sprang the first people, the children of the Sun, the Uchees.

The people wished to find their medicine. A great monster serpent destroyed the people. They cut his head from his body. The next day the body and head were together. They again slew the monster. His head again grew to his body.

Then they cut off his head and placed it on top of a tree, so that the body could not reach it. The next morning the tree was dead and the head was united to the body. They again severed it and put it upon another tree. In the morning the tree was dead and the head and body were reunited.

The people continued to try all the trees in the forest. At last they placed the head over the Tar, the cedar tree, and in the morning the head was dead. The cedar was alive, but covered with blood, which had trickled down from the head.

Thus the Great Medicine was found.

Fire was made by boring with a stick into a hard weed.

The people selected a second family. Each member of this family had engraved on his door a picture of the sun.

In the beginning all the animals could talk, and but one language was used. All were at peace. The deer lived in a cave, watched over by a keeper and the people were hungry. He selected a deer and killed it. But finally the deer were set free and roved over the entire earth.

All animals were set free from man, and names were given to them, so that they could be known.

Yuchi

THE FIRST FIRE

IN THE BEGINNING there was no fire, and the world was cold, until the Thunders sent their lightning and put fire into the bottom of a hollow sycamore tree which grew on an island. The animals knew it was there, because they could see the smoke coming out at the top, but they could not get to it on account of the water, so they held a council to decide what to do. This was a long time ago.

Every animal that could fly or swim was anxious to go after the fire. The Raven offered, and because he was so large and strong they thought he could surely do the work, so he was sent first. He flew high and far across the water and alighted on the sycamore tree, but while he was wondering what to do next, the heat had scorched all his feathers black, and he was frightened and came back without the fire. The little Screech Owl volunteered to go, and reached the place safely, but while he was looking down into the hollow tree a blast of hot air came up and nearly burned out his eyes. He managed to fly home as best he could, but it was a long time before he could see well, and his eyes are red to this day. Then the Hooting Owl and the Horned Owl went, but by the time they got to the hollow tree the fire was burning so fiercely that the smoke nearly blinded them, and the ashes carried up by the wind made white rings about their eyes. They had to come home again without the fire, but with all their rubbing they were never able to get rid of the white rings.

Now no more of the birds would venture, and so the little Uksu'hi snake, the black racer, said he would go through the water and bring back some fire. He swam across to the island and crawled through the grass to the tree, and went in by a small hole at the bottom. The heat and smoke were too much for him, too, and after dodging about blindly over the hot ashes until he was almost on fire himself he managed by good luck to get out again at the same hole, but his body had been scorched black, and he has ever since had the habit of darting and doubling on his track as if trying to escape from close quarters. He came back, and the great blacksnake, Gule'gi, "The Climber," offered to go for fire. He swam over to the island and climbed up the tree on the outside, as the blacksnake always does, but when he put his head down into the hole the smoke choked him so that he fell into the burning stump, and before he could climb out again he was as black as the Uksu'hi.

Now they held another council, for still there was no fire, and the world was cold, but birds, snakes, and four-footed animals, all had some excuse for not going, because they were all afraid to venture near the burning sycamore, until at last the Water Spider said she would go. This is not the water spider that looks like a mosquito, but the other one, with black downy hair and red stripes on her body. She can run on top of the water or dive to the bottom, so there would be no trouble to get over to the island, but the question was, how could she bring back the fire? "I'll manage that," said the Water Spider; so she spun a thread from her body and wove it into a *tusti* bowl, which she fastened on her back. Then she crossed over to the island and through the grass to where the fire was still burning. She put one little coal of fire into her bowl, and came back with it, and ever since we have had fire, and the Water Spider still keeps her *tusti* bowl.

Cherokee

THE ORIGIN OF GAME AND CORN

WHEN I WAS A BOY this is what the old men told me they had heard when they were boys.

Long years ago, soon after the world was made, a hunter and his wife lived at Pilot Knob with their only child, a little boy. The father's name was Kana'ti (The Lucky Hunter), and his wife was called Selu (Corn). No matter when Kana'ti went into the wood, he never failed to bring back a load of game, which his wife would cut up and prepare, washing off the blood from the meat in the river near the house. The little boy used to play down by the river every day, and one morning the old people thought they heard laughing and talking in the bushes as though there were two children there. When the boy came home at night his parents asked him who had been playing with him all day. "He comes out of the water," said the boy, "and he calls himself my elder brother. He says his mother was cruel to him and threw him into the river." Then they knew that the strange boy had sprung from the blood of the game which Selu had washed off at the river's edge.

Every day when the little boy went out to play the other would join him, but as he always went back again into the water the old people never had a chance to see him. At last one evening Kana'ti said to his son, "Tomorrow, when the other boy comes to play, get him to wrestle with you, and when you have your arms around him hold on to him and call for us." The boy promised to do as he was told, so the next day as soon as his playmate appeared he challenged him to a wrestling match. The other agreed at once, but as soon as they had their arms around each other, Kana'ti's boy began to scream for his father.

The old folks at once came running down, and as soon as the Wild Boy saw them he struggled to free himself and cried out, "Let me go; you threw me away!" but his brother held on until the parents reached the spot, when they seized the Wild Boy and took him home with them. They kept him in the house until they had tamed him, but he was always wild and artful in his disposition, and was the leader of his brother in every mischief. It was not long until the old people discovered that he had magic powers, and they called him I'nage-utasun'hi (He-who-grew-up-wild).

Whenever Kana'ti went into the mountains he always brought back a fat buck or doe, or maybe a couple of turkeys. One day the Wild Boy said to his brother, "I wonder where our father gets all that game; let's follow him next time and find out." A few days afterward Kana'ti took a bow and some feathers in his hand and started off toward the west. The boys waited a little while and then went after him, keeping out of sight until they saw him go into a swamp where there were a great many of the small reeds that hunters use to make arrowshafts. Then the Wild Boy changed himself into a puff of bird's down, which the wind took up and carried until it alighted upon Kana'ti's shoulder just as he entered the swamp, but Kana'ti knew nothing about it. The old man cut reeds, fitted the feathers to them and made some arrows, and the Wild Boy—in his other shape—thought, "I wonder what those things are for?" When Kana'ti had his arrows finished he came out of the swamp and went on again. The wind blew the down from his shoulder, and it fell in the woods, when the Wild Boy took his right shape again and went back and told his brother what he had seen. Keeping out of sight of their father, they followed him up the mountain until he stopped at a certain place and lifted a large rock. At once there ran out a buck, which Kana'ti shot, and then lifting it upon his back he started for home again. "Oho!" exclaimed the boys, "he keeps all the deer shut up in that hole, and whenever he wants meat he just lets one out and kills it with those things he made in the swamp." They hurried and reached home before their father, who had the heavy deer to carry, and he never knew that they had followed.

A few days later the boys went back to the swamp, cut some reeds, and made seven arrows, and then started up the mountain to where their father kept the game. When they got to the place, they raised the rock and a deer came running out. Just as they drew back to shoot it, another came out, and then another and another, until the boys got confused and forgot what they were about. In those days all the deer had their tails hanging down like other animals, but as a buck was running past the Wild Boy struck its tail with his arrow so that it pointed upward. The boys thought this good sport, and when the next one ran past the Wild Boy struck its tail so that it stood straight up, and his brother struck the next one so hard with his arrow that the deer's tail was almost curled over his back. The deer carries his tail this way ever since. The deer came running past until the last one had come out of the hole and escaped into the forest. Then came droves of raccoons, rabbits, and all the other four-footed animals—all but the bear, because there was no bear then. Last came great flocks of turkeys, pigeons, and partridges that darkened the air like a cloud and made such a noise with their wings that Kana'ti, sitting at home, heard the sound like distant thunder on the mountains and said to himself, "My bad boys have got into trouble; I must go and see what they are doing."

So he went up the mountain, and when he came to the place where he kept the game he found the two boys standing by the rock, and all the birds and animals were gone. Kana'ti was furious, but without saying a word he went down into the cave and kicked the covers off four jars in one corner, when out swarmed bedbugs, fleas, lice, and gnats, and got all over the boys. They screamed with pain and fright and tried to beat off the insects, but the thousands of vermin crawled over them and bit and stung them until both dropped down nearly dead. Kana'ti stood looking on until he thought they had been punished enough, when he knocked off the vermin and made the boys a talk. "Now," said he, "you have always had plenty to eat and never had to work for it. Whenever you were hungry all I had to do was to come up here and get a deer or a turkey and bring it home for your mother to cook; but now you have let out all the animals, and after this when you want a deer to eat you will have to hunt all over the woods for it, and then maybe not find one. Go home now to your mother, while I see if I can find something to eat for supper."

When the boys got home again they were very tired and hungry and asked their mother for something to eat. "There is no meat," said Selu, "but wait a little while and I'll get you something." So she took a basket and started out to the storehouse. This storehouse was built upon poles high up from the ground, to keep it out of the reach of animals, and there was a ladder to climb up by, and one door, but no other opening. Every day when Selu got ready to cook the dinner she would go out to the storehouse with a basket and bring it back full of corn and beans. The boys had never been inside the storehouse, and so they wondered where all the corn and beans could come from, as the house was not a very large one; so as soon as Selu went out of the door the Wild Boy said to his brother, "Let's go and see what she does." They ran around and climbed up at the back of the storehouse and pulled out a piece of clay from between the logs, so that they could look in. There they saw Selu standing in the middle of the room with the basket in front of her on the floor. Leaning over the basket, she rubbed her stomach—so—and the basket was half full of corn. Then she rubbed under her armpits—so—and the basket was full to the top with beans. The boys looked at each other and said, "This will never do; our mother is a witch. If we eat any of that it will poison us. We must kill her."

When the boys came back into the house, she knew their thoughts before they spoke. "So you are going to kill me?" said Selu. "Yes," said the boys, "you are a witch." "Well," said their mother, "when you have killed me, clear a large piece of ground in front of the house and drag my body seven times around the circle. Then drag me seven times over the ground inside the circle, and stay up all night and watch, and in the morning you will have plenty of corn." The boys killed her with their clubs, and cut off her head and put it up on the roof of the house with her face turned to the west, and told her to look for her husband. Then they set to work to clear the ground in front of the house, but instead of clearing the whole piece they cleared only seven little spots. This is why corn now grows only in a few places instead of over the whole world. They dragged the body of Selu around the circle, and wherever her blood fell on the ground the corn sprang up. But instead of dragging her body seven times across the ground they dragged it over only twice, which is the reason the Indians still work their crop but twice. The two brothers sat up and watched their corn all night, and in the morning it was full grown and ripe.

When Kana'ti came home at last, he looked around, but could not see Selu anywhere, and asked the boys where was their mother. "She was a witch, and we killed her," said the boys; "there is her head up there on top of the house." When he saw his wife's head on the roof, he was very angry, and said, "I won't stay with you any longer; I am going to the Wolf people." So he started off, but before he had gone far the Wild Boy changed himself again to a tuft of down, which fell on Kana'ti's shoulder. When Kana'ti reached the settlement of the Wolf people, they were holding a council in the townhouse. He went in and sat down with the tuft of bird's down on his shoulder, but he never noticed it. When the Wolf chief asked him his business, he said: "I have two bad boys at home, and I want you to go in seven days from now and play ball against them." Although Kana'ti spoke as though he wanted them to play a game of ball, the Wolves knew that he meant for them to go and kill the two boys. They promised to go. Then the bird's down blew off from Kana'ti's shoulder, and the smoke carried it up through the hole in the roof of the townhouse. When it came down on the ground outside, the Wild Boy took his right shape again and went home and told his brother all that he had heard in the townhouse. But when Kana'ti left the Wolf people, he did not return home, but went on farther.

The boys then began to get ready for the Wolves, and the Wild Boy—the magician—told his brother what to do. They ran around the house in a wide circle until they had made a trail all around it excepting on the side from which the Wolves would come, where they left a small open space. Then they made four large bundles of arrows and placed them at four different points on the outside of the circle, after which they hid themselves in the woods and waited for the Wolves. In a day or two a whole party of Wolves came and surrounded the house to kill the boys. The Wolves did not notice the trail around the house, because they came in where the boys had left the opening, but the moment they went inside the circle the trail changed to a high brush fence and shut them in. Then the boys on the outside took their arrows and began shooting them down, and as the Wolves could not jump over the fence they were all killed, excepting a few that escaped through the opening into a great swamp close by. The boys ran around the swamp, and a circle of fire sprang up in their tracks and set fire to the grass and bushes and burned up nearly all the other Wolves. Only two or three got away, and from these have come all the wolves that are now in the world.

Soon afterward some strangers from a distance, who had heard that the brothers had a wonderful grain from which they made bread, came to ask for some, for none but Selu and her family had ever known corn before. The boys gave them seven grains of corn, which they told them to plant the next night on their way home, sitting up all night to watch the corn, which would have seven ripe ears in the morning. These they were to plant the next night and watch in the same way, and so on every night until they reached home, when they would have corn enough to supply the whole people. The strangers lived seven days' journey away. They took the seven grains and watched all through the darkness until morning, when they saw seven tall stalks, each stalk bearing a ripened ear. They gathered the ears and went on their way. The next night they planted all their corn, and guarded it as before until daybreak, when they found an abundant increase. But the way was long and the sun was hot, and the people grew tired. On the last night before reaching home they fell asleep, and in the morning the corn they had planted had not even sprouted. They brought with them to their settlement what corn they had left and planted it, and with care and attention were able to raise a crop. But ever since the corn must be watched and tended through half the year, which before would grow and ripen in a night.

As Kana'ti did not return, the boys at last concluded to go and find him. The Wild Boy took a gaming wheel and rolled it toward the Darkening Land. In a little while the wheel came rolling back, and the boys knew their father was not there. He rolled it to the south and to the north, and each time the wheel came back to him, and they knew their father was not there. Then he rolled it toward the Sunland, and it did not return. "Our father is there," said the Wild Boy, "let us go and find him." So the two brothers set off toward the east, and after traveling a long time they came upon Kana'ti walking along with a little dog by his side. "You bad boys," said their father, "have you come here?" "Yes," they answered, "we always accomplish what we start out to do—we are men." "This dog overtook me four days ago," then said Kana'ti, but the boys knew that the dog was the wheel which they had sent after him to find him. "Well," said Kana'ti, "as you have found me, we may as well travel together, but I shall take the lead."

Soon they came to a swamp, and Kana'ti told them there was something dangerous there and they must keep away from it. He went on ahead, but as soon as he was out of sight the Wild Boy said to his brother, "Come and let us see what is in the swamp." They went in together, and in the middle of the swamp they found a large panther asleep. The Wild Boy got out an arrow and shot the panther in the side of the head. The panther turned his head and the other boy shot him on that side. He turned his head away again and the two brothers shot together—*tust, tust, tust!* But the panther was not hurt by the arrows and paid no more attention to the boys. They came out of the swamp and soon overtook Kana'ti, waiting for them. "Did you find it?" asked Kana'ti. "Yes," said the boys, "we found it, but it never hurt us. We are men." Kana'ti was surprised, but said nothing, and they went on again.

After a while he turned to them and said, "Now you must be careful. We are coming to a tribe called the *Anada'duntaski* ('Roasters,' i.e., cannibals), and if they get you they will put you in a pot and feast on you." Then he went on ahead. Soon the boys came to a tree which had been struck by lightning, and the Wild Boy directed his brother to gather some of the splinters from the tree and told him what to do with them. In a little while they came to the settlement of the cannibals, who, as soon as they saw the boys, came running out, crying, "Good, here are two nice fat strangers. Now we'll have a feast!" They caught the boys and dragged them into the townhouse, and sent word to all the people of the settlement to come to the feast. They made up a great fire, put water into a large pot and set it to boiling, and then seized the Wild Boy and put him down into it. His brother was not in the least frightened and made no attempt to escape, but quietly knelt down and began putting the splinters into the fire, as if to make it burn better. When the cannibals thought the meat was about ready they lifted the pot from the fire, and that instant a blinding light filled the townhouse, and the lightning began to dart from one side to the other, striking down the cannibals until not one of them was left alive. Then the lightning went up through the smoke-hole, and the next moment there were the two boys standing outside the town-house as though nothing had happened. They went on and soon met Kana'ti, who seemed much surprised to see them, and said, "What! are you here again?" "O, yes, we never give up. We are great men!" "What did the cannibals do to you?" "We met them and they brought us to their townhouse, but they never hurt us." Kana'ti said nothing more, and they went on.

He soon got out of sight of the boys, but they kept on until they came to the end of the world, where the sun comes out. The sky was just coming down when they got there, but they waited until it went up again, and then they went through and climbed up on the other side. There they found Kana'ti and Selu sitting together. The old folk received them kindly and were glad to see them, telling them they might stay there a while, but then they must go to live where the sun goes down. The boys stayed with their parents seven days and then went on toward the Darkening Land, where they are now. We call them *Anisga'ya Tsunsdi'* (The Little Men), and when they talk to each other we hear low rolling thunder in the west.

Cherokee

MAN'S ACQUISITION OF CORN

IN ANCIENT TIMES there was a village situated on the banks of a river. The chief source of food for the people was game and fish, berries and various edible roots.

There came a day when the people dwelling in this village were told by an old woman that she heard the voice of a woman singing on the river; and she told them further that the words used by this strange singer were: "Fair and fine are the planted fields where I dwell, going to and fro. Fair and fine are the planted fields which we have planted. My grandmother and my ancestors have planted them."

After hearing this singing for ten nights the old woman said to her family and neighbors: "Let us go out to see what this singing means. Perhaps some woman has fallen into the water, and it may be she who is singing in the middle of the river." They did go to the river bank, but saw nothing.

On the tenth night following, the woman again began to sing, seemingly from the middle of the river not very far from the village. Again she sang: "Fair and fine are the planted fields where I dwell, going to and fro. Fair and fine are the planted fields which we have planted. My grandmother and my ancestors have planted them." Then the women of the village, going to the river bank for three nights, sang songs of welcome and recognition. On the third night these women perceived that the singer on the river had drawn nearer to them. On the fourth night the women watching with their children on the river bank, and singing in response to the singing on the river, were surprised to see coming toward them a large number of women. Thereupon one of the girls exclaimed: "Oh, grandmother, do not let these women seize us," and the children fled from the place. But the spokeswoman, who was the eldest person present, said: "I alone shall remain here to await whatever may befall me, and I do so because my granddaughter, who is coming, is in need of pity and aid."

At this the midstream singer exclaimed: "Oh, my grandmother! take me hence. I am not able to go where you now are." Then the grandmother placed her canoe of birch bark in the stream and soon by rapid paddling reached the side of the young woman who had been singing in midstream. She found her lying on the back of a beaver, which held her above the water. The granddaughter was the first to speak, saying: "Oh, my grandmother! take me hence." The grandmother at once placed her granddaughter in the canoe, after which she headed for the shore of the stream, paddling to the landing place in a short time. When they had landed, the young woman said: "Oh, grandmother! now leave me here. I will remain here, and you must come after me in the morning. Nothing shall happen to me in the meantime." The grandmother at once returned to her own lodge, where she told what had taken place.

Early the next morning she returned to the landing place where she had left her granddaughter. There she saw only the growing stalk of a plant. Drawing near to this she found growing on the stalk an ear of corn, and breaking it off she carried it back to her lodge, where she hung it up on a roof-supporting pole by the fireplace.

It came to pass during the following night that the grandmother had a dream or vision, in which the young woman who had been singing in midstream said to her, "Oh, my grandmother, you should unhang me from this place. It is indeed too hot here. You should place me in the ground—plant me—and then leave me there. I will provide for you and your people. So kindly place me under the ground." This dream came to the old woman three nights in succession. So she took down the ear of corn, and after shelling it she planted the grains of corn in the ground just as she had been instructed to do by the dream.

But on the following night the grandmother again dreamed, and the young woman in the dream said to her, "You and your people must care for me. You must not permit weeds to kill me. You shall see me sprout and grow to maturity; and it is a truth that in the future all the people who shall be born will see that I will provide for their welfare. So you must take great care of me. You will see, you and your people, a great multitude of people who are about to arrive here. You will see, I say, that I will provide for all during the time the earth shall be in existence. You shall now learn what is a truth—that I am corn; I am native corn; I am sweet corn. I am the first corn that came or was delivered to this earth."

For three successive nights the grandmother had this same dream or vision. She came to regard it as a command to her regarding what she must do with the corn on the ear which she had found on the bank of the river. She planted the corn in the ground as directed. She followed carefully the directions of the Corn Maiden as to the care required by the growing corn to enable it to mature and to prevent it being choked to death by weeds.

In the autumn the old woman harvested her corn, and taking it into her lodge she divided it into as many portions as there were families in the village of her people. Then she gave a portion to the chief matron in each lodge, telling each that the corn should be used in the spring for seed and also how it should be planted and cultivated. Afterward she returned to her own lodge. She was very happy at the prospect of her people having something which would supply them with a regular food, if they would only properly care for it.

In a short time after reaching her own lodge she lay down on her couch to rest for the night; but she had hardly fallen asleep before she had another dream of the Corn Maiden. In this dream the Corn Maiden said to her: "You must tell my children that they must not waste in any manner the corn which shall grow to maturity in the future. It is well known that those who do not honor and properly care for me always come to want. Unless they act so toward me, when I leave I shall take all the corn and other seed away. And, grandmother, you must tell all these things to your people and kindred."

Seneca

MYTH OF THE EARTH GRASPER

NOW AT THAT TIME Earth Grasper turned himself around and he went toward a mountain standing in the distance. And there he met a man-being and that one said, "From whence do you come?" Then Earth Grasper said, "Yonder there floats an island. I come from there. I am going about to see what is taking place on the earth." Earth Grasper again spoke, and said another thing, "Now you have asked me, so now in my turn I ask you, from whence do you come?" The man-being said, "I come from the direction of the sun's setting, and I too am going about examining the earth. It is known that I myself possess it; I myself completed all."

Now at that time Earth Grasper said, "What then do they call you?" The man-being replied, "Hadui, I myself am called." (And the meaning of this name was Disease and Death.) The man-being Death said, "What do they call you?" "I am called He-Who-Grasps-The-Earth-With-Two-Hands. I completed the bodies of human beings who live on the earth. Now I wish to see how much power you have. For you continue to say, 'I myself have completed the earth present here.'"

Now at that time Hadui held a rattle which was made of the shell of the great turtle. Now he shook his rattle to cause it to give sounds; it made a loud sound. All the various kinds of animals which were traveling about were frightened.

Now at that time the Earth Grasper said, "Perhaps it would satisfy my mind to see that you could cause the mountain standing yonder in the distance to come hither; just to move itself hither."

Hadui said, "Thus it shall come to pass."

Hadui said, "Come. Let us two face about." They two now faced about. Both faced one certain way. Now at that time Hadui said, "Come! come hither, mountain standing yonder. You shall come close up to this place where we two stand, at our backs." Now at this time he said to the Earth Grasper, "Listen, you and I shall stop breathing as long as we can hold our breaths."

When they had held their breaths as long as they could, then Hadui said, "Come, now let us two face about again." So at that time they faced about. They saw that the mountain standing in the distance had changed its place but slightly.

Now at that time the Earth Grasper said, "It has become clear that you are not able to cause the mountain standing yonder to move hither. So it is not you who finished the earth here present. So now I myself, at this time, will cause the mountain yonder to move hither. The mountain standing yonder will move itself hither when I speak. Truly I myself completed the earth. So now let us two face about."

When his voice died away in saying, "Come hither, mountain standing yonder! Stand here at our backs," then they faced about. Now also he said, "Let us two hold our breaths. So it will be decided by the length of time you can hold your breath. That will decide it."

They kept still while they held their breaths. Then Hadui became aware that some kind of thing seemingly grazed against his back, so he turned around again; that is, he thought, "So, let me see what kind of thing is this that is taking place." And because he turned his head quickly in turning himself around, his face struck the mountain edge there. Then the Earth Grasper said, "Now, you and I will face about again." And the mountain stood at that very place—at their backs.

Now the Earth Grasper looked at Hadui and he saw that his nose had become twisted, also his mouth. And the Earth Grasper said, "Listen, I myself am master here on this earth. I myself have completed it."

Then Hadui said, "It is certain that you have great power. You were able to cause the mountain standing yonder to move hither. And I thought that I would see what manner of thing grazed my shoulder; so I turned around and I struck my face against the mountain standing there. Verily, then it became the truth to me that you finished the earth because you could control the standing mountain.

"It is true that you formed and completed all the things which the earth contains. So then I have decided at once to humble myself low before you. Have mercy on me, that I should continue to live humbly. You say that human beings are about to settle on the earth present here and it is true. I will give aid to your mankind.

"It is a fact that *orenda* (magic power) dwells in my flesh. I have infected with this *orenda* the earth present here. It is I who was the first to wander to and fro on the earth.

Soon it will be that human beings will be vexed by visions as they go to and fro here on the earth. The hunch-backed form of my body will be imitated. Their faces will be as my face is, when they become ill. Human beings will be bewitched as they go about from place to place.

"Because of me, they will recover health when they are ill. And I am going to say another thing. I believe that I shall be able to continue to aid the human beings whom you have formed. O-ha-a, your evil twin brother who hates your purposes, will try all manner of things in his attempts to destroy your work. That is why people shall become ill and people shall suffer in mind. It will result only in putting an end to the days of human beings. So then I will attempt to continue to aid human beings without ceasing. I will remove away illness, that they may still have some remaining days. But they must remember me in order that I should aid them. They must continue to call me, 'My Dear Grandfather.' And when customarily they will talk about me, then they must say, 'Our Dear Grandfather.' By that name shall human beings continue to designate me. So then I myself will continue to call them 'My Grandchildren.' "

Now then the Earth Grasper said, "I will accept your word that you will continue to aid mankind, and in the next place the game animals. Just one thing I think perhaps would not result in good; that you reveal yourself or your power to them. You would frighten them should they see you and your manner of doing."

Now at that time Hadui was pleased and now he said, "I accept. Now then I will tell you what shall come to pass. I shall dwell in the places where the ground is rough and there are stone cliffs; where there are tall rocks and also high banks. Then no one will see me; there I will continue to abide as long as the earth shall continue to be in this place. It is true that it would not result in good that the human beings whom you have formed should meet with me, and in the next place the game animals and all the kinds of things which grow on the earth. That shall come to pass. But there is nothing to prevent them making something that shall resemble my humble body and also my face.

"From a certain tree, whose life is very hardy, and which is called basswood, shall be taken the timber from which they shall make something which shall resemble the form of my face to-day. And they shall use it as a means when they call on me to blow upon one who is ill. There is no objection if a human being should impersonate me. One of them must cover his face with the thing which is made to resemble the shape of my body, and will go to the several lodges of the people.

"As soon as they arrive there then they shall begin, and they shall blow repeatedly on the person who is ill. It will be just the same as if I myself had blown on that one repeatedly.

"So then native tobacco shall be one of the principal things there, that they whom I greet as 'My Dear Grandchildren' will pledge their words with it. Customarily one shall hold in his hand that which I regard highly, native tobacco.

"And one will cast the native tobacco on the fire, that smoke may arise. At that time it will be possible that I myself shall draw in the smoke. And that shall be one of the

54

principal things that they will continue to use as a means, and someone will continue to impersonate me. And from the fire kindled by mankind, one will take up hot ashes, and blow repeatedly over the entire body of the person who is sick. Then at that time the disease, the sickness, will go away.

"In the next place, one of the main things provided when they will call upon me, and which I highly prize, will be parched corn-mush; they must prepare a kettle of it when they begin the rite. So thus it shall continue to be. And no matter at what time of the year. So may one who is ill recover health."

Onondaga

THE ORIGIN AND USE OF WAMPUM

ACCORDINGLY, THEN, whenever they held a council there were shamans there. And according to their strength among these shamans it was known who was the most powerful. After they held their council they lighted their pipes and smoked. In the case of an exceedingly great shaman every time he drew upon his pipe, wampum fell from his mouth. If the wampum was white, then it denoted that the shaman was of medium power. If the wampum was half white and half reddish it denoted the least powerful shaman. But if, in the case of a shaman, his wampum was almost black, then he would win over these shamans, the others who had the most wampum, after the shamans had smoked their pipes. And so whenever these two nations wanted to make a treaty they gave wampum to each other as a payment, the beads woven into a belt designed with two hands, meaning that they had agreed to the treaty and would fight no more and forever would not hunt one another down again. And that is all.

Wawenock

3

THE FOREST AND THE SEA

THE GREAT AREA of semi-Arctic land that stretches across Canada from Hudson Bay to the Rockies is the home of the caribou hunters. To the eastward, they are Algonquin-speaking tribes; to the westward, Athapascan. The tribes of central Canada rely on the caribou almost as completely as the Plains tribes relied on the buffalo. They are hunters of small game also, and of the moose. Berries and fish and edible roots supplement their meat diet. They do no farming and are mostly nomads.

They live in skin or bark-covered tipis, in dome-shaped huts and, in the Northwest, in log houses. Their utensils are made of bark or wood. Their clothing is tailored from skins. They travel in summer by means of bark canoes, and in winter on dog sleds, toboggans and snowshoes.

These are the few, outstanding traits of this vast area; but, as there has always been a good deal of give and take between them and bordering tribes, many variants may be found. The tribes east and south of Hudson Bay have much in common with the Great Lakes and Eastern Woodland groups; the south-central tribes have affinities with the men of the Plains. The northern tribes exchange ideas with the Eskimos, and the far western tribes have been influenced by the North Pacific peoples. Their art is a limited one, but their porcupine quill and moosehair embroidery, and their woven quillwork are outstanding in both abstract and floral designs. In our day, it has been superseded by beadwork on cloth. Their stories and myths are poor stuff, not to be compared with the work either of the Eskimos or the story-tellers of the Plains. The tale of the culture hero, "Crow Head" is typical.

The Eskimo lives on the treeless, frozen coast that extends some six thousand miles from Greenland to Siberia. It was long thought that the Eskimos were the last group to cross to America from Asia, but this is not the case. The Eskimo has been here some two or three thousand years.

The three designs on the lower center of Plate 22 are examples of early work. They show a fine relation of line to the form and surface decorated. The early Eskimos, like their descendants, were excellent carvers. Pictographic art, like the walrus-ivory pipe also on Plate 22, is later work. In it, the design is incidental, for the picture is a record of a whale hunt. This style apparently had its origin in the east, and was carried later to Alaska.

The Eskimo is a very ingenious person. The people are dependent on mammals, birds, and fish for most of their needs. They make clothing, and well-tailored it is, from the skins of the caribou and seal. Waterproof garments are devised from the intestines of sea mammals. The dog sled and the kayak were Eskimo inventions. Since they had no firewood, they made a blubber-burning lamp with a moss wick. Their tools, and their hunting and fishing equipment were made of walrus-ivory. In summer, they live in skin huts. In winter, their homes are underground huts built of earth and driftwood. East of Point Barrow, Alaska, winter houses are built of snow. In Alaska, where wood is available, the Eskimos carve masks, bowls and boxes. The mask on Plate 22 represents a seal and its spirit; the half-face being the spirit.

The Eskimo legends given here are brooding and sad, but they are good stories. It should be noted particularly that they are more realistic than the legends previously cited; they make fewer attempts to explain the basic forces of nature, though they manifest an equal awe.

Along the North Pacific coast of North America, the Indian lives in a dramatic setting. High mountains rise abruptly from the sea. There are big trees; there are sea mammals, big fish, big game. The Indian here responded to his environment in a big way. He took the big trees and made of them great communal houses, occupied by a large number of families. He fronted his house with a tree, his totem pole, his emblem of family pride. He wasted none of the tree. He wove the cedar bark into mats and clothing, including waterproof ponchos. He built sea-going canoes capable of carrying fifty or sixty men. Even its sails were made of wood. Large wooden boxes held his thousands of blankets and furs—his wealth.

Carrying the figure of bigness to its extreme, the North Pacific Indian *talked* big. He staged dramatic ceremonies, acted out by fantastically masked figures. He dramatized himself and his own importance at the "potlatch." This term, which originally meant "giving" has too many ramifications to explain fully in this brief space. In short, a potlatch is a party, given by some chief or great man. The host tells his guests what a great man he is, and then distributes many presents to them. He can well afford to be generous. For the recipient of the fifty blankets (blankets being the basic unit of exchange), must, in order to save face give another potlatch at which he returns a hundred blankets. And so on, with respect to all other items distributed by the party-giver.

Like "Raven" in the Tlingit story on page 64, the Indians of the North Pacific area could do many things. They were expert navigators. They worked wood and wove fabrics in styles superior to any others north of Mexico. The art of the totem poles, for instance. In these graphic representations of the owner's social position, the animals represented are shown as they appeared in the native myths. For this reason, the myths relating to several prominent North Pacific families have been cited in the stories which follow. The representations on Plate 24 will take on added meaning in the light of the myths.

Any unusual incident in the life of the owner of a pole was incorporated in the design, as well as a detailed reckoning of his descent from great progenitors. If these ancestors, symbolized as animals, were actual people the totem animal is given a human face. It is possible, also, to distinguish men from animals by the erect ears given the latter and set upon the top of their heads. Bird totems may be recognized by beaks, sometimes set on a human face. Family crests are placed at the top, bottom and middle of the pole.

The totem poles and the masks are comparatively recent work, carved since the makers became acquainted with steel tools. But the art itself and the forms employed are old. In simpler styles, they were used originally on memorial columns and on interior house posts.

The ceremonial carved and painted masks reach a high degree of mechanical and artistic excellence. Many of them, though cast in the form of the human face, represent supernatural beings or monsters out of the myths. There are also clan masks which represent the totem of individual clans. Some are double masks, representing when closed an animal or bird, and when open representing man as the animal or bird. The double-headed serpent mask on Plate 27 is of this type. In the dances, or dramatic presentations of the tribal myths, these masks are worn by the actors.

The Tlingit and Chilkat blankets, whose manner of weaving has been already explained in the INTRODUCTION, hold a unique position in textile design. The patterns are painted designs which have been adapted to the technique of weaving. Hence these blankets use curved forms ordinarily absent in Indian weaving designs. Since women are not considered to understand the religious significance of the designs, they are first painted by men on pattern boards. Design units used in building up these patterns may be seen on Plate 27. The Chilkat design on Plate 30, which has geometric form, is much older than the animal patterns.

Feast dishes are conceived of as being animate and are carved in the forms of men or animals. Note the wooden dish representing the Raven shown on Plate 26.

Basketry executed by the Tlingit, and by the Thompson and Lillooet, has been noticed in the INTRODUCTION. The basket-weaving area extends down the coast as far as California. These California basket-weavers, a complex group made up of many small tribes, do not share the North Pacific culture. Among them, the Pomos make the best baskets. Their work possesses the greatest variety of design arrangement, an outstanding feature being the use of interwoven feathers. These are sometimes used to outline the design which had been worked out in the weaving of the basket, or, where the feathers completely cover the basket, the arrangement of feathers constitutes the design.

In contrast to the brawling, boasting, naturalistic stories of the North Pacific tribes, the legends and myths of the California Indians are gentle and oddly pathetic in their simple telling. Our example of the innumerable legends told of the culture-hero, Coyote, is taken from their mythology.

CROW-HEAD

SOON AFTER CROW-HEAD'S birth, his father died. Crow-Head knew nothing about him. Once the other Indians were fishing, and there were several medicinemen among them. It was in the evening, and the setting sun presented a bloodshot appearance. One medicineman pointed at it and asked the boy, "Do you see that red sky? That is your father's blood." This made Crow-head suspect that one of the medicinemen had killed his father. He went home, where he was living with his grandmother, and began to cry. "Why are you crying?" "I heard those men talking about my father." "There is no use crying, you will be a man some day." The next day the people were fishing. Crow-head punched a hole in the ice and began angling with a hook. The Indians caught nothing, only Crow-head caught a large trout. He pulled out its soft parts, and hid the bones under his deerskin capote. He started towards the medicineman who had killed his father, pulled out the fish spine, and broke it over him. When the people went home that evening, they missed the medicineman. They did not know what was the matter with him. One man went out and found him lying dead by his fishing rod. This was the first time Crow-head ever killed anyone. By breaking the fish spine, he had broken that of his enemy and thus killed him.

Crow-head was living with a little orphan, whom he called his grandchild. He used to wear a crow-skin cape, which warned him of the approach of enemies and constituted his medicine. Two girls in the camp once made fun of his crow-skin garment. Crow-head was displeased and said to his grandson, "We will make a birchbark canoe and leave." In a coulée they found fine birchbark. Some Indians from the rocks on either side pelted them with snowballs. "Some bad Indians are pelting us with snow," said the orphan. "That's nothing," replied Crow-head. They took the bark for the canoe and returned. In the meantime the bad Indians, who were Cree, had killed all the Chipewyan. Crow-head piled all the corpses together in a heap. He was a great medicineman. He began to make a canoe. Worms began to come to the corpses. Then he took his crow-skin, laid it on the dead bodies, and told the boy not to wake him until the next day at noon. While he was sleeping, worms crawled into his nose, ears, and mouth.

Crow-head woke up and started off in his canoe. In the Barren Grounds he made many small lodges, and with his medicine declared that all the dead should be in those lodges. He left and lay down on the worms. The people all came to life again, and nothing remained in place of their corpses save their rotten garments. The Cree started homewards, but Crow-head, lying on the maggots, caused them by his magic to return to the same place. The little boy cried, thinking his grandfather was dead. He pushed the old man, but Crow-head pretended to be dead. At last, the boy pulled him by his beard, then Crow-head awoke and beheld the Cree. The Cree was surprised to get back to their starting point and, seeing the two survivors, decided to kill them also. Crow-head rose, walked to the river, shaved off the bark of a rotten birch, made peep-holes in the tree, hid the boy in the hollow, and ordered him to watch.

Crow-head was a dwarf. He went to the river with the crow-skin on his back and a blanket over it, pretending to mourn his lost relatives. The Cree, thinking he was but a child, said, "There is no use killing a child like that with a pointed arrow." So they shot at him with blunt points, but all the arrows grazed off. Then they pulled ashore, and Crow-head fled to the brush, pursued by the enemy. When far from the canoes, he threw off his blanket, took a deer horn which he carried for a weapon, and ran among the enemy, breaking each man's right arm and left leg. Then they said, "This is Crow-head." They retreated towards their canoes, but Crow-head smashed every one of them. Then he summoned his grandson from his hiding place. The Cree had spears, and Crow-head told the boy to take them and kill their enemies. The boy did as he was bidden. The Cree said to the boy, "If it were only you, you could not do this to us." And they made a "crooked finger" at him.

Crow-head left his grandson. He was gone for many days. The boy cried, not knowing what was the matter. Up the river he heard waves beating against the bank. Going thither, he found his grandfather washing himself. Crow-head asked the boy, "What are you crying for?" "I thought you were lost." "There is no use crying, all our people are alive again." They started to join the resuscitated Indians. They heard some one playing ball, laughing and singing. Putting ashore, they heard the noise of crying. They went into a lodge and asked what the crying was about. "Two friends of ours are lost, they have been killed by the Cree." Then they recognized Crow-head and his grandson.

The two girls who made fun of Crow-head's crow-skin were not restored to life by him.

Late in the fall, when the Chipewyan were going to a lake to fish and it was commencing to freeze, two boys came running and told the people that two giants taller than pine trees had killed all their friends. The Chipewyan were camping on the edge of a big lake. None of them slept that night for fear of the giants. The next morning the giants were seen approaching. Crow-head said, "There is no use in running away, they will kill me first." He put on his crow-skin and went towards them on the ice. The first giant wished to seize him, and with long fingers shaped like bear claws he tore Crow-head's crow feathers. The giants fought for the possession of Crow-head, each wishing to eat him up. Crow-head hit both of them with his deer horn, and killed them. He walked homeward. He was so angry that he could neither speak nor sleep. His eyes were like fire. He went to the lake and, beginning at one point, he commenced to hammer along the edge until he got back to his starting place. There he fell dead, for his heart was under the nail of his little finger and by hammering the ice he had injured it.

Chipewyan

61

ORIGIN OF LIVING THINGS

PREVIOUS TO A TIME when water covered the earth, the people lived on such food as they could always find prepared for them in abundance. They did not know of any animals at that time on the land or in the water. The water finally went away and the seaweeds became trees, shrubs, bushes, and grass. The long seaweeds were the trees and the smaller kinds became the bushes and grass. The grass, however, was in some manner put in various places by a walrus at a later date than the appearance of the trees.

A woman who had lost her husband lived among strangers. As they desired to change the place of their habitation, they resolved to journey to another point of land at a distance. The woman who was depending on charity had become a burden of which they wished to rid themselves. So they put all their belongings into the *umiak* and when they were on the way they seized the woman and cast her overboard. She struggled to regain the side of the boat, and when she seized it, the others cut off her fingers which fell into the water and changed to seals, walrus, whales, and white bears. The woman in her despair, screamed her determination to have revenge for the cruelty perpetrated upon her. The thumb became a walrus, the first finger a seal, and the middle finger a white bear. When the former two animals see a man they try to escape lest they be served as the woman was.

The white bear lives both on the land and in the sea, but when he perceives a man revengeful feelings fill him, and he determines to destroy the person who mutilated the woman from whose finger he sprang.

Eskimo

AURORAS

AURORAS ARE BELIEVED to be the torches held in the hands of spirits seeking the souls of those who have just died, to lead them over the abyss at the edge of the world. A narrow pathway leads across it to the land of brightness and plenty, where disease and pain are no more, and where food of all kinds is always ready in abundance. To this place none but the dead and the Raven can go. When the spirits wish to communicate with the people of the earth they make a whistling noise and the earth people answer only in a whispering tone. The Eskimo say that they are able to call the aurora and converse with it. They send messages to the dead through these spirits.

Eskimo

SEDNA AND THE FULMAR

ONCE UPON A TIME there lived on a solitary shore an Inung with his daughter Sedna. His wife had been dead for some time and the two led a quiet life. Sedna grew up to be a handsome girl and the youths came from all around to sue for her hand, but none of them could touch her proud heart. Finally, at the breaking up of the ice in the spring a fulmar flew from over the ice and wooed Sedna with enticing song. "Come to me," it said; "come into the land of the birds, where there is never hunger, where my tent is made of the most beautiful skins. You shall rest on soft bearskins. My fellows, the fulmars, shall bring you all your heart may desire; their feathers shall clothe you; your lamp shall always be filled with oil, your pot with meat." Sedna could not long resist such wooing and they went together over the vast sea. When at last they reached the country of the fulmar, after a long and hard journey, Sedna discovered that her spouse had shamefully deceived her. Her new home was not built of beautiful pelts, but was covered with wretched fishskins, full of holes, that gave free entrance to wind and snow. Instead of soft reindeer skins her bed was made of hard walrus hides and she had to live on miserable fish, which the birds brought her. Too soon she discovered that she had thrown away her opportunities when in her foolish pride she had rejected the Inuit youth. In her woe she sang: "Aja. O father, if you knew how wretched I am you would come to me and we would hurry away in your boat over the waters. The birds look unkindly upon me the stranger; cold winds roar about my bed; they give me but miserable food. O come and take me back home. Aja."

When a year had passed and the sea was again stirred by warmer winds, the father left his country to visit Sedna. His daughter greeted him joyfully and besought him to take her back home. The father hearing of the outrages wrought upon his daughter determined upon revenge. He killed the fulmar, took Sedna into his boat, and they quickly left the country which had brought so much sorrow to Sedna. When the other fulmars came home and found their companion dead and his wife gone, they all flew away in search of the fugitives. They were very sad over the death of their poor murdered comrade and continue to mourn and cry until this day.

Having flown a short distance they discerned the boat and stirred up a heavy storm. The sea rose in immense waves that threatened the pair with destruction. In this mortal peril the father determined to offer Sedna to the birds and flung her overboard. She clung to the edge of the boat with a death grip. The cruel father then took a knife and cut off the first joints of her fingers. Falling into the sea they were transformed into whales, the nails turning into whalebone. Sedna holding on to the boat more tightly, the second finger joints fell under the sharp knife and swam away as seals; when the father cut off the stumps of the fingers they became ground seals. Meantime the storm subsided, for the fulmars thought Sedna was drowned. The father then allowed her to come into the boat again. But from that time she cherished a deadly hatred against him and swore bitter revenge. After they got ashore, she called her dogs and let them gnaw off the feet and hands of her father while he was asleep. Upon this he cursed himself, his daughter, and the dogs which had maimed him; whereupon the earth opened and swallowed the hut, the father, the daughter, and the dogs. They have since lived in the land of Adlivun, of which Sedna is the mistress.

Central Eskimo (Okomiut and Akudnirmiut)

RAVEN

IN OLDEN TIMES only high-caste people knew the story of Raven properly because only they had time to learn it.

At the beginning of things there was no daylight and the world lay in blackness. Then there lived in a house at the head of Nass river a being called Raven-At-The-Head-Of-Nass, the principal deity to whom the Tlingit formerly prayed but whom no one had seen; and in his house were all kinds of things including sun, moon, stars, and daylight. He was addressed in prayers as My Creator and Invisible-Rich-Man. With him were two old men called Old-Man-Who-Foresees-All-Troubles-In-The-World and He-Who-Knows-Everything-That-Happens. Next to Raven-At-The-Head-Of-Nass, they prayed to the latter of these. Under the earth was a third old person, Old-Woman-Underneath, placed under the world by Raven-At-The-Head-Of-Nass. Raven-At-The-Head-Of-Nass was unmarried and lived alone with these two old men, and yet he had a daughter, a thing no one is able to explain. Nor do people know what this daughter was. The two old persons took care of her like servants, and especially they always looked into the water before she drank to see that it was perfectly clean.

First of all beings Raven-At-The-Head-Of-Nass created the Heron as a very tall and very wise man, and after him the Raven, who was also a very good and very wise man at that time.

Raven came into being in this wise. His first mother had many children, but they all died young, and she cried over them continually. According to some, this woman was Raven-At-The-Head-Of-Nass' sister and it was Raven-At-The-Head-Of-Nass who was doing this because he did not wish her to have any male children. By and by Heron came to her and said, "What is it that you are crying about all the time?" She answered, "I am always losing my children. I can not bring them up." Then he said, "Go down on the beach when the tide is lowest, get a small, smooth stone, and put it into the fire. When it is red hot, swallow it. Do not be afraid." She said, "All right." Then she followed Heron's directions and gave birth to Raven. Therefore Raven's name was really Itcaku, the name of a very hard rock. This is why Raven was so tough and could not easily be killed.

Heron and Raven both became servants to Raven-At-The-Head-Of-Nass, but he thought more of Raven and made him head man over the world. Then Raven-At-The-Head-Of-Nass made some people.

Raven-At-The-Head-Of-Nass tried to make human beings out of a rock and out of a leaf at the same time, but the rock was slow while the leaf was very quick. Therefore human beings came from the leaf. Then he showed a leaf to the human beings and said, "You see this leaf. You are to be like it. When it falls off the branch and rots there is nothing left of it." That is why there is death in the world. If men had come from the rock there would be no death. Years ago people used to say when they were getting old, "We are unfortunate in not having been made from a rock. Being made from a leaf, we must die."

Raven-At-The-Head-Of-Nass also said, "After people die, if they are not witches, and do not lie or steal, there is a good place for them to go to." Wicked people are to be dogs and such low animals hereafter. The place for good people is above, and, when one comes up there, he is asked, "What were you killed for?" or "What was your life in the world?" The place he went to was governed by his reply. So people used to say to their children, "Do not lie. Do not steal. For the Maker will see you."

Some time afterward a man died, and Raven, coming into the house, saw him there with his wife and children weeping around him. So he raised the dead man's blanket with both hands, held it over the body, and brought him back to life.

After that both Raven and her husband told this woman that there was no death, but she disbelieved them. Then Raven said to her, "Lie down and go to sleep." And, as she slept, she thought she saw a wide trail with many people upon it and all kinds of fierce animals around. Good people had to pass along this trail in order to live again. When she came to the end of the trail there was a great river there, and a canoe came across to her from the other side of it. She entered this and crossed. There some people came to her and said, "You better go back. We are not in a good place. There is starvation here, we are cold, and we get no water to drink."

This is why people burn the bodies of the dead and put food into the fire for them to eat. Burning their bodies makes the dead comfortable. If they were not burned their spirits would be cold. This is why they invite all those of the opposite clan as well as the nearest relations of the dead man's wife, seating them together in one place, and burn food in front of them. It is because they think that the dead person gets all of the property destroyed at the feast and all of the food then burned up. It is on account of what Raven showed them that they do so.

Petrel was one of the first persons created by Raven-At-The-Head-Of-Nass. He was keeper of the fresh water, and would let none else touch it. The spring he owned was on a rocky island outside of Kuiu, called Fort-far-out, where the well may still be seen. Raven stole a great mouthful of this water and dropped it here and there as he went along. This is the origin of the great rivers of the world, the Nass, Skeena, Stikine, Chilkat, and others. He said, "This thing that I drop here and there will whirl all the time. It will not overflow the world, yet there will be plenty of water." Before this time Raven is said to have been pure white, but, as he was flying up through the smoke hole with Petrel's water, the latter said, "Spirits, hold down my smoke hole." So they held him until he was turned black by the smoke.

After this Raven saw a fire far out at sea. Tying a piece of pitchwood to a chicken hawk's bill, he told him to go out to this fire, touch it with the pitchwood, and bring it back. When he had brought it to him Raven put it into the rock and the red cedar saying, "This is how you are to get your fire, from this rock and this red cedar," and that is the way they formerly did.

Thus Raven went about among the natives of Alaska telling them what to do, but Raven-At-The-Head-Of-Nass they never saw. Raven showed all the Tlingit what to do for a living, but he did not get to be such a high person as Raven-At-The-Head-Of-Nass, and he taught the people much foolishness. At that time the world was full of dangerous animals and fish. Raven also tied up some witches, and so it was through him that the people believed in witchcraft. Then he told the people that some wild animals were to be their friends (i.e., their crest animals) to which they were to talk.

Once he gave a feast and invited persons to it from other places. He had two slaves after that, named Gidzaget and Gidzanuqiu. This is why the natives here had slaves. It was on account of his example. There was a man who had no arm, so Raven thought he would be a shaman and cure him. This is how the Tlingit came to have shamans. After there was death he showed them how to dance over the body placed in the middle of the floor.

Raven also taught the people how to make halibut hooks, and went out fishing with them. He had names for the halibut hooks and talked to them before he let them down into the sea. That is why the natives do so now. He also taught them to be very quick when they went out halibut fishing or they would catch nothing.

He also made different kinds of fish traps and taught the people how to use them. He made the small variety and a big trap, shaped like a barrel, for use in the Stikine. He taught them how to make the seal spear. It has many barbs, and there are different kinds. One is called *tsa-caxictdzas*. It is provided with some attachment that hits the seal upon the head whenever it comes to the surface, driving its head under water until it dies, and that is what the name signifies. Then he showed them how to make a canoe. This he did on the Queen Charlotte islands. At first the people were afraid to get into it, but he said, "The canoe is not dangerous. People will seldom get drowned."

He taught them how to catch a salmon called *icqen*, which requires a different kind of hook from that used for halibut. The place where he taught people how to get different kinds of shellfish is a beach on the Queen Charlotte islands called Raven's beach to this day.

After he was through teaching the people these things, he went under the ocean, and when he came back, taught them that the sea animals are not what we think they are, but are like human beings. First he went to the halibut people. They have a chief who invited him to eat, and he had dried devilfish and other kinds of dried fish brought out. He was well liked everywhere he went under the sea because he was a very smart man. After that he went to see the sculpin people, who were very industrious and had all kinds of things in their houses. The killer-whale people seemed to live on hair-seal meat, fat, and oil. Their head chief was named Gonaqadet, and even to this day the natives say that the sight of him brings good fortune.

While he was under the ocean he saw some people fishing for halibut, and he tried to tease them by taking hold of their bait. They, however, caught him by the bill and pulled him up as far as the bottom of their canoe, where he braced himself so that they pulled his bill out. Then Raven went from house to house inquiring for his bill until he came to the house of the chief. Upon asking for it there, they handed it to him wrapped in eagle down. Then he put it back into its place and flew off through the smoke hole.

Raven left that town and came to another. There he saw a king salmon jumping about far out at sea. He got it ashore and killed it. Because he was able to do everything, the natives did all that he told them. He was the one who taught all things to the natives, and some of them still follow his teachings. After that he got all kinds of birds for his servants. It was through these that people found out he was the Raven.

Once he went to a certain place and told the people to go and fight others. He said, "You go there and kill them all, and you will have all the things in that town." This was the beginning of war.

After having been down among the fish teaching them, Raven went among the birds and land animals. He said to the grouse, "You are to live in a place where it is wintry, and you will always look out for a place high up so that you can get plenty of breeze." Then he handed the grouse four white pebbles, telling him to swallow them so that they might become his strength. "You will never starve," he said, "so long as you have these four pebbles." He also said, "You know that Sealion is your grandchild. You must be generous, get four more pebbles and give them to him." That is how the sealion came to have four large pebbles. It throws these at hunters, and, if one strikes a person, it kills him. From this story it is known that the grouse and the sealion can understand each other.

Raven said to the ptarmigan: "You will be the maker of snowshoes. You will know how to travel in snow." It was from these birds that the Athapascans learned how to make snowshoes, and it was from them that they learned how to put their lacings on.

Next Raven came to the "wild canary," which is found in the Tlingit country all the year round, and said: "You will be head among the very small birds. You are not to live on what human beings eat. Keep away from them."

Then he went to the robin and said: "You will make the people happy by letting them hear your whistle. You will be a good whistler."

Then he said to the flicker: "You will be the head one among the birds next in size. You will not be found in all places. You will be very seldom seen."

Then he came to the snipes and said to them: "You will always go in flocks. You will never go out alone." Therefore we always see them in flocks.

He came to the crows and said: "You will make lots of noise. You will be great talkers." That is why, when you hear one crow, you hear a lot of others right afterward.

He came to the humming bird and said: "A person will enjoy seeing you. If he sees you once, he will want to see you again."

He said to the eagle: "You will be very powerful and above all birds. Your eyesight will be very good. What you want will be very easy for you." He put talons on the eagle and said that they would be very useful to him.

And so he went on speaking to all the birds.

Then he said to the land otter: "You will live in the water just as well as on land." He and the land otter were good friends, so they went halibut fishing together. The land otter was a fine fisherman. Finally he said to the land otter: "You will always have your house on a point where there is plenty of breeze from either side. Whenever a canoe capsizes with people in it you will save them and make them your friends." The land-otter-man originated from Raven telling this to the land otter. All Alaskans know about the land-otter-man but very few tell the story of Raven correctly.

If the friends of those who have been taken away by the land otters get them back, they become shamans, therefore it was through the land otters that shamans were first known. Shamans can see one another by means of the land-otter spirits although others can not.

After leaving the land otters, Raven appeared at Taku. There is a cliff at the mouth of that inlet where the North Wind used to live, and Raven stayed there with him. The North Wind was proud and shone all over with what the Indians thought were icicles. So the Indians never say anything against the North Wind, however long it blows, because it has power. Years ago people thought that there were spirits in all the large cliffs upon the islands, and they would pray to those cliffs. They had this feeling toward them because Raven once lived in this cliff with the North Wind.

Raven observed certain regulations very strictly when he was among the rivers he had created. He told people never to mention anything that lives in the sea by its right name while they were there, but to call a seal a rabbit, for instance, and so with the other animals. This was to keep them from meeting with misfortune among the rapids. Formerly the Indians were very strict with their children when they went up the rivers, but nowadays all that has been forgotten.

After this Raven went to Chilkat and entered a sweat house along with the chief of the killer whales who tried to roast him. Raven, however, had a piece of ice near him and every now and then put part of it into his mouth. Then he would tell the killer whale that he felt chilly and make him feel ashamed. "If I did not belong to the Ganaxtedi family," said Raven, "I could not have stood that sweat house." For this reason the Ganaxtedi now claim the raven as an emblem and think they have more right to it than anybody else.

It was from Raven that people found out there are Athapascan Indians. He went back into their country. So the Chilkat people to this day make their money by going thither. He also showed the Chilkat people how to make *tcil*, secret storehouses maintained some distance out of town, and he taught them how to put salmon into these and keep them frozen there over winter. So the Chilkat people got their name from *tcil*, "storehouse," and *xat*, "salmon."

Raven also showed the Chilkat people the first seeds of the Indian tobacco and taught them how to plant it. After it was grown up, he dried it, gathered clam shells, roasted them until they were very soft, and pounded them up with the tobacco. They used to chew this, and it was so good that it is surprising they gave it up. They made a great deal of money at Chilkat by trading with this among the interior Indians, but nowadays it is no longer planted.

Tlingit

THE BEAVER OF KILLISNOO

SOME PEOPLE BELONGING to the Decitan family captured a small beaver, and, as it was cunning and very clean, they kept it as a pet. By and by, however, although it was well cared for, it took offense at something and began to compose songs. Afterward one of the beaver's masters went through the woods to a certain salmon creek and found two salmon-spear handles, beautifully worked, standing at the foot of a big tree. He carried these home, and, as soon as they were brought into the house, the beaver said, "That is my make." Then something was said that offended it again. Upon this the beaver began to sing just like a human being and surprised the people very much. While it was doing this it seized a spear and threw it straight through its master's chest, killing him instantly. Then it threw its tail down upon the ground and the earth on which that house stood dropped in. They found out afterward that the beaver had been digging out the earth under the camp so as to make a great hollow. It is from this story that the Decitan claim the beaver and have the beaver hat. They also have songs composed by the beaver.

Tlingit

STORY OF THE KILLER-WHALE CREST

THERE WAS A MAN called Natsilane *(the name of a worm that appears on dried salmon)* who was continually quarreling with his wife. He had many brothers-in-law, who became very much ashamed of this discord but had to stay around to protect their sister. One day his brothers-in-law took him to an island far out at sea, named Katseuxti, and talked very kindly to him. But, while he was out of sight upon the island, they left him. Then he began thinking, "What can I do for myself?" As he sat there he absent-mindedly whittled killer whales out of cottonwood bark, which works easily. The two he had made he put into the water, and, as he did so, he shouted aloud as shamans used to do on such occasions. Then he thought they looked as if they were swimming, but, when they came up again, they were nothing but bark. After a while he made two more whales out of alder. He tried to put his clan's spirits into them as was often done by shamans, and, as he put them in, he whistled four times like the spirit, "Whu, whu, whu, whu." But they, too, floated up. Now he tried all kinds of wood—hemlock, red cedar, etc. Finally he tried pieces of yellow cedar, which swam right away in the form of large killer whales. They swam out for a long distance, and, when they came back, again turned into wood. Then he made holes in their dorsal fins, seized one of them with each hand and had the killer whales take him out to sea. He said, "You see my brothers-in-law traveling about in canoes. You are to upset them." After he had gone out for some distance between the whales they returned to land and became wood once more. He took them up and put them in a certain place.

The next time he saw his brothers-in-law coming along in their canoes he put his spirits into the water again, and they smashed the canoes and killed those in them. Then

Natsilane said to his killer whales, "You are not to injure human beings any more. You must be kind to them." After that they were the canoes of spirits, and, if shamans are lucky, they get these spirit canoes. It is through this story that the Daqlawedi family claim the killer whale.

Tlingit

THE IMAGE THAT CAME TO LIFE

A YOUNG CHIEF on the Queen Charlotte islands married, and soon afterwards his wife fell ill. Then he sent around everywhere for the very best shamans. If there were a very fine shaman at a certain village he would send a canoe there to bring him. None of them could help her, however, and after she had been sick for a very long time she died.

Now the young chief felt very badly over the loss of his wife. He went from place to place after the best carvers in order to have them carve an image of his wife, but no one could make anything to look like her. All this time there was a carver in his own village who could carve much better than all the others. This man met him one day and said, "You are going from village to village to have wood carved like your wife's face, and you can not find anyone to do it, can you? I have seen your wife a great deal walking along with you. I have never studied her face with the idea that you might want some one to carve it, but I am going to try if you will allow me."

Then the carver went after a piece of red cedar and began working upon it. When he was through, he went to the young chief and said, "Now you can come along and look at it." He had dressed it just as he used to see the young woman dressed. So the chief went with him, and, when he got inside, he saw his dead wife sitting there just as she used to look. This made him very happy, and he took it home. Then he asked the carver, "What do I owe you for making this?" and he replied, "Do as you please about it." The carver had felt sorry to see how this chief was mourning for his wife, so he said, "It is because I felt badly for you that I made that. So don't pay me too much for it." He paid the carver very well, however, both in slaves and in goods.

Now the chief dressed this image in his wife's clothes and her marten-skin robe. He felt that his wife had come back to him and treated the image just like her. One day, while he sat mourning very close to the image, he felt it move. His wife had also been very fond of him. At first he thought that the movement was only his imagination, yet he examined it every day, for he thought that at some time it would come to life. When he ate he always had the image close to him.

After a while the whole village learned that he had this image and all came in to see it. Many could not believe that it was not the woman herself until they had examined it closely.

One day, after the chief had had it for a long, long time, he examined the body and found it just like that of a human being. Still, although it was alive, it could not move or speak. Some time later, however, the image gave forth a sound from its chest like that of crackling wood, and the man knew that it was ill. When he had some one move it away from the place where it had been sitting they found a small red-cedar tree growing there on top of the flooring. They left it until it grew to be very large, and it is because of this that cedars on the Queen Charlotte islands are so good. When people up this way look for red cedars and find a good one they say, "This looks like the baby of the chief's wife."

Every day the image of the young woman grew more like a human being, and, when they heard the story, people from villages far and near came in to look at it and at the young cedar tree growing there, at which they were very much astonished. The woman moved around very little and never got to talk, but her husband dreamed what she wanted to tell him. It was through his dreams that he knew she was talking to him.

Tlingit

KUMUSH AND HIS DAUGHTER

CHARACTERS

Kumush . . . *The Creator, according to Indian myths*
Skoks . . . . *A Spirit*

KUMUSH LEFT TULA LAKE and wandered over the earth. He went to the edge of the world and was gone a great many years; then he came back to Nihlaksi, where his sweat-house had been; where Látkakáwas brought the disk; where the body of the beautiful blue man was burned, and where Isis was saved.

Kumush brought his daughter with him from the edge of the world. Where he got her, no one knows. When he came back, Isis and all the people he had made were dead; he and his daughter were alone. The first thing he did was to give the young girl ten dresses, which he made by his word. The finest dress of all was the burial dress; it was made of buckskin, and so covered with bright shells that not a point of the buckskin could be seen.

The first of the ten dresses was for a young girl; the second was the maturity dress, to be worn while dancing the maturity dance; the third was the dress to be put on after coming from the sweat-house, the day the maturity dance ended; the fourth was to be worn on the fifth day after the dance; the fifth dress was the common, everyday dress; the sixth was to wear when getting wood; the seventh when digging roots; the eighth was to be used when on a journey; the ninth was to wear at a ball game; the tenth was the burial dress.

When they came to Nihlaksi, Kumush's daughter was within a few days of maturity. In the old time, when he was making rules for his people, Kumush had said that at maturity a girl should dance five days and five nights, and while she was dancing an old woman, a good singer, should sing for her. When the five days and nights were over she should bathe in the sweat-house, and then carry wood for five days. If the girl grew sleepy while she was dancing, stopped for a moment, nodded and dreamed, or if she fell asleep while in the sweat-house and dreamed of some one's death, she would die herself.

Kumush was the only one to help his daughter; he sang while she danced. When the dance was over and the girl was in the sweat-house, she fell asleep and dreamed of some one's death. She came out of the sweat-house with her face and hands and body painted with the color of a red root. As she stood by the fire to dry the paint, she said to her father: "While I was in the sweat-house I fell asleep and I dreamed that as soon as I came out some one would die."

"That means your own death," said Kumush. "You dreamed of yourself."

Kumush was frightened; he felt lonesome. When his daughter asked for her burial dress he gave her the dress to be worn after coming from the sweat-house, but she wouldn't take it. Then he gave her the dress to be worn five days later, and she refused it. One after another he offered her eight dresses—he could not give her the one she had worn when she was a little girl, for it was too small. He held the tenth dress tight under his arm; he did not want to give it to her, for as soon as she put it on the spirit would leave her body.

"Why don't you give me my dress?" asked she. "You made it before you made the other dresses, and told me what it was for; why don't you give it to me now? You made everything in the world as you wanted it to be."

He gave her the dress, but he clung to it and cried. When she began to put it on he tried to pull it away. She said: "Father, you must not cry. What has happened to me is your will; you made it to be this way. My spirit will leave the body and go west."

At last Kumush let go of the dress, though he knew her spirit would depart as soon as she had it on. He was crying as he said: "I will go with you; I will leave my body here, and go."

"No," said the daughter, "my spirit will go west without touching the ground as it goes. How could you go with me?"

"I know what to do," said Kumush. "I know all things above, below, and in the world of ghosts; whatever is, I know."

She put on the dress, Kumush took her hand, and they started, leaving their bodies behind. Kumush was not dead but his spirit left the body.

As soon as the daughter died, she knew all about the spirit world. When they started she said to her father: "Keep your eyes closed; if you open them you will not be able to follow me, you will have to go back and leave me alone."

The road they were traveling led west to where the sun sets. Along that road were three nice things to eat: goose eggs, wild cherries and crawfish. If a spirit ate of the wild cherries it would be sent back to this world, a spirit without a body, to wander about homeless, eating wild cherries and other kinds of wild fruit. If it ate of the goose eggs, it would wander around the world, digging goose eggs out of the ground, like roots. It would have to carry the eggs in a basket without a bottom, and would always be trying to mend the basket with plaited grass. If it ate of the crawfish it would have to dig crawfish in the same way.

A Skoks offered Kumush's daughter these three harmful things, but she did not look at them; she went straight on toward the west, very fast.

After a time Kumush asked: "How far have we gone now?"

"We are almost there," said the girl. "Far away I see beautiful roses. Spirits that have been good in life take one of those roses with the leaves, those that have been bad do not see the roses."

Again Kumush asked: "How far are we now?"

"We are passing the place of roses."

Kumush thought: "She should take one of those roses."

The girl always knew her father's thoughts. As soon as that thought came into his mind, she put back her hand and, without turning, pulled a rose and two leaves. Kumush did not take one. He could not even see them, for he was not dead.

After a time they came to a road so steep that they could slide down it. At the beginning of the descent there was a willow rope. The girl pulled the rope and that minute music and voices were heard. Kumush and his daughter slipped down and came out on a beautiful plain with high walls all around it. It was a great house, and the plain was its floor. That house is the whole underground world, but only spirits know the way to it.

Kumush's daughter was greeted by spirits that were glad to see her, but to Kumush they said "Sonk!" *(raw, not ripe)*, and they felt sorry for him that he was not dead.

Kumush and his daughter went around together, and Kumush asked: "How far is it to any side?"

"It is very far, twice as far as I can see. There is one road down,—the road we came,—and another up. No one can come in by the way leading up, and no one can go up by the way leading down."

The place was beautiful and full of spirits; there were so many that if every star of the sky, and all the hairs on the head of every man and all the hairs on all the animals were counted they would not equal in number the spirits in that great house.

When Kumush and his daughter first got there they couldn't see the spirits though they could hear voices, but after sunset, when darkness was in the world above, it was light in that house below.

"Keep your eyes closed," said Kumush's daughter. "If you open them, you will have to leave me and go back."

At sunset Kumush made himself small, smaller than any thing living in the world. His daughter put him in a crack, high up in a corner of the broad house, and made a mist before his eyes.

When it was dark, Wus-Kumush, the keeper of the house, said: "I want a fire!" Right away a big, round, bright fire sprang up in the center, and there was light everywhere in the house. Then spirits came from all sides, and there were so many that no one could have counted them. They made a great circle around Kumush's daughter, who stood by the fire, and then they danced a dance not of this world, and sang a song not of this world. Kumush watched them from the corner of the house. They danced each night, for five nights. All the spirits sang, but only those in the circle danced. As daylight came they disappeared. They went away to their own places, lay down and became dry, disjointed bones.

Wus-Kumush gave Kumush's daughter goose eggs and crawfish. She ate them and became bones. All newcomers became bones, but those who had been tried for five years, and hadn't eaten anything the Skoks gave them, lived in shining settlements outside, in circles around the big house. Kumush's daughter became bones, but her spirit went to her father in the corner.

On the sixth night she moved him to the eastern side of the house. That night he grew tired of staying with the spirits; he wanted to leave the underground world, but he wanted to take some of the spirits with him to people the upper world. "Afterward," said he, "I am going to the place where the sun rises. I shall travel on the sun's road till I come to where he stops at midday. There I will build a house."

"Some of the spirits are angry with you," said Wus-Kumush. "Because you are not dead they want to kill you; you must be careful."

"They may try as hard as they like," said Kumush; "they can't kill me. They haven't the power. They are my children; they are all from me. If they should kill me it would only be for a little while. I should come to life again."

The spirits, though they were bones then, heard this, and said: "We will crush the old man's heart out, with our elbows."

Kumush left Wus-Kumush and went back to the eastern side of the house. In his corner was a pile of bones. Every bone in the pile rose up and tried to kill him, but they couldn't hit him, for he dodged them. Each day his daughter moved him, but the bones knew where he was, because they could see him. Every night the spirits in the form of living people danced and sang; at daylight they lay down and became disconnected bones.

"I am going away from this place," said Kumush, "I am tired of being here." At daybreak he took his daughter's bones, and went around selecting bones according to their quality, thinking which would do for one tribe and which for another. He filled a basket with them, taking only shin-bones and wrist-bones. He put the basket on his back and started to go up the eastern road, the road out. The path was steep and slippery, and his load was heavy. He slipped and stumbled but kept climbing. When he was half-way up, the bones began to elbow him in the back and neck, struggling to kill him. When near the top the strap slipped from his forehead and the basket fell. The bones became spirits, and, whooping and shouting, fell down into the big house and became bones again.

"I'll not give up," said Kumush; "I'll try again." He went back, filled the basket with bones and started a second time. When he was half-way up he said: "You'll see that I will get to the upper world with you bones!" That minute he slipped, his cane broke and he fell. Again the bones became spirits and went whooping and shouting back to the big house.

Kumush went down a second time, and filled the basket. He was angry, and he chucked the bones in hard. "You want to stay here," said he, "but when you know my place up there, where the sun is, you'll want to stay there always and never come back to this place. I feel lonesome when I see no people up there; that is why I want to take you there. If I can't get you up now, you will never come where I am."

When he put the basket on his back the third time, he had no cane, so he thought: "I wish I had a good, strong cane." Right away he had it. Then he said: "I wish I could get up with this basketful of bones."

When half-way up the bones again tried to kill him. He struggled and tugged hard. At last he got near the edge of the slope, and with one big lift he threw the basket up on to level ground. "Maklaksûm káko!" *(Indian bones)* said he.

He opened the basket and threw the bones in different directions. As he threw them, he named the tribe and kind of Indians they would be. When he named the Shastas he said: "You will be good fighters." To the Pitt River and the Warm Spring Indians he said: "You will be brave warriors, too." But to the Klamath Indians he said: "You will be like women, easy to frighten." The bones for the Modoc Indians he threw last, and he said to them: "You will eat what I eat, you will keep my place when I am gone, you will be bravest of all. Though you may be few, even if many and many people come against you, you will kill them." And he said to each handful of bones as he threw it: "You must find power to save yourselves, find men to go and ask the mountains for help. Those who go to the mountains must ask to be made wise, or brave, or a doctor. They must swim in the *gauwams* and dream. When you are sure that a doctor has tried to kill some one, or that he won't put his medicine in the path of a spirit and turn it back, you will kill him. If an innocent doctor is killed, you must kill the man who killed him, or he must pay for the dead man."

Then Kumush named the different kinds of food those people should eat,—catfish, salmon, deer and rabbit. He named more than two hundred different things, and as he named them they appeared in the rivers and the forests and the flats. He thought, and they were there. He said: "Women shall dig roots, get wood and water, and cook. Men shall hunt and fish and fight. It shall be this way in later times. This is all I will tell you."

When he had finished everything Kumush took his daughter, and went to the edge of the world, to the place where the sun rises. He traveled on the sun's road till he came to the middle of the sky; there he stopped and built his house, and there he lives now.

Modoc

ORIGIN OF DEATH

PEOPLE GREW IN THIS WORLD in the beginning. There were many people here and there. They became numerous. Then one died. Cricket's child died. The people were talking about it. "What shall we do?" said they. All the people gathered together. They did not know what to do. Some said, "Let us have people come to life again. Let us not bury them!" —"Stop!" said others. "Go and tell Coyote. He does not know what has happened." So some one went to tell him. Coyote came. "What do you think!" said they, "we were saying that the dead should come back again."—"Why are you saying that?" said Coyote. "Bury him. He is dead. If people come back, then they will fill up everything. Around this world there is water. They will fill the world up, and push us into the water." So they buried Cricket's child, and cried.

Now, five days after this they finished the sweating. They felt sad. They thought, "Would that Coyote's child might die!" So it died, and Coyote cried. He said, "My child is dead. Let us have people come back to life."—"No!" they said. "If he should come back to life, my child that died before would not smell good. He has decayed. You said we must bury people. You said that the dead would otherwise fill up the world." So he buried him, and cried. That is the way the first people died. That was the first death.

Shasta

COYOTE AND THE YELLOW-JACKETS

PEOPLE WERE LIVING AT ÍHIWE'YAX. There was a fish-weir there on the river, and people were drying lots of salmon. Coyote was living at Utci'yagig; and he thought, "I had better go and get some salmon." So he went to get salmon. He came to the fish-weir, and the people gave him a great pile of salmon. So he went back; he lifted the load with difficulty and put it on his back, then he went off.

By and by he thought, "I guess I will rest. There is all day in which to rest. I will take a nap." So he went to sleep. By and by he awoke, and it was still only midday. Without looking, he took his pack of salmon, which he had used as a pillow while he slept, and took a bite. But while he was asleep the Yellow-Jackets had thought of him. "May he sleep soundly!" they said, and he did. Then they blew smoke towards him to work him harm, and took away his pack of salmon that he had carried. In its place they put a bundle of pine-bark, tied up. They put this under his head. So when he seized what he thought was salmon in his mouth, his face came against the bark.

He jumped up. "Who is it that has done this?" he said. He looked for tracks, but could not find them. "I'll fix that man, whoever he may be," said Coyote. Then he ran back to the fish-weir. "Coyote is running hither," the people said. "What can be the trouble with him?" He got there, and said, "I rested there at Utci'yagig. I was tired and went to sleep there. When I woke up, I missed something,—missed that that I had carried. Some one took every bit of it away." So he stayed over night; and in the morning they gave him much salmon, as before, and he went away, loaded down.

Again, in the same place, he laid down his pack and rested. "I wonder what will happen!" he thought. "I wonder who will come!" Then he slept, he feigned sleep. Now the Yellow-Jackets came. He didn't think they were the ones. "They always light on salmon that way," he thought. So they lighted on the salmon, on the pack he was leaning on. They almost lifted it. Coyote was looking at them as they moved it. Then they lifted it up from the ground, and dropped it again. "I wish you would help me!" they said to each other. They lifted it, they flew away with it. "Not too fast!" said they. They flew away, and took his salmon from him, the salmon he was carrying home. Coyote watched them as they flew, he followed them; but just there he grew tired, and gave out.

Then he went back to tell to the people at the fish-weir all that had happened. "Oh! here comes Coyote again," said they. He got there. "It was an evil being who took it from me, who took the salmon I carried away from here. He went in that direction." Everywhere this was reported among the people. They all gathered together, and heard about it. Then they got ready. Now, again Coyote went off carrying salmon. He rested in the same place; the other people sat about here and there, waiting to see the Yellow-Jackets take the salmon away. While they waited, Turtle came up. Coyote laughed, "He-he-he! Who ever told you to come?" Turtle said nothing, but sat apart by himself. "Why did you come?" said Coyote. "You ought not to have come," and he laughed at him. But Turtle sat there, and paid no attention to Coyote, who laughed at him.

Now the Yellow-Jackets came. As before, they lifted the load up a little ways and down again; then they just lifted it, it was so heavy, and flew away with it. The people followed them when they flew. They flew in that direction, to where Mount Shasta stands. Thither they went in a straight line. The people followed them up the valley and the river, straight to Mount Shasta. Coyote got tired not far from where he started. Here and there the others dropped out, tired, and formed a line of those unable to go on. Turtle, of whom Coyote had made fun, was still running. "I'm not really running yet," said Turtle, as he passed them. By and by all had given out but Turtle. They were scattered all along, but Turtle still kept on. The Yellow-Jackets still flew with the salmon. They went up the mountain, and Turtle followed. Then at the very top of Mount Shasta they took it in through a hole. Coyote was the first to get tired; but Turtle, at whom he had laughed, was the only one who went on up the mountain.

Coyote saw him. "He-he-he!" said he. "Who thought he could do anything, and there he is, the one who has overtaken all the rest." Now all the people came up, and arrived at the place. They tried to smoke the Yellow-Jackets out, and the smoke came up far away there in the valley. Coyote ran fast, so as to stop up the hole; but the smoke came out again in another place. So Coyote ran fast, and stopped it up. The people fanned the smoke into the house of the Yellow-Jackets; but the smoke rose here and there, coming out at many places all over the valley. So they gave it up. They could not smoke the Yellow-Jackets out. Then the people scattered about everywhere from there. That is what the story says happened long ago.

Shasta

PLATES 1-32

THE PLAINS AND THE LAKES

THE FOREST AND THE RIVERS

THE FOREST AND THE SEA

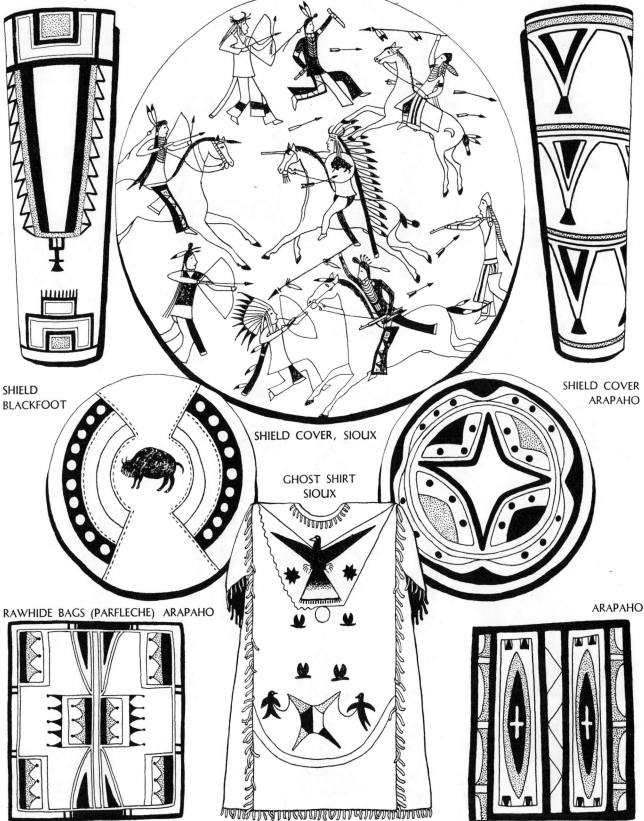

MEDICINE CASE, COMANCHE

MEDICINE CASE, ARAPAHO

SHIELD
BLACKFOOT

SHIELD COVER, SIOUX

GHOST SHIRT
SIOUX

SHIELD COVER
ARAPAHO

RAWHIDE BAGS (PARFLECHE) ARAPAHO

ARAPAHO

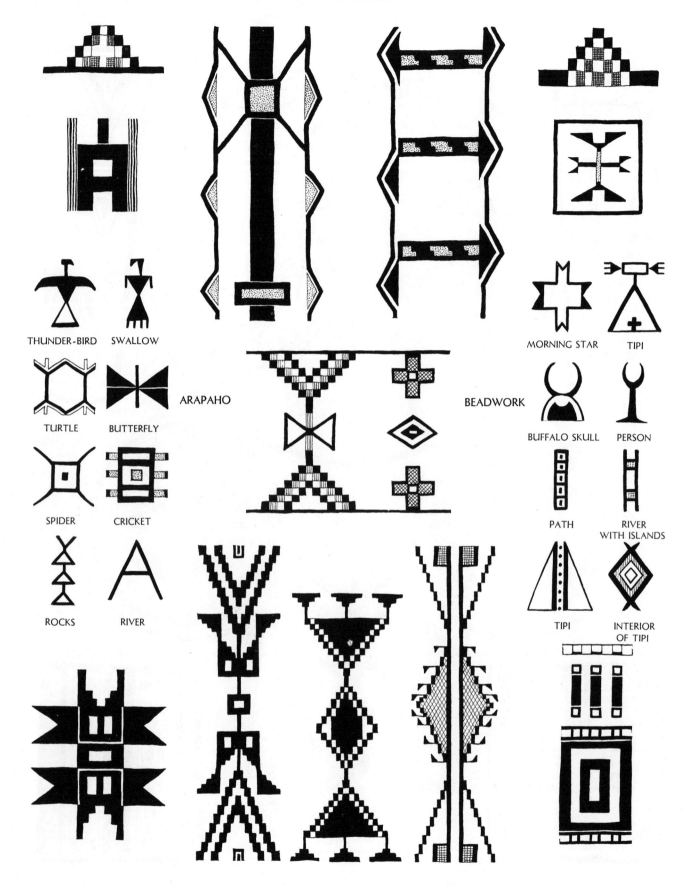

THUNDER-BIRD   SWALLOW

ARAPAHO

BEADWORK

MORNING STAR   TIPI

TURTLE   BUTTERFLY

BUFFALO SKULL   PERSON

SPIDER   CRICKET

PATH   RIVER
WITH ISLANDS

ROCKS   RIVER

TIPI   INTERIOR
OF TIPI

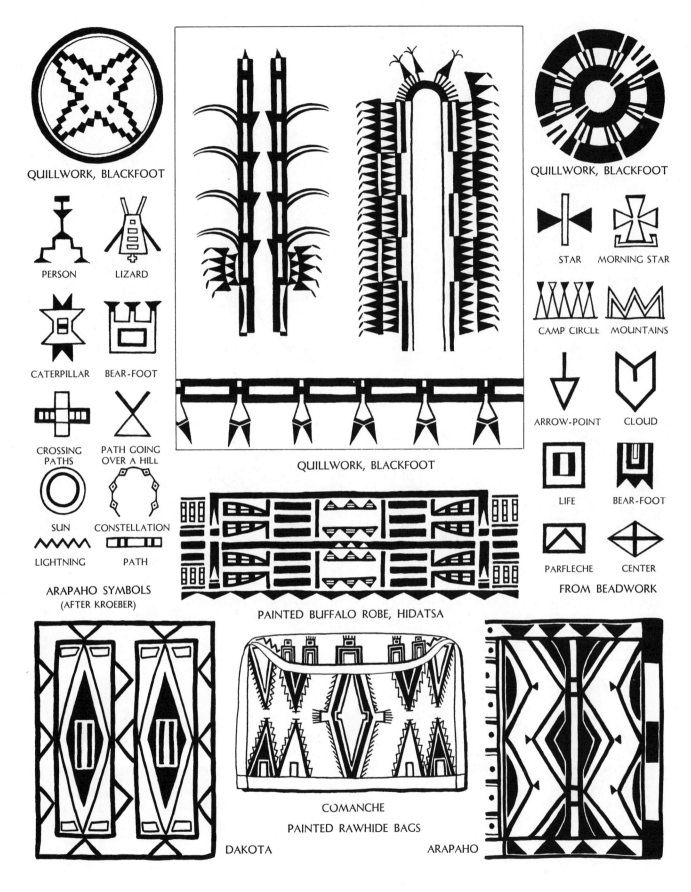

QUILLWORK, BLACKFOOT

QUILLWORK, BLACKFOOT

QUILLWORK, BLACKFOOT

PERSON

LIZARD

CATERPILLAR

BEAR-FOOT

CROSSING PATHS

PATH GOING OVER A HILL

SUN

CONSTELLATION

LIGHTNING

PATH

ARAPAHO SYMBOLS
(AFTER KROEBER)

STAR   MORNING STAR

CAMP CIRCLE   MOUNTAINS

ARROW-POINT   CLOUD

LIFE   BEAR-FOOT

PARFLECHE   CENTER

FROM BEADWORK

PAINTED BUFFALO ROBE, HIDATSA

COMANCHE

PAINTED RAWHIDE BAGS

DAKOTA

ARAPAHO

DAKOTA

DAKOTA

CROW

DAKOTA

BLACKFOOT

ARAPAHO

BEADED MOCCASINS   BEADED KNIFE-CASES   BEADED MOCCASINS

DAKOTA   RAWHIDE BAGS   ARAPAHO

QUILLWORK   BLACKFOOT

BEADWORK   BEADWORK

DAKOTA   ARAPAHO   ARAPAHO   BLACKFOOT

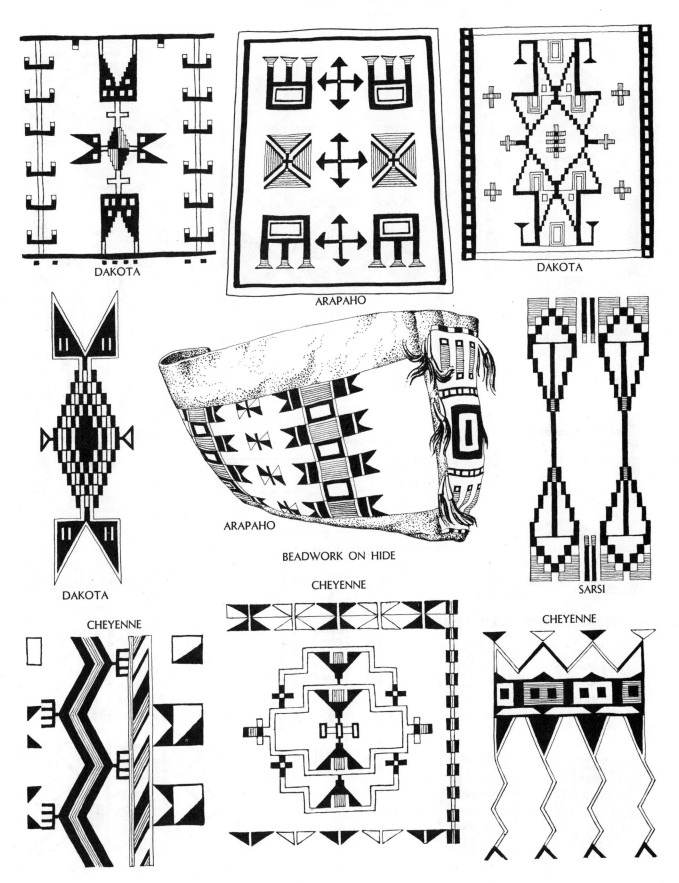

DAKOTA

ARAPAHO

DAKOTA

DAKOTA

ARAPAHO

BEADWORK ON HIDE

CHEYENNE

SARSI

CHEYENNE

CHEYENNE

BEADWORK ON HIDE

UTE

UTE

NEZ PERCÉ

NEZ PERCÉ

SHOSHONE

WOVEN BAGS, NEZ PERCÉ

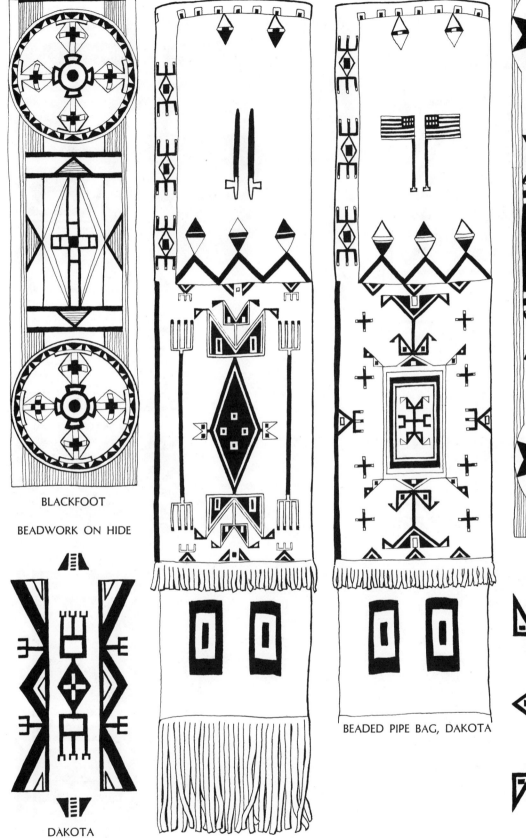

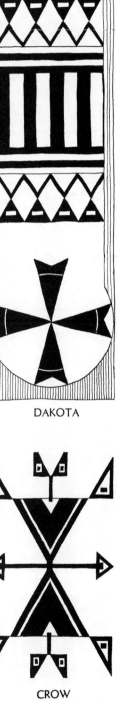

BLACKFOOT

BEADWORK ON HIDE

BEADED PIPE BAG, DAKOTA

DAKOTA

DAKOTA

CROW

MENOMINI

MENOMINI   THUNDER-BIRD

POTAWATOMI

PANTHER   MENOMINI

OJIBWAY

POTAWATOMI

OJIBWAY

WOVEN BAGS

POTAWATOMI

MENOMINI

MENOMINI

SAUK & FOX

SILK APPLIQUE, MENOMINI

QUILLWORK ON BUCKSKIN BAG, OJIBWAY

BEADWORK, OJIBWAY

BEADWORK, POTAWATOMI

SILK APPLIQUE, MENOMINI

BEADWORK, MENOMINI

BEADWORK, WINNEBAGO

BEADWORK, SAUK & FOX

BEADWORK OJIBWAY

MENOMINI

BEADWORK

BEADWORK

MENOMINI

MEDICINE BAG, MENOMINI

SAUK & FOX

MENOMINI

POTAWATOMI

SAUK & FOX

ENGRAVED SHELL
TENNESSEE

INCISED POTTERY
LOUISIANA

INCISED POTTERY,   LOUISIANA

INCISED POTTERY, ARKANSAS

CARVED FROM DIORITE, ALABAMA

INCISED AND
PAINTED POTTERY, ARKANSAS

STONE PIPE, OHIO

INCISED POTTERY
ALABAMA

EMBOSSED COPPER,   GEORGIA

STONE PIPE, OHIO

STONE PIPE, OHIO

ENGRAVED SHELL, TENNESSEE

INCISED POTTERY, ARKANSAS

ENGRAVED SHELL, GEORGIA

ENGRAVED SHELL, ILLINOIS

POTTERY PIPE, GEORGIA

ENGRAVED STONE, MISSISSIPPI

POTTERY PIPE, GEORGIA

POTTERY PIPE, GEORGIA

STONE, MISSISSIPPI

INCISED POTTERY, SOUTHERN APPALACHIAN

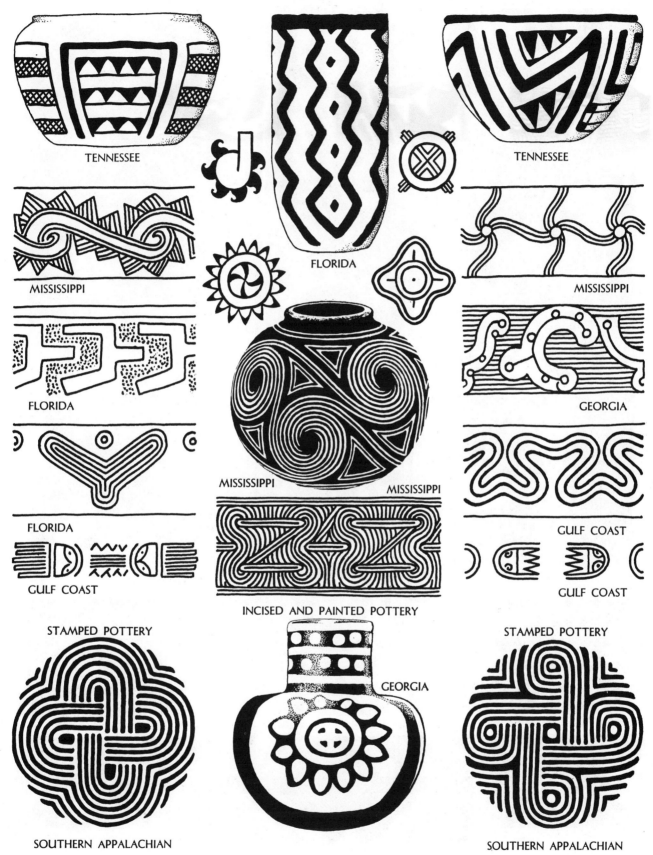

TENNESSEE

FLORIDA

TENNESSEE

MISSISSIPPI

MISSISSIPPI

FLORIDA

GEORGIA

FLORIDA

MISSISSIPPI

GULF COAST

GULF COAST

MISSISSIPPI

GULF COAST

STAMPED POTTERY

INCISED AND PAINTED POTTERY

GEORGIA

STAMPED POTTERY

SOUTHERN APPALACHIAN

SOUTHERN APPALACHIAN

SEMINOLE

CREEK

ALIBAMU

BEAD EMBROIDERY AND WEAVING

ALIBAMU

CREEK

YUCHI

CENTIPEDE   YUCHI

BEADWORK

SEMINOLE

YUCHI   CENTIPEDE

STORM CLOUDS

CLOUDS AND MOON

MILKY WAY

RAINBOW

OTTER

SUN AND MOON
OR MOON AND
STAR SYMBOL

TRIBAL SIGN

(AFTER SPECK)

SEMINOLE

SILK APPLIQUE, CHEROKEE

SILK APPLIQUE, CHEROKEE

INCISED POTTERY, CHEROKEE

16 THE FOREST AND THE RIVERS

CHITIMACHA

CHOCTAW

CHITIMACHA

CHITIMACHA

BASKET WEAVES

CHOCTAW

CHOCTAW

CHOCTAW

CHEROKEE

CHOCTAW

CHEROKEE

SILVERWORK   IROQUOIS

IROQUOIS   SILVERWORK

IROQUOIS

WOODEN MASKS

SENECA

INTERWOVEN BEADS

QUILLWORK

INCISED POTTERY

INCISED POTTERY PIPES

POTTERY PIPE,

INCISED POTTERY   IROQUOIS

POTTERY PIPE

SLATE PIPE

WASHINGTON COVENANT BELT, IROQUOIS
USED AS A COVENANT OF PEACE BETWEEN THE 13 ORIGINAL COLONIES AND THE SIX NATIONS

HIAWATHA BELT, IROQUOIS
RECORD OF THE FORMATION OF THE IROQUOIS LEAGUE OF THE FIVE NATIONS

WAMPUM BELTS

TO-TA-DA-HO BELT, ONONDAGA

MOHAWK

SENECA

IROQUOIS

DELAWARE

PASSAMAQUODDY (NECKBAND)

DELAWARE

IROQUOIS

BEADWORK   MICMAC   ON CLOTH

MALECITE

PENOBSCOT   PENOBSCOT

BARK BOXES, MONTAGNAIS

PAINTED HIDE, NASKAPI

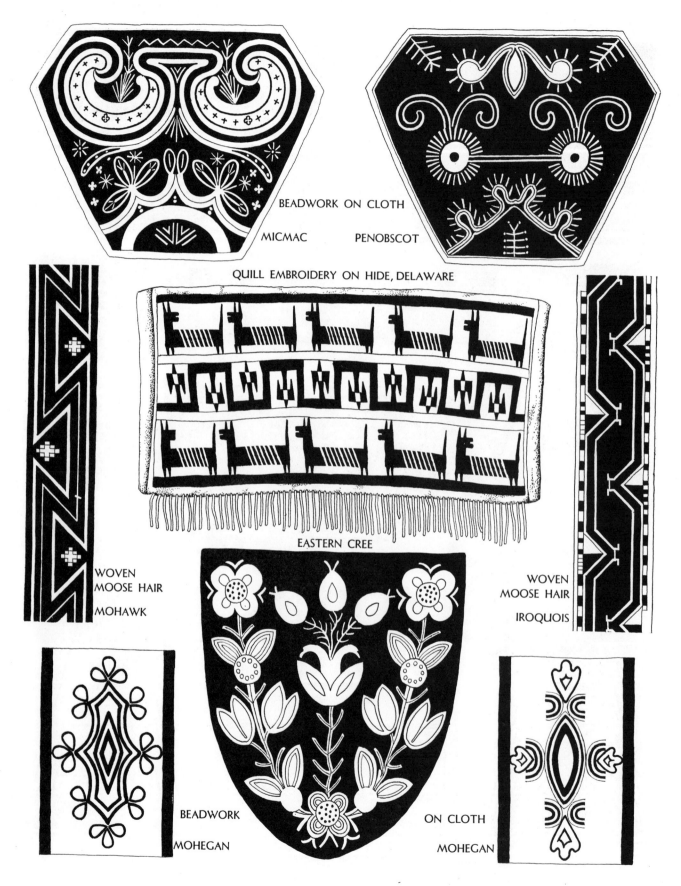

BEADWORK ON CLOTH

MICMAC   PENOBSCOT

QUILL EMBROIDERY ON HIDE, DELAWARE

WOVEN MOOSE HAIR MOHAWK

EASTERN CREE

WOVEN MOOSE HAIR IROQUOIS

BEADWORK MOHEGAN

ON CLOTH MOHEGAN

BEADWORK ON CLOTH, DÉNÉ

DÉNÉ, BEADWORK ON CLOTH

QUILLWORK, ATHAPASCAN

BEADWORK ON CLOTH, DÉNÉ

ATHAPASCAN, QUILLWORK

QUILLWORK, SLAVEY

SLAVEY, QUILLWORK

QUILLWORK, CHIPEWYAN

MOOSE HAIR EMBROIDERY, KASKA
QUILLWORK BORDER

TINNE, QUILLWORK

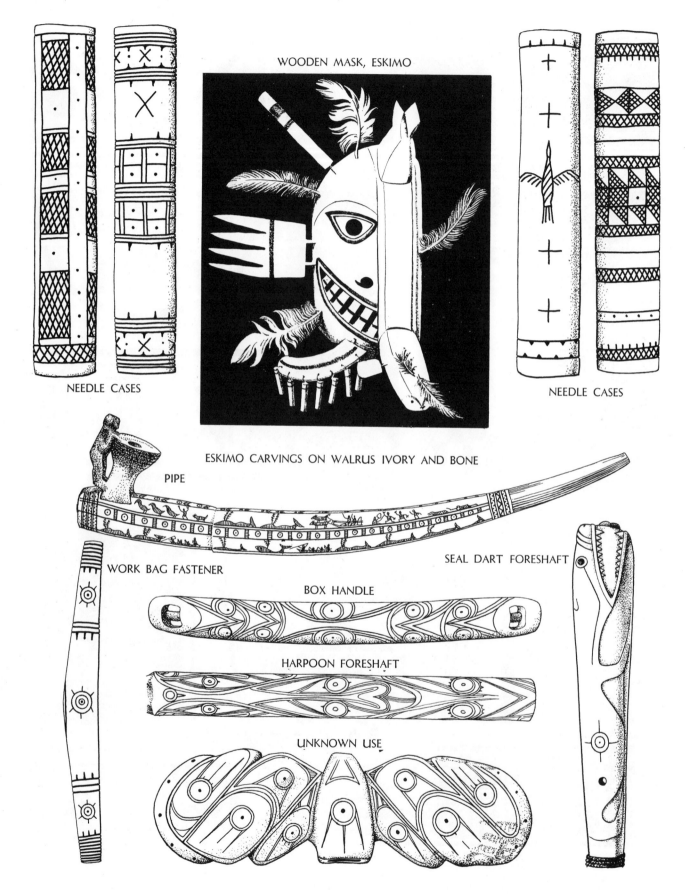

NEEDLE CASES

WOODEN MASK, ESKIMO

NEEDLE CASES

ESKIMO CARVINGS ON WALRUS IVORY AND BONE

PIPE

WORK BAG FASTENER

SEAL DART FORESHAFT

BOX HANDLE

HARPOON FORESHAFT

UNKNOWN USE

BEAR-TRACKS

RAINBOW

FOOT-PRINT

HAWK

RAVEN

CROSS

GOOSE-TRACK

BEAK CURVED
UNTIL TIP RESTS ON MOUTH

BEAK STRAIGHT

SCOOP-NET

TADPOLE

EAGLE

SHARK

CROSSINGS

BACKBONE

BEAK CURVED

VAULTED FOREHEAD
WITH THREE CRESCENTS

HALF-CROSS

WAVE

SPLIT-STICK

RAVEN-TAIL

BEAVER

BEAR

FIRE-WEED

BUTTERFLY

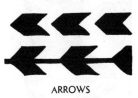

ARROWS

SAND-HILLS

SALMON BERRIES

DESIGN UNITS USED IN
BASKETRY, TLINGIT

(AFTER EMMONS)

LARGE INCISOR TEETH,
STICK, AND SCALY TAIL

PROTRUDING TONGUE

SHAMAN'S HAT

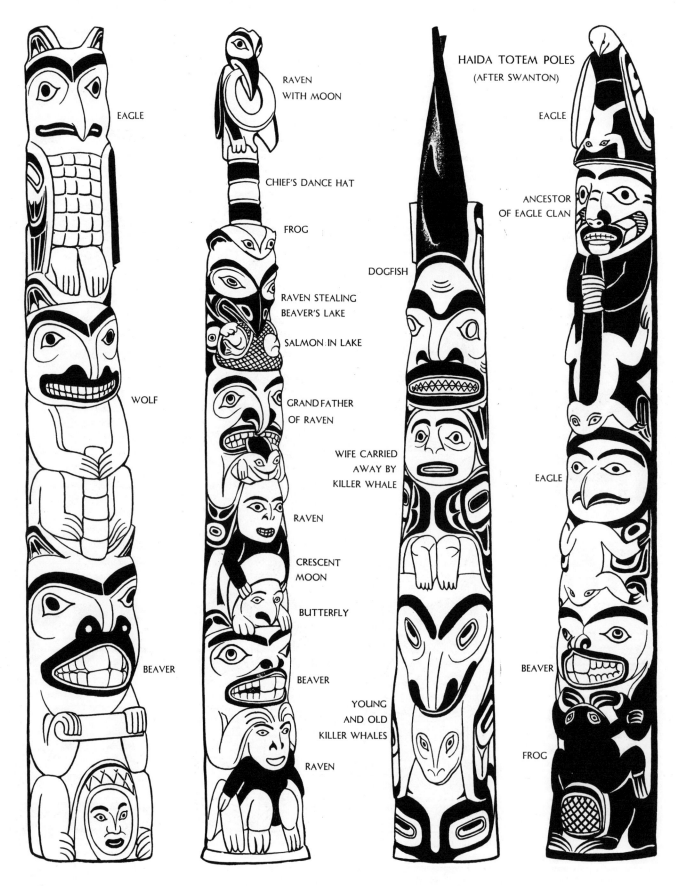

EAGLE

RAVEN
WITH MOON

CHIEF'S DANCE HAT

FROG

RAVEN STEALING
BEAVER'S LAKE

SALMON IN LAKE

WOLF

GRANDFATHER
OF RAVEN

DOGFISH

WIFE CARRIED
AWAY BY
KILLER WHALE

RAVEN

CRESCENT
MOON

BUTTERFLY

BEAVER

BEAVER

YOUNG
AND OLD
KILLER WHALES

RAVEN

HAIDA TOTEM POLES
(AFTER SWANTON)

EAGLE

ANCESTOR
OF EAGLE CLAN

EAGLE

BEAVER

FROG

INTERIOR
HOUSE POST
HAIDA

INTERIOR
HOUSE POST
TSIMSHIAN

HAIDA HOUSE

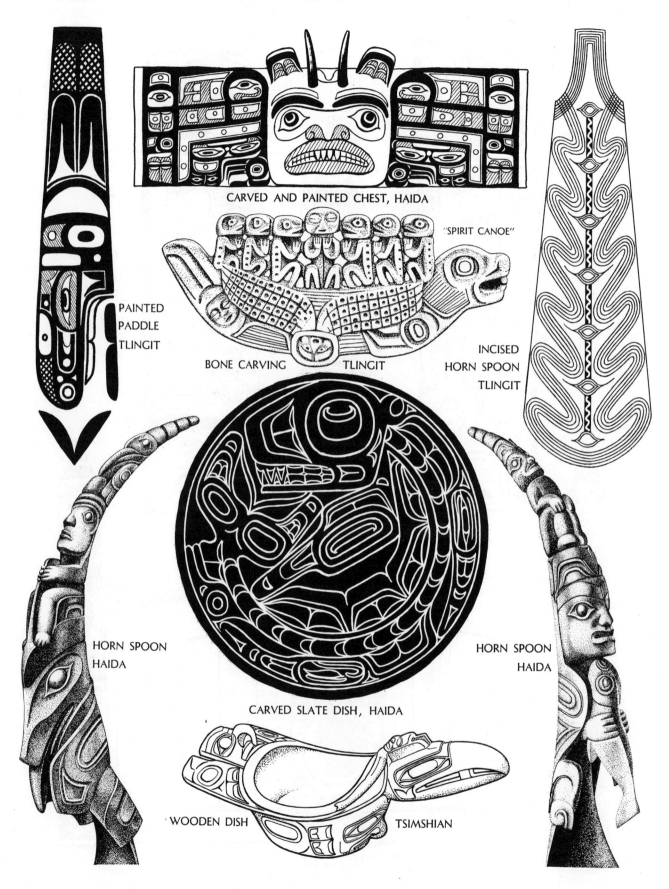

CARVED AND PAINTED CHEST, HAIDA

"SPIRIT CANOE"

PAINTED
PADDLE
TLINGIT

BONE CARVING   TLINGIT

INCISED
HORN SPOON
TLINGIT

HORN SPOON
HAIDA

HORN SPOON
HAIDA

CARVED SLATE DISH, HAIDA

WOODEN DISH   TSIMSHIAN

MASK, DOUBLE-HEADED SERPENT, KWAKIUTL

FULL MOON

MASK, BELLA COOLA

PAINTED DRUM HEAD   TSIMSHIAN

RAINBOW

MASK, BELLACOOLA

UNITS USED IN PAINTED DESIGNS AND CHILKAT BLANKETS

HAND, PAW, OR FOOT

EYE

MAN'S HEAD

DOUBLE-EYE

FEATHER

NOSTRIL

MOUTH

EAR

CHILKAT

CARVED AND PAINTED BOX

BONE WITH SHELL INLAY, KITKSAN

HEADDRESS, TSIMSHIAN

HEADDRESS, HAIDA

PAINTED HIDE, HAIDA

WOODEN RATTLE, TLINGIT

MASK, BELLACOOLA

MASK, BELLACOOLA

MASK, KWAKIUTL

MASK, KWAKIUTL

BEAR WITH YOUNG

CHILKAT BLANKETS

BEAR WITH TWO KILLER-WHALES

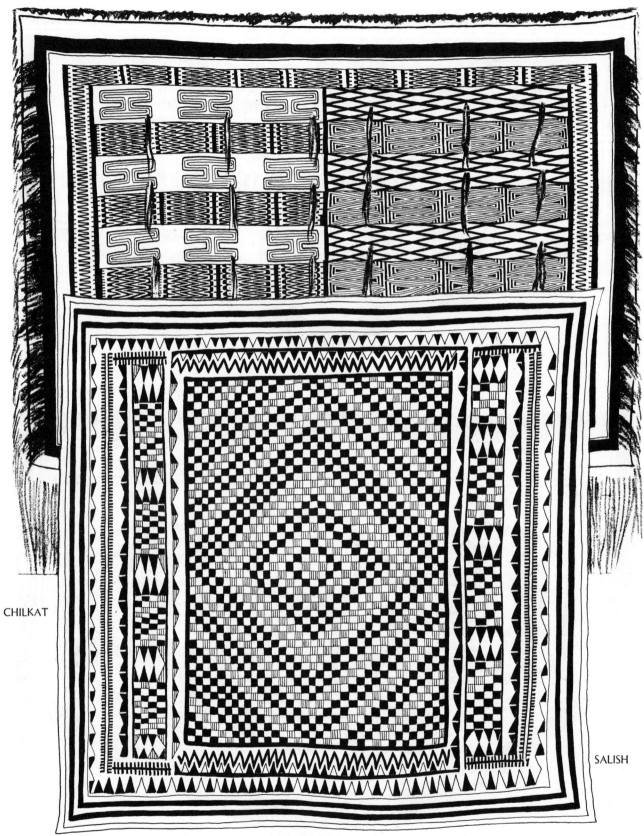

CHILKAT

SALISH

CEREMONIAL BLANKETS

BASKET DESIGNS, TLINGIT

DANCING-SHIRT, CHILKAT

BASKET DESIGNS, TLINGIT

DANCING-APRON, TLINGIT

SALISH

LILLOOET
BASKETRY

SALISH

STONE-HAMMER

LILLOOET

MOUTH

GROUSE-TRACK

FLYING-GOOSE

MOUNTAINS WITH LAKES
LILLOOET

SALISH

WAVES OR RIPPLES
LILLOOET

TSIMSHIAN

TSIMSHIAN

4

MOUNTAIN AND MESA

"IT IS A LITTLE VILLAGE, looking as if it had been crumpled all up together." So did Hawikuh, pueblo of the Zuni in New Mexico, look to Coronado's men in 1540. There was no gold for the Spaniards to take, but there was corn. The Spaniards seized on the corn and departed.

Forty years later, Spanish settlers began arriving in the area. Revolts, suffering, changes in masters followed with monotonous regularity; yet, despite it all, the Indian is still in his ancient home, holding fast to his ancient traditions.

The present-day Indians of the Southwest are the descendants of many tribes which invaded the country from north, south and east. First to come, so far as we know, were Basket Makers who lived in caves and brush huts. They were hunters and farmers. Corn was their principal crop.

Next came the Cliff Dwellers. Just as we have seen that the Mound-builders were no mysterious race of beings, so it was with the Cliff Dwellers. They were Pueblo Indians, as we call them, ancestors of the present groups so-called; but they were also in their time the greatest architects north of Mexico, the builders of the great communal apartment dwellings whose ruins are still to be seen and marvelled at. The ancestors of the present-day Pomos and Papagos were another invading group who arrived at about the same time as the Cliff Dwellers and built the first irrigation canals in the Southwest.

Then came the nomads—the Apaches, the Navaho and the Comanches, to name the best-known of them. These were hunters and seed-gatherers, always on the move. Their many different languages indicate their origin. Some were from the Plains; some were from the east; some were from Mexico.

The black and white pottery, with its geometric and rectilinear designs, shown on Plate 35, comes from the ruins of the Cliff Dwellings and pueblos. Most of these designs show the influence of basket and textile weaving. In startling contrast is the pottery from the Mimbres Valley on Plate 37. Realism is so rare in early work that the style developed there is truly unique. Pottery from Casas Grandes shows bird and animal forms and effigy vessels, indicating Mexican influence from the Nahua and Aztec groups. The Cochiti legend, "The Institution of Pottery," will be found a valuable clue to the purposes of the designers.

Pre-historic Hopi and Zuni potters also used bird motives, some realistic, others so highly conventionalized that it is difficult to identify the forms unless one is acquainted with the historic changes. Plate 34 shows a representative range of bird forms.

A typical modern Zuni design uses the deer enclosed in a panel of leaf-like forms and free scrolls, called the "deer's house." The deer is invariably painted with his heart showing—the same symbolism that is expressed by leaving a break in an encircling line of a design in order that the soul of the vessel may not be imprisoned. Since the Indian believes his baskets and bowls have life, it would be fatal to the maker to close the break.

The prayer meal bowls illustrated on Plate 38 show true symbolism, cloud and rain symbols and life forms associated with water. Symbolism is expressed in the highest degree in the Navaho sand paintings (Plate 42) which are really prayers to cure the sick. By destroying the painting the medicine man destroys the illness of the patient. The Navaho story of "The Floating Logs" on page 115 explains the origin and symbolism of sandpainting. The Navaho's blanket designs are not symbolic, but under pressure of white ideas they are using patterns that probably cause their ancestors to turn in their graves (Plate 45). The center blanket, with *Yei,* a male god, was copied by the weaver from a sand painting.

Ancient symbolical designs are embroidered on ceremonial garments by the Hopi. Those shown on Plates 43 and 45 with clouds, rain streaks, butterflies, and so forth, are particularly fine in design. Rain symbols are found on the mask of one of the Kachina dancers on Plate 41.

Among the Pueblo groups the Hopi are the only ones who do any amount of decorated basketry. The Apaches are expert basket makers. The designs are mostly geometrical but not symbolic (Plate 40).

The well-known silver work of the Navaho and Zuni was derived from the Spanish as many of the forms indicate, although most of the design elements are original with the Indian.

The legends and myths of the Southwest tribes are, perhaps, the best-known of Indian stories to the average reader. The Navaho legends and ceremonial chants, the Zuni origin myth and its concomitant chant-poems make stirring reading; and do not forget that the clue to the symbolism of color and of the graphic designs will be found in their explanations of the supernatural.

THE FLOATING LOGS

A MAN SAT THINKING, "Let me see; my songs are too short; I want more songs; where shall I go to find them?" Hasjelti appeared and, perceiving his thoughts, said, "I know where you can go to get more songs." "Well, I much want to get more, and I will follow you."

When they reached a certain point in a box canyon in the Big Colorado River they found four gods (the Hostjobokon) at work hewing logs of cottonwood. Hasjelti said, "This will not do; cottonwood becomes water-soaked; you must use pine instead of cottonwood." The Hostjobokon then began boring the pine with flint, when Hasjelti said, "That is slow work," and he commanded the whirlwind to hollow the log. A Jerusalem cross was formed with one solid log and a hollow one. The song-hunter entered the hollow log and Hasjelti closed the end with a cloud, that the water of the river might not enter when the logs were launched upon the great waters. The Hostjobokon, accompanied by their wives, rode upon the logs, a couple sitting on the end of each cross arm. These were accompanied by Hasjelti, Hostjoghon, and two Naaskiddi, who walked on the banks to ward the logs off from the shore. Hasjelti carried a squirrel skin filled with tobacco from which to supply the gods on their journey. Hostjoghon carried a staff ornamented with eagle and turkey plumes and a gaming ring with two hummingbirds tied to it with white cotton cord. The two Naaskiddi carried staffs of lightning. After floating a long distance down the river they came to waters that had a shore on one side only, and they landed. Here they found people like themselves. These people, on learning of the song-hunter's wish, gave to him many songs and they painted pictures on a cotton blanket and said, "These pictures must go with the songs. If we give this blanket to you you will lose it. We will give you white earth and black coals which you will grind together to make black paint, and we will give you white sand, yellow sand, and red sand, and for the blue paint you will take white sand and black coals with a very little red and yellow sand. These together will give you blue."

The song-hunter remained with these people until the corn was ripe. There he learned to eat corn and he carried some back with him to the Navaho, who had not seen corn before, and he taught them how to raise it and how to eat it.

As the logs would not float upstream the song-hunter was conveyed by four sunbeams, one attached to each end of the cross-logs, to the box canyon whence he emerged. Upon his return he separated the logs, placing an end of the solid log into the hollow end of the other and planted this great pole in the river, where to this day it is to be seen by those so venturesome as to visit this point.

Navaho

GAME STORY

THERE WAS A MAN who, while playing the hoop game and the game of seven wooden dice, lost all his property, including a very good house. He also lost the beads that belonged to his niece. Because of this his brothers resolved to kill him. A necklace of mixed beads was hanging in the center of the house. The niece told her uncle he might wager that also. "All right, niece," he replied, and took the white shell, the turquoise, the abalone, the coral, the jet; he took five of them off one by one. He also provided himself with specular iron ore, pollen of larkspur and of cat-tails. With these he walked away to the corn pits which were full. From these he took one ear each of the five colors. He patted these together until they were small. "Well, little mother," he said to his niece, "they speak of killing me. It may be you and I will see each other again. Goodbye."

Then he put a tree into the water with himself (inside of it). He floated in the tree down where the stream enters the Colorado River. He got out of the tree there and walked along the shore. He felt lonesome there. He planted the corn he had brought with him in the form of a cross, putting the seed in, one by one. Each stalk had two ears projecting opposite each other. There were twelve stalks with two ears each.

He stayed there four years and then started to return to his home. After many days he got back, arriving early in the morning at his home which was called *te'ineisk'it*. He went to the corn storage pits, but they were entirely empty. He put four ears in them and blew on them four times. After that he went where his niece was sitting. They were having a famine. "Prepare food for me, my little mother," he said to her. "There is none," she replied. "Four days after you left, the corn was all gone. I do not know how it happened." She sat there crying. "I cannot cook food for you, my uncle." "Go and get something," he said again. "Do not say that, uncle, there is none, none." When they had spoken to each other four times she went to the pits.

When she got there the pits were full. "Thanks, uncle," she called as she ran back with the corn. The girl then ran to the men and told them her uncle had come and that the corn pits were full again.

"Welcome," they said, when they came in and they then embraced him. "You are the only one, younger brother. In the future we will not speak evil of you. Something has happened to the game animals. We hunt in vain."

Wondering what had happened, the returned brother hunted for days in vain. One day when he was hunting he went to the top of a mountain. Below a cliff he saw a deer standing. He ran around and crept up where the deer had been, but it had vanished. He examined the ground, but the soil had not been disturbed. The next day he climbed the mountain again and there the deer stood again. This time he walked directly toward it trying to keep it in sight; but where it had been standing there was nothing but some deer dung. A little distance from where he stood there had been a spruce tree, but when he turned his head away and then looked in that direction again a god stood there. "What is it, grandchild?" he asked. "A deer which was standing right there has vanished," he replied. "Have you white shell, grandson?" "I have them all, grandfather." "My grandson has everything. We will do it," the god said. [*They went up to the god's house.*]

He found the door fronts were darkness, daylight, the moon, and the sun. Inside, shadow gods were sitting on either side, facing each other. "Well, go on, my grandson," the first god said. He took steps on the right side of the house four times, blowing as he did so, and four footprints appeared. He discovered that the first god had pets which he kept far in the interior. He heard from inside someone say, "Ho, I smell earth people. The polite master has brought in a human being." "Do not say that; he has everything," the god said. Back of the fire a male deer was lying. On him lay a feathered arrow with a red shaft. It had just been pulled out.

The man took a seat in the center. He put down one each of white shell, turquoise, coral, abalone, jet, specular iron ore, blue pollen, cat-tail pollen, and then covered them with a blanket. He stepped over these four times and they became a great heap.

The god was sorrowful and said, "I do not think we can give you a fair equivalent." He found out afterward that he stayed there in the house of the game animals four days. The shadow gods distributed the precious objects. They gave each of those present fifteen pieces, then thirteen, then nine, then seven, then five, then three, and all had been given out.

"This is the way deer should be skinned. Break the legs here at the wrist joint, but let them hang by the tendons. Leave the skin on the nose and lips. Draw the skin carefully from under the eyes. Do not cut through the bladder. Turn the hide back to the hips. If you do this way you will always kill game. Put the head toward the center, but do not let the eyes burn or the teeth. You must not cook it by burying it in the ashes. Game animals must not be thrown away. Sickness will result if you do not observe these things. If the teeth are burned the hunter's teeth will hurt. You earth people will have a cure for it, grandson," the god told him.

He had everything prepared. "What did you come for, grandson?" Small Whirlwind told him that on that side were images of the game animals standing side by side. On the east side was the paunch of an animal in which were deer songs. The man pointed to these. The god looked down and said, "All right, grandson. It was for these you came."

Being *xactc'eyalti* I came up.
To the abode of the deer I came up.
To the door post of darkness I came up.
To the door post of daylight I came up.
To the door post of moon I came up.
To the door post of sun I came up.
To the place where *xactc'eyalti* with *xactc'ejin* sat facing each other, I came up.
To where the black bow and the feathered arrows with red shaft lie across each other, I came up.
Over there they lie across each other, red with the mouth blood of a male deer.
Over there the deer I killed likes me.

He sang only one deer song.
They were here when I was hunting them in vain he thought to himself. "Shoot them in the brush," he told him. This is where they are.

I being *xactc'eyalti.*
On the trail to the top of Black Mountain,
On the trail among the flowers,
Male deer are there,
The pollen of herbs I will put in its mouth,
The male deer steps along in the dew of the vegetation.
I kill him but he likes me.

He returned home. He shot into the brush and a deer rolled over with the arrow in him. He shot into another kind of brush and a fawn rolled over with the arrow in him. He shot into another kind of brush and a yearling rolled over with the arrow.

"I have done something important," he thought to himself as he ran back. They found he had killed them all. That is why when they get away we track them.

There are very many game songs. If one does not know them he does not hunt. We are afraid about these things because they are pets of the gods.

Navaho

THE CREATION OF THE HORSE

SOMETHING WAS SPREAD over it. It moved and became alive. It whimpered. Woman-Who-Changes began to sing:—

Changing Woman I am, I hear.
In the center of my house behind the fire, I hear.
Sitting on jewels spread wide, I hear.
In a jet basket, in a jet house, there now it lies.
Vegetation with its dew in it, it lies.
Over there,
It increases, not hurting the house now with it it lies,
　　inside it lies.

Its feet were made of mirage. They say that, because a horse's feet have stripes. Its gait was a rainbow, its bridle of sun strings. Its heart was made of red stone. Its intestines were made of water of all kinds, its tail of black rain. Its mane was a cloud with a little rain. Distant lightning composed its ears. A big spreading twinkling star formed its eye and striped its face. Its lower legs were white. At night it gives light in front because its face was made of vegetation. Large beads formed its lips; white shell, its teeth, so they would not wear out quickly. A black flute was put into its mouth for a trumpet. Its belly was made of dawn, one side white, one side black. That is why it is called "half white."

A white-shell basket stood there. In it was the water of a mare's afterbirth. A turquoise basket stood there. It contained the water of the afterbirth. An abalone basket full of the eggs of various birds stood there. A jet basket with eggs stood there. The baskets stand for quadrupeds, the eggs for birds. Now as Changing Woman began to sing, the animals came up to taste. The horse tasted twice; hence mares sometimes give birth to twins. One ran back without tasting. Four times, he ran up and back again. The last time he said, "Sh!" and did not taste. "She will not give birth. Long-ears (Mule) she will be called," said Changing Woman. The others tasted the eggs from the different places. Hence there are many feathered people. Because they tasted the eggs in the abalone and jet baskets many are black.

Navaho

THE GREAT SHELL OF KINTYEL

KINTYEL, BROAD HOUSE, AND KINDOTLIZ, Blue House, are two pueblo houses in the Chaco Canyon. They are ruins now; but in the days when Kinniki lived on earth many people dwelt there. Not far from the ruins is a high cliff called Tse'dezá, or Standing Rock. Near these places the rite of *yói hatál,* or the bead chant, was first practised by the Navaho, and this is the tale of how it first became known to man:—

Two young men, one from Kintyel and one from Kindotliz, went out one day to hunt deer. About sunset, as they were returning to Kindotliz, weary and unsuccessful, they observed a war-eagle soaring overhead, and they stopped to watch his flight. He moved slowly away, growing smaller and smaller to their gaze until at length he dwindled to a black speck, almost invisible; and while they strained their sight to get a last look he seemed to them to descend on the top of Standing Rock. In order to mark the spot where they last saw him they cut a forked stick, stuck it in the ground fork upward, and arranged it so that when they should look over it again, crouching in a certain position, their sight would be guided to the spot. They left the stick standing and went home to Kindotliz.

In those days eagles were very scarce in the land; it was a wonder to see one; so when the young men got home and told the story of their day's adventures, it became the subject of much conversation and counsel, and at length the people determined to send four men, in the morning, to take sight over the forked stick, in order to find out where the eagle lived.

Next morning early, the four men designated went to the forked stick and sighted over it, and all came to the conclusion that the eagle lived on the point of Tse'dezá. They went at once to the rock, climbed to the summit, and saw the eagle and its young in a cleft on the face of the precipice below them. They remained on the summit all day and watched the nest.

At night they went home and told what they had seen. They had observed two young eagles of different ages in the nest. Of the four men who went on the search, two were from Kintyel and two were from Kindotliz, therefore people from the two pueblos met in counsel in an estufa, and there it was decided that Kindotliz should have the elder of the two eaglets and that Kintyel should have the younger.

The only way to reach the nest was to lower a man to it with a rope; yet directly above the nest was an overhanging ledge which the man, descending, would be obliged to pass. It was a dangerous undertaking, and no one could be found to volunteer for it. Living near the pueblos was a miserable Navaho beggar who subsisted on such food as he could pick up. When the sweepings of the rooms and the ashes from the fireplaces were thrown out on the kitchen heap, he searched eagerly through them and was happy if he could find a few grains of corn or a piece of paper bread. He was called Nahoditáhe, or He Who Picks Up (like a bird). They concluded to induce this man to make the dangerous descent.

They returned to the pueblo and sent for the poor Navaho to come to the estufa. When he came they bade him be seated, placed before him a large basket of paper bread, bowls of boiled corn and meat, with all sorts of their best food, and told him to eat his fill. He ate as he had never eaten before, and after a long time he told his hosts that he was satisfied. "You shall eat," said they, "of such abundance all your life, and never more have to scrape for grains of corn among the dirt, if you will do as we desire." Then they told him of their plan for catching the young eagles, and asked him if he were willing to be put in a basket and lowered to the nest with a rope. He pondered and was silent. They asked him again and again until they had asked him four times, while he still sat in meditation. At last he answered: "I lead but a poor life at best. Existence is not sweet to a man who always hungers. It would be pleasant to eat such food for the rest of my days, and some time or other I must die. I shall do as you wish."

On the following morning they gave him another good meal; they made a great, strong carrying-basket with four corners at the top; they tied a strong string to each corner, and, collecting a large party, they set out for the rock of Tse'dezá.

When the party arrived at the top of the rock they tied a long, stout rope to the four strings on the basket. They instructed the Navaho to take the eaglets out of the nest and drop them to the bottom of the cliff. The Navaho then entered the basket and was lowered over the edge of the precipice. They let the rope out slowly till they thought they had lowered him far enough and then they stopped; but as he had not yet reached the nest he called out to them to lower him farther. They did so, and as soon as he was on a level with the nest he called to the people above to stop.

He was just about to grasp the eaglets and throw them down when Wind whispered to him: "These people of the Pueblos are not your friends. They desire not to feed you with their good food as long as you live. If you throw these young eagles down, as they bid you, they will never pull you up again. Get into the eagles' nest and stay there." When he heard this, he called to those above: "Swing the basket so that it may come nearer to the cliff. I cannot reach the nest unless you do." So they caused the basket to swing back and forth. When it touched the cliff he held fast to the rock and scrambled into the nest, leaving the empty basket swinging in the air.

The Pueblos saw the empty basket swinging and waited, expecting to see the Navaho get back into it again. But when they had waited a good while and found he did not return they began to call to him as if he were a dear relation of theirs. "My son," said the old men, "throw down those little eagles." "My elder brother! My younger brother!" the young men shouted, "throw down those little eagles." They kept up their clamor until nearly sunset; but they never moved the will of the Navaho. He sat in the cleft and never answered them, and when the sun set they ceased calling and went home.

In the cleft or cave, around the nest, four dead animals lay; to the east there was a fawn; to the south a hare; to the west the young of a Rocky Mountain sheep, and to the north a prairie-dog. From time to time, when the eaglets felt hungry, they would leave the nest and eat of the meat; but the Navaho did not touch it.

Early next day the Pueblo people returned and gathered in a great crowd at the foot of the cliff. They stayed there all day repeating their entreaties and promises, calling the Navaho by endearing terms, and displaying all kinds of tempting food to his gaze; but he heeded them not and spoke not.

They came early again on the third day, but they came in anger. They no longer called him by friendly names; they no longer made fair promises to him; but, instead, they shot fire-arrows at the eyry in hopes they would burn the Navaho out or set fire to the nest and compel him to throw it and the eaglets down. But he remained watchful and active, and whenever a fire-arrow entered the cave he seized it quickly and threw it out. Then they abused him and reviled him, and called him bad names until sunset, when again they went home.

They came again on the fourth day and acted as they had done on the previous day; but they did not succeed in making the Navaho throw down the little eagles. He spoke to the birds, saying: "Can you not help me?" They rose in the nest, shook their wings, and threw out many little feathers, which fell on the people below. The Navaho thought the birds must be scattering disease on his enemies. When the latter left at sunset they said: "Now we shall leave you where you are, to die of hunger and thirst." He was then altogether three nights and nearly four days in the cave. For two days the Pueblos had coaxed and flattered him; for two days they had cursed and reviled him, and at the end of the fourth day they went home and left him in the cave to die.

When his tormentors were gone he sat in the cave hungry and thirsty, weak and despairing, till the night fell. Soon after dark he heard a great rushing sound which approached from one side of the entrance to the cave, roared a moment in front, and then grew faint in the distance at the other side. Thus four times the sound came and went, growing louder each time it passed, and at length the male Eagle lit on the eyry. Soon the sounds were repeated, and the female bird, the mother of the eaglets, alighted. Turning at once toward the Navaho, she said: "Greeting, my child! Thanks, my child! You have not thrown down your younger brother, Doniki." The male Eagle repeated the same words. They addressed the Navaho by the name of Doniki, but afterwards they named him Kinniki, after the chief of all the Eagles in the sky. He only replied to the Eagles: "I am hungry. I am thirsty."

The male Eagle opened his sash and took out a small white cotton cloth which contained a little corn meal, and he took out a small bowl of white shell no bigger than the palm of the hand. When the Indian saw this he said: "Give me water first, for I am famishing with thirst." "No," replied the Eagle; "eat first and then you shall have something to drink." The Eagle then drew forth from his tail feathers a small plant which has many joints and grows near streams. The joints were all filled with water. The Eagle mixed a little of the water with some of the meal in the shell and handed the mixture to the Navaho. The latter ate and ate, until he was satisfied, but he could not diminish in the least the contents of the shell vessel. When he was done eating there was as much in the cup as there was when he began. He handed it back to the Eagle, the latter emptied it with one sweep of his finger, and it remained empty. Then the Eagle put the jointed plant to the Navaho's lips as if it were a wicker bottle, and the Indian drank his fill.

On the previous nights, while lying in the cave, the Navaho had slept between the eaglets in the nest to keep himself warm and shelter himself from the wind, and this plan had been of some help to him; but on this night the great Eagles slept one on each side of him, and he felt as warm as if he had slept among robes of fur. Before the Eagles lay down to sleep each took off his robe of plumes, which formed a single garment, opening in front, and revealed a form like that of a human being.

The Navaho slept well that night and did not waken till he heard a voice calling from the top of the cliff: "Where are you? The day has dawned. It is growing late. Why are you not abroad already?" At the sound of this voice the Eagles woke too and put on their robes of plumage. Presently a great number of birds were seen flying before the opening of the cave and others were heard calling to one another on the rock overhead. There were many kinds of Eagles and Hawks in the throng. Some of all the large birds of prey were there. Those on top of the rock sang:—

> Kinnakíye, there he sits.
> When they fly up,
> We shall see him.
> He will flap his wings.

One of the Eagles brought a dress of eagle plumes and was about to put it on the Navaho when the others interfered, and they had a long argument as to whether they should dress him in the garment of the Eagles or not; but at length they all flew away without giving him the dress. When they returned they had thought of another plan for taking him out of the cave. Laying him on his face, they put a streak of crooked lightning under his feet, a sunbeam under his knees, a piece of straight lightning under his chest, another under his outstretched hands, and a rainbow under his forehead.

An Eagle then seized each end of these six supports,—making twelve Eagles in all,— and they flew with the Navaho and the eaglets away from the eyry. They circled round twice with their burden before they reached the level of the top of the cliff. They circled round twice more ascending, and then flew toward the south, still going upwards. When they got above the top of Tsótsil (Mt. Taylor), they circled four times more, until they almost touched the sky. Then they began to flag and breathed hard, and they cried out: "We are weary. We can fly no farther." The voice of one, unseen to the Navaho, cried from above: "Let go your burden." The Eagles released their hold on the supports, and the Navaho felt himself descending swiftly toward the earth. But he had not fallen far when he felt himself seized around the waist and chest, he felt something twining itself around his body, and a moment later he beheld the heads of two Arrow-snakes looking at him over his shoulders. The Arrow-snakes bore him swiftly upwards, up through the sky-hole, and landed him safely on the surface of the upper world above the sky.

When he looked around him he observed four pueblo dwellings, or towns; a white pueblo in the east, a blue pueblo in the south, a yellow pueblo in the west, and a black pueblo in the north. Wolf was the chief of the eastern pueblo, Blue Fox of the southern, Puma of the western, and Big Snake of the northern. The Navaho was left at liberty to go where he chose, but Wind whispered into his ear and said: "Visit, if you wish, all the pueblos except that of the north. Chicken Hawk and other bad characters dwell there."

Next he observed that a war party was preparing, and soon after his arrival the warriors went forth. What enemies they sought he could not learn. He entered several of the houses, was well treated wherever he went, and given an abundance of paper bread and other good food to eat. He saw that in their homes the Eagles were just like ordinary people down on the lower world. As soon as they entered their pueblos they took off their feather suits, hung these up on pegs and poles, and went around in white suits which they wore underneath their feathers when in flight. He visited all the pueblos except the black one in the north. In the evening the warriors returned. They were received with loud wailing and with tears, for many who went out in the morning did not return at night. They had been slain in battle.

In a few days another war party was organized, and this time the Navaho determined to go with it. When the warriors started on the trail he followed them. "Whither are you going?" they asked. "I wish to be one of your party," he replied. They laughed at him and said: "You are a fool to think you can go to war against such dreadful enemies as those that we fight. We can move as fast as the wind, yet our enemies can move faster. If they are able to overcome us, what chance have you, poor man, for your life?" Hearing this, he remained behind, but they had not travelled far when he hurried after them. When he overtook them, which he soon did, they spoke to him angrily, told him more earnestly than before how helpless he was, and how great his danger, and bade him return to the villages. Again he halted; but as soon as they were out of sight he began to run after them, and he came up with them at the place where they had encamped for the night. Here they gave him of their food, and again they scolded him, and sought to dissuade him from accompanying them.

In the morning, when the warriors resumed their march, he remained behind on the camping-ground, as if he intended to return; but as soon as they were out of sight he proceeded again to follow them. He had not travelled far when he saw smoke coming up out of the ground, and approaching the smoke he found a smoke-hole, out of which stuck an old ladder, yellow with smoke, such as we see in the pueblo dwellings to-day. He looked down through the hole and beheld, in a subterranean chamber beneath, a strange-looking old woman with a big mouth. Her teeth were not set in her head evenly and regularly, like those of an Indian; they protruded from her mouth, were set at a distance from one another, and were curved like the claws of a bear. She was Nastsé Estsán, the Spider Woman. She invited him into her house, and he passed down the ladder.

When he got inside, the Spider Woman showed him four large wooden hoops,—one in the east colored black, one in the south colored blue, one in the west colored yellow, and one in the north white and sparkling. Attached to each hoop were a number of decayed, ragged feathers. "These feathers," said she, "were once beautiful plumes, but now they are old and dirty. I want some new plumes to adorn my hoops, and you can get them for me. Many of the Eagles will be killed in the battle to which you are going, and when they die you can pluck out the plumes and bring them to me. Have no fear of the enemies. Would you know who they are that the Eagles go to fight? They are only the bumblebees and the tumble-weeds." She gave him a long black cane and said: "With this you can gather the tumble-weeds into a pile, and then you can set them on fire. Spit the juice of scare-weed at the bees and they cannot sting you. But before you burn up the tumble-weeds gather some of the seeds, and when you have killed the bees take some of their nests. You will need these things when you return to the earth." When Spider Woman had done speaking the Navaho left to pursue his journey.

He travelled on, and soon came up with the warriors where they were hiding behind a little hill and preparing for battle. Some were putting on their plumes; others were painting and adorning themselves. From time to time one of their number would creep cautiously to the top of the hill and peep over; then he would run back and whisper: "There are the enemies. They await us." The Navaho went to the top of the hill and peered over; but he could see no enemy whatever. He saw only a dry, sandy flat, covered in one place with sunflowers, and in another place with dead weeds; for it was now late in the autumn in the world above.

Soon the Eagles were all ready for the fray. They raised their war-cry, and charged over the hill into the sandy plain. The Navaho remained behind the hill, peeping over to see what would occur. As the warriors approached the plain a whirlwind arose; a great number of tumble-weeds ascended with the wind and surged around madly through the air; and, at the same time, from among the sunflowers a cloud of bumblebees arose. The Eagles charged through the ranks of their enemies, and when they had passed to the other side they turned around and charged back again. Some spread their wings and soared aloft to attack the tumble-weeds that had gone up with the whirlwind. From time to time the Navaho noticed the dark body of an Eagle falling down through the air. When the combat had continued some time, the Navaho noticed a few of the Eagles running toward the hill where he lay watching. In a moment some more came running toward him, and soon after the whole party of Eagles, all that was left of it, rushed past him, in a disorderly retreat, in the direction whence they had come, leaving many slain on the field. Then the wind fell;

the tumble-weeds lay quiet again on the sand, and the bumblebees disappeared among the sunflowers.

When all was quiet, the Navaho walked down to the sandy flat, and, having gathered some of the seeds and tied them up in a corner of his shirt, he collected the tumble-weeds into a pile, using his black wand. Then he took out his fire-drill, started a flame, and burnt up the whole pile. He gathered some scare-weed, as the Spider Woman had told him, chewed it, and went in among the sunflowers. Here the bees gathered around him in a great swarm, and sought to sting him; but he spat the juice of the scare-weed at them and stunned with it all that he struck. Soon most of them lay helpless on the ground, and the others fled in fear. He went around with his black wand and killed all that he could find. He dug into the ground and got out some of their nests and honey; he took a couple of the young bees and tied their feet together, and all these things he put into the corner of his blanket. When the bees were conquered he did not forget the wishes of his friend, the Spider Woman; he went around among the dead Eagles, and plucked as many plumes as he could grasp in both hands.

He set out on his return journey, and soon got back to the house of Spider Woman. He gave her the plumes and she said: "Thank you, my grandchild, you have brought me the plumes that I have long wanted to adorn my walls, and you have done a great service to your friends, the Eagles, because you have slain their enemies." When she had spoken, he set out again on his journey.

He slept that night on the trail, and next morning he got back to the towns of the Eagles. As he approached he heard from afar the cries of the mourners, and when he entered the place the people gathered around him and said: "We have lost many of our kinsmen, and we are wailing for them; but we have been also mourning for you, for those who returned told us you had been killed in the fight."

He made no reply, but took from his blanket the two young bumblebees and swung them around his head. All the people were terrified and ran, and they did not stop running till they got safely behind their houses. In a little while they got over their fear, came slowly from behind their houses, and crowded around the Navaho again. A second time he swung the bees around his head, and a second time the people ran away in terror; but this time they only went as far as the front walls of their houses, and soon they returned again to the Navaho. The third time that he swung the bees around his head they were still less frightened, ran but half way to their houses, and returned very soon. The fourth time that he swung the bees they only stepped back a step or two. When their courage came back to them, he laid the two bees on the ground; he took out the seeds of the tumble-weeds and laid them on the ground beside the bees, and then he said to the Eagle People: "My friends, here are the children of your enemies; when you see these you may know that I have slain your enemies." There was great rejoicing among the people when they heard this, and this one said: "It is well. They have slain my brother," and that one said: "It is well. They have slain my father," and another said: "It is well. They have slain my sons." Then Great Wolf, chief of the white pueblo, said: "I have two beautiful maiden daughters whom I shall give to you." Then Fox, chief of the blue pueblo in the south, promised him two more maidens, and the chiefs of the other pueblos promised him two each, so that eight beautiful maidens were promised to him in marriage.

The chief of the white pueblo now conducted the Navaho to his house and into a large and beautiful apartment, the finest the poor Indian had ever seen. It had a smooth wall, nicely coated with white earth, a large fireplace, mealing-stones, beautiful pots and water-jars, and all the conveniences and furniture of a beautiful pueblo home. And the chief said to him: "Sadáni, my son-in-law, this house is yours."

The principal men from all the pueblos now came to visit him, and thanked him for the great service he had done for them. Then his maidens from the yellow house came in bringing corn meal; the maidens from the black house entered bringing soap-weed, and the maidens of the white house, where he was staying, came bearing a large bowl of white shell. A suds of the soap-weed was prepared in the shell bowl. The maidens of the white house washed his head with the suds; the maidens of the black house washed his limbs and feet, and those of the yellow house dried him with corn meal. When the bath was finished the maidens went out; but they returned at dark, accompanied this time by the maidens of the blue house. Each of the eight maidens carried a large bowl of food, and each bowl contained food of a different kind. They laid the eight bowls down before the Navaho, and he ate of all till he was satisfied. Then they brought in beautiful robes and blankets, and spread them on the floor for his bed.

Next morning the Navaho went over to the sky-hole, taking with him the young bees and the seeds of the tumble-weeds. To the former he said: "Go down to the land of the Navaho and multiply there. My people will make use of you in the days to come; but if you ever cause them sorrow and trouble, as you have caused the people of this land, I shall again destroy you." As he spoke, he flung them down to the earth. Then taking the seeds of the tumble-weeds in his hands, he spoke to them as he had spoken to the bees, and threw them down through the sky-hole. The honey of the bees and the seeds of the tumble-weeds are now used in the rites of the bead chant.

The Navaho remained in the pueblos of the Eagle People twenty-four days, during which time he was taught the songs, prayers, ceremonies, and sacrifices of the Eagles, the same as those now known to us in the rite of the bead chant; and when he had learned all, the people told him it was time for him to return to the earth, whence he had come.

They put on him a robe of eagle plumage, such as they wore themselves, and led him to the sky-hole. They said to him: "When you came up from the lower world you were heavy and had to be carried by others. Henceforth you will be light and can move through the air with your own power." He spread his wings to show that he was ready; the Eagles blew a powerful breath behind him; he went down through the sky-hole, and was wafted down on his outstretched wings until he lit on the summit of Tsótsil.

He went back to his own relations among the Navahos; but when he went back everything about their lodge smelt ill; its odors were intolerable to him, and he left it and sat outside. They built for him then a medicine-lodge where he might sit by himself. They bathed his younger brother, clothed him in new raiment, and sent him, too, into the lodge, to learn what his elder brother could tell him. The brothers spent twelve days in the lodge together, during which the elder brother told his story and instructed the younger in all the rites and songs learned among the Eagles.

After this he went to visit the pueblo of Kintyel, whose inmates had before contemplated such treachery to him; but they did not recognize him. He now looked sleek and well fed. He was beautifully dressed and comely in his person, for the Eagles had moulded in beauty, his face and form. The Pueblo people never thought that this was the poor beggar whom they had left to die in the eagles' nest. He noticed that there were many sore and lame in the pueblo. A new disease, they told him, had broken out among them. This was the disease which they had caught from the feathers of the eaglets when they were attacking the nest. "I have a brother," said the Navaho, "who is a potent shaman. He knows a rite that will cure this disease." The people of the pueblo consulted together and concluded to employ his brother to perform the ceremony over their suffering ones.

The Navaho said that he must be one of the first dancers, and that in order to perform the rite properly he must be dressed in a very particular way. He must, he said, have strings of fine beads—shell and turquoise—sufficient to cover his legs and forearms completely, enough to go around his neck, so that he could not bend his head back, and great strings to pass over the shoulder and under the arm on each side. He must have the largest shell basin to be found in either pueblo to hang on his back, and the one next in size to hang on his chest. He must have their longest and best strings of turquoise to hang to his ears. The Wind told him that the greatest shell basin they had was so large that if he tried to embrace it around the edge, his finger-tips would scarcely meet on the opposite side, and that this shell he must insist on having. The next largest shell, Wind told him, was but little smaller.

Three days after this conference, people began to come in from different pueblos in the Chaco Canyon and from pueblos on the banks of the San Juan,—all these pueblos are now in ruins—and soon a great multitude had assembled. Meantime, too, they collected shells and beads from the various pueblos in order to dress the first dancer as he desired. They brought him some great shell basins and told him these were what he wanted for the dance; but he measured them with his arms as Wind had told him, and, finding that his hands joined easily when he embraced the shells, he discarded them. They brought him larger and larger shells, and tried to persuade him that such were their largest; but he tried and rejected all. On the last day, with reluctance, they brought him the great shell of Kintyel and the great shell of Kindotliz. He clasped the first in his arms; his fingers did not meet on the opposite side. He clasped the second in his arms, and the tips of his fingers just met. "These," said he, "are the shells I must wear when I dance."

Four days before that on which the last dance was to occur, the Pueblo people sent out messengers to the neighboring camps of Navahos, to invite the latter to witness the exhibition of the last night and to participate in it with some of their *alíli* (dances or dramas). One of the messengers went to the Chelly Canyon and there he got Ganaskidi, with his son and daughter, to come and perform a dance. The other messengers started for the Navaho camp at the foot of Tsótsil on the south (near where Cobero is now). On his way he met an *akáninili,* or messenger, coming from Tsótsil to invite the people of the Chaco Canyon to a great Navaho ceremony. The messengers exchanged bows and quivers as a sign they had met one another, and the messenger from Kintyel returned to his people without being able to get the Navahos to attend. This is the reason that, on the last night of the great ceremony of the bead chant, there are but few different dances or shows.

On the evening of the last day they built a great circle of branches, such as the Navahos build now for the rites of the mountain chant, and a great number of people crowded into the inclosure. They lighted the fires and dressed the first dancer in all their fine beads and shells just as he desired them to dress him. They put the great shell of Kintyel on his back, and the great shell of Kindotliz on his chest, and another fine shell on his forehead. Then the Navaho began to dance, and his brother, the medicine-man, began to sing, and this was the song he sang:—

The white-corn plant's great ear sticks up.
Stay down and eat.

The blue-corn plant's great ear sticks up.
Stay down and eat.

The yellow-corn plant's great ear sticks up.
Stay down and eat.

The black-corn plant's great ear sticks up.
Stay down and eat.

All-colored corn's great ear sticks up.
Stay down and eat.

The round-eared corn's great ear sticks up.
Stay down and eat.

This seemed a strange song to the Pueblo people, and they all wondered what it could mean; but they soon found out what it meant, for they observed that the dancing Navaho was slowly rising from the ground. First his head and then his shoulders appeared above the heads of the crowd; next his chest and waist; but it was not until his whole body had risen above the level of their heads that they began to realize the loss that threatened them. He was rising toward the sky with the great shell of Kintyel, and all the wealth of many pueblos in shell-beads and turquoise on his body. Then they screamed wildly to him and called him by all sorts of dear names—father, brother, son—to come down again, but the more they called the higher he rose. When his feet had risen above them they observed that a streak of white lightning passed under his feet like a rope, and hung from a dark cloud that gathered above. It was the gods that were lifting him; for thus, the legends say, the gods lift mortals to the sky. When the Pueblos found that no persuasions could induce the Navaho to return, some called for ropes that they might seize him and pull him down; but he was soon beyond the reach of their longest rope. Then a shout was raised for arrows that they might shoot him; but before the arrows could come he was lost to sight in the black cloud and was never more seen on earth.

Navaho

THE INSTITUTION OF POTTERY

IN THE BEGINNING Itc'tinaku considered how the people should live. She said to herself, "My old father and my old mother must go down to the people and be Clay Old Woman and Clay Old Man." In Shipap* she made the old man and woman into Clay Old Woman and Clay Old Man. The old woman began to mix the clay with sand and soften it with water. When she had finished she made it into a ball and wrapped it in a white manta. She began to coil a pot with her clay, and Clay Old Man danced beside her singing while she worked. All the people gathered in the village and watched her all day long. When she had made her pot so high *(about eighteen inches)* and the old man was singing and dancing beside her, he kicked it with his foot and it broke in many pieces. The old woman picked up his stick and chased him all around the plaza. She overtook him in the middle of the kiva. They made friends again and she took the broken pot and rolled it into a ball again. The old man took the pot and gave a piece of it to everybody in the village. They each took it and made pottery as Clay Old Woman had made it. This was the time they learned to make pottery. Clay Old Man told them never to forget to make pottery. In those days they only indented it with the marks of their fingers. Ever since, when we do not make pottery, these two masked dancers come with the dance to remind us of the clay they gave to the people. They tell us not to forget our grinding stones and always to grind our own corn flour.

*The underworld; the place from which people first emerged.

Cochiti

HELUTA PLANTS THE DEER

THEY WERE LIVING IN COCHITI. They challenged each other to a display of their crops, and they asked Heluta to come to compete. They fasted for four days, and on the fourth day they sent to Heluta and said, "It is time to come to our village." All the people of Cochiti gathered together but Heluta did not come. They sent a messenger again to hurry him. All the people had brought their harvests but Heluta did not bring any corn or musk-melons or gourds. They made fun of him and said, "What has he got to show off? He has not brought anything." He came into the house where all the men were eating. The east room was filled with white corn, and the north room was filled with yellow corn; the west room was filled with blue corn, and the south room was filled with red corn, and the middle room was filled with spotted corn and with watermelons and muskmelons and all kinds of gourds. When they had looked at everything Heluta said, "Is this all?" "Yes." "Now it is my turn to show you how I live." He opened his little fawn-skin bag and took out a piece of cob with two or three kernels sticking to it. "This is what I live by." They laughed at him. "What kind of a living is that? No melons and only a few little corn kernels!" Heluta said, "Wait. You will see which one makes the best living; you by all your work, or the man who has the power himself." He went back to Shipap and he said, "In four days (years) you will find out." The people tried to make him turn back, but they could not.

Next spring the people began to plant. Their corn and melons grew well, but there was no rain. By the middle of the summer everything was dried up and dead. The next year it was the same. For four years they planted, but every year the rain failed them and their crops were burned up by the sun.

In four years they were starving. They chose the fly as messenger and sent him to Shipap, to Heluta. He came into the center of the first room. In that room the *sk'akuts katcinas* were roasting corn. Whenever one of the kernels popped they all jumped. The fly flew past them into the second room and the third room and came to the fourth room. Heluta said to him, "What is it you have come to ask?" "They sent me to talk to you." "You are foolish. You mustn't come to find me whenever those people tell you to come to me. Come close." The fly flew close to him. "Stick out your tongue." He stuck out his tongue and Heluta pulled it out by the root. "Now go back and tell your people that you found me. I am not coming back to the village. I have told them already it is their own fault."

Fly went back to the village. He tried to tell them what Heluta had said. He could not because he had lost his tongue. After that he could only say "buzz." Heluta had said, "You will never talk anymore, you have no tongue." The people said, "How can he tell us? He has no tongue. What shall we do?" "We will send Hummingbird to find Heluta." They called Hummingbird and said, "Go and find Heluta and bring him back to the village." Hummingbird went to Shipap. He flew into the first room where the *sk'akuts katcinas* were roasting corn. He flew into the second room and the third room. He came to Heluta. Heluta said to him, "What is it you have come to ask?" "I have come to bring you back to the village. The people need you. They want you to forgive what they have done to you. The children are dying of hunger and thirst. Now they have learned that it is by your power that they live." Heluta said to Hummingbird, "Yes, my son, I will go back to the village. I am sorry for them. First they must hunt and bring me a deer from the north side of the mountains where the sun has never shone upon him. When they have taken this deer, send for me." The people went hunting and caught a deer from the north side of the mountain upon whom the sun had never shone. They sent for Heluta and brought him to the village. They laid the deer before him. Heluta took it to Shipap. The clouds began to come up with thunder and lightning, and it rained. Since then there has always been rain in this country.

Heluta told them, "My seed is dewclaws. Whenever you kill a deer, do not throw these away, because these are my seed. Watch me, and you will see my field." He took a great bunch of dewclaws and dug in the ground. He put each one in a hole in the earth. When he had finished, the first he had planted were already coming up above the ground. The people saw the small antlers of the deer. They watched them grow until they were full size and ran off to the mountains. Heluta called them all together and took them to Shipap and shut them up there. When they were full grown he opened the door and let them out over the mountains. So he is the father of all the deer.

Cochiti

THE BIRTH OF MEN AND THE CREATURES

ANON IN THE NETHERMOST of the four cave-wombs of the world, the seed of men and the creatures took form and increased; even as within eggs in warm places worms speedily appear, which growing, presently burst their shells and become as may happen, birds, tadpoles or serpents, so did men and all creatures grow manifoldly and multiply in many kinds. Thus the lowermost womb or cave-world, which was *Anosin tehuli* (the womb of sooty depth or of growth-generation, because it was the place of first formation and black as a chimney at night time, foul too, as the internals of the belly), thus did it become overfilled with being. Everywhere were unfinished creatures, crawling like reptiles one over another in filth and black darkness, crowding thickly together and treading each other, one spitting on another or doing other indecency, insomuch that loud became their murmurings and lamentations, until many among them sought to escape, growing wiser and more manlike.

Then came among men and the beings, it is said, the wisest of wise men and the foremost, the all-sacred master, Poshaiyankya, he who appeared in the waters below, even as did the Sun-father in the wastes above, and who arose from the nethermost sea, and pitying men still, won upward, gaining by virtue of his wisdom-knowledge issuance from that first world-womb through ways so dark and narrow that those who, seeing somewhat, crowded after, could not follow, so eager were they and so mightily did they strive with one another! Alone, then, he fared upward from one womb *(cave)* to another out into the great breadth of daylight. There the earth lay, like a vast island in the midst of the great waters, wet and unstable. And alone fared he forth dayward, seeking the Sun-father and supplicating him to deliver mankind and the creatures there below.

Then did the Sun-father take counsel within himself, and casting his glance downward espied, on the great waters, a Foam-cap near to the Earth-mother. With his beam he impregnated and with his heat incubated the Foam-cap, whereupon she gave birth to Uanam Achi Piahkoa, the Beloved Twain who descended; first, Uanam Ehkona, the Beloved Preceder, then Uanam Yaluna, the Beloved Follower, Twin brothers of Light, yet Elder and Younger, the Right and the Left, like to question and answer in deciding and doing. To them the Sun-father imparted, still retaining, control-thought and his own knowledge-wisdom, even as to the offspring of wise parents their knowingness is imparted and as to his right hand and his left hand a skillful man gives craft freely, surrendering not his knowledge. He gave them, of himself and their mother the Foam-cap, the great cloud-bow, and for arrows the thunderbolts of the four quarters, and for buckler the fog-making shield, which (spun of the floating clouds and spray and woven, as of cotton we spin and weave) supports as on wind, yet hides (as a shadow hides) its bearer, defending also. And of men and all creatures he gave them the fathership and dominion, also as a man gives over the control of his work to the management of his hands.

Well instructed of the Sun-father, they lifted the Sky-father with their great cloud-bow into the vault of the high zenith, that the earth might become warm and thus fitter for their children, men and the creatures. Then along the trail of the sun-seeking Poshaiyankya, they sped backward swiftly on their floating fog-shield, westward to the Mountain of Generation. With their magic knives of the thunderbolt they spread open the uncleft depths of the mountain, and still on their cloud-shield—even as a spider in her web descendeth—so descended they unerringly, into the dark of the under-world. There they abode with men and the creatures, attending them, coming to know them, and becoming known of them as masters and fathers, thus seeking the ways for leading them forth.

Now there were growing things in the depths, like grasses and crawling vines. So now the Beloved Twain breathed on the stems of these grasses (growing tall, as grass is wont to do toward the light, under the opening they had cleft and whereby they had de-scended), causing them to increase vastly and rapidly by grasping and walking round and round them, twisting them upward until lo! they reach forth even into the light. And where successively they grasped the stems, ridges were formed and thumb-marks whence sprang branching leaf-stems. Therewith the two formed a great ladder whereon men and creatures might ascend to the second cave-floor, and thus not be violently ejected in after-time by the throes of the Earth-mother, and thereby be made demoniac and deformed.

Up this ladder, into the second cave-world, men and the beings crowded, following closely the Two Little but Mighty Ones. Yet many fell back and, lost in the darkness, peopled the under-world, whence they were delivered in after-time amid terrible earth shak-ings, becoming the monsters and fearfully strange beings of olden time. Lo! in this second womb it was dark as is the night of a stormy season, but larger of space and higher than had been the first, because it was nearer the navel of the Earth-mother, hence named *Kolin tehuli* (the Umbilical-womb, or the Place of Gestation). Here again men and the beings increased and the clamor of their complainings grew loud and beseeching. Again the Two, augmenting the growth of the great ladder, guided them upward, this time not all at once, but in successive bands to become in time the fathers of the six kinds of men (the yellow, the tawny gray, the red, the white, the mingled, and the black races), and with them the gods and creatures of them all. Yet this time also, as before, multitudes were lost or left behind. The third great cave-world, whereunto men and the creatures had now ascended, being larger than the second and higher, was lighter, like a valley in starlight, and named *Awisho tehuli*—the Vaginal-womb, or the Place of Sex-generation or Gestation. For here the various peoples and beings began to multiply apart in kind one from another; and as the nations and tribes of men and the creatures thus waxed numerous as before, here, too, it became overfilled. As before, generations of nations now were led out successively (yet many lost, also as hitherto) into the next and last world-cave, *Tepahaian tehuli*, the Womb of Parturition.

Here it was light like the dawning, and men began to perceive and to learn variously according to their natures, wherefore the Twain taught them to seek first of all our Sun-father, who would, they said, reveal to them wisdom and knowledge of the ways of life—wherein also they were instructing them as we do little children. Yet, like the other cave-worlds, this too became, after long time, filled with progeny; and finally, at periods, the Two led forth the nations of men and the kinds of being, into this great upper world, which is called *Tekohaian ulahnane*, or the World of Disseminated Light and Knowledge or Seeing.

Eight years made the span of four days and four nights when the world was new. It was while yet such days and nights continued that men were led forth, first in the night, that it might be well. For even when they saw the great star, which since then is spoken of as the lying star, they thought it the Sun himself, so burned it their eyeballs! Men and the creatures were nearer alike then than now: black were our fathers the late-born of creation, like the caves from which they came forth; cold and scaly their skins like those of mud-creatures; goggled their eyes like those of an owl; membranous their ears like those of cave-bats; webbed their feet like those of walkers in wet and soft places; and according as they were elder or younger, they had tails, longer or shorter. They crouched when they walked, often indeed, crawling along the ground like toads, lizards and newts; like infants who still fear to walk straight, they crouched, as before-time they had in their cave-worlds, that they might not stumble and fall, or come to hurt in the uncertain light thereof. And when the morning star rose they blinked excessively as they beheld its brightness and cried out with many mouth-motionings that surely now the Father was coming; but it was only the elder of the Bright Ones, gone before with elder nations and with his shield of flame, heralding from afar (as we herald with wet shell scales or crystals) the approach of the Sun-father! And when, low down in the east the Sun-father himself appeared, what though shrouded in the midst of the great world waters, they were so blinded and heated by his light and glory that they cried out to one another in anguish and fell down wallowing and covering their eyes with their bare hands and arms. Yet ever anew they looked afresh to the light and anew struggled toward the sun as moths and other night creatures seek the light of a camp fire; yea, and though burned, seek ever anew that light!

Thus ere long they became used to the light, and to this high world they had entered. Wherefore, when they arose and no longer walked bended, lo! it was then that they first looked full upon one another and in horror of their filthier parts, strove to hide these, even from one another, with girdles of bark and rushes; and when by thus walking only upon their hinder feet the same became bruised and sore, they sought to protect them with plaited sandals of yucca fiber.   *Zuni*

THE ORIGIN OF PRIESTS AND OF KNOWLEDGE

IT WAS THUS, by much devising of ways, that men began to grow knowing in many things, and were instructed by what they saw, and so became wiser and better able to receive the words and gifts of their fathers and elder brothers, the gods, Twain and others, and priests. For already masters-to-be were amongst them. Even in the dark of the under-worlds such had come to be; as had, indeed, the various kinds of creatures-to-be, so these. And according to their natures they had found and cherished things, and had been granted gifts by the gods; but as yet they knew not the meaning of their own powers and possessions, even as children know not the meanings and right uses of the precious or needful things given them; nay nor yet the functions of their very parts! Now in the light of the Sun-father, persons became known from persons, and these things from other things; and thus the people came to know their many fathers among men, to know them by themselves or by the possessions they had.

Now the first and most perfect of all these fathers among men after Poshaiyankya was Yanauluha, who brought up from the under-world the water of the inner ocean, and seeds of life-production and growing things; in gourds he brought these up, and also things containing the "of-doing-powers."

He who was named Yanauluha carried ever in his hand a staff which now in the daylight appeared plumed and covered with feathers of beautiful colors—yellow, blue-green, and red, white, black, and varied. Attached to it were shells and other potent contents of the under-world. When the people saw all these things and the beautiful baton, and heard the song-like tinkle of the sacred shells, they stretched forth their hands like little children and cried out, asking many questions.

Yanauluha, and other priests having been made wise by teaching of the masters of life with self-magic-knowing replied: "It is a staff of extension, wherewith to test the hearts and understandings of children." Then he balanced it in his hand and struck with it a hard place and blew upon it. Amid the plumes appeared four round things, seeds of moving beings, mere eggs were they, two blue like the sky; two dun-red like the flesh of the Earth-mother.

Again the people cried out with wonder and ecstasy, and again asked they questions, many.

"These be," said he who was named Yanauluha, "the seed of living things; both the cherishers and annoyancers, of summer time; choose ye without greed which ye will have for to follow! For from one twain shall issue beings of beautiful plumage, colored like the verdure and fruitage of summer; and whither they fly and ye follow, shall be everlastingly manifest summer, and without toil, the pain whereof ye ken not, fields full fertile of food

134

shall flourish there. And from the other twain shall issue beings evil, uncolored, black, piebald with white; and whither these two shall fly and ye follow, shall strive winter with summer; fields furnished only by labor such as ye wot not of shall ye find there, and contended for between their offspring and yours shall be the food-fruits thereof."

"The blue! the blue!" cried the people, and those who were most hasty and strongest strove for the blue eggs, leaving the other eggs for those who had waited. "See," said they as they carried them with much gentleness and laid them, as one would the new-born, in soft sand on the sunny side of a cliff, watching them day by day, "precious seed!" And "Yea verily!" said they when the eggs cracked and worms issued, presently becoming birds with open eyes and with pinfeathers under their skins, "Verily we chose with understanding, for see! yellow and blue, red and green are their dresses, even seen through their skins!" So they fed the pair freely of the food that men favor—thus alas! cherishing their appetites for food of all kinds! But when their feathers appeared they were black with white bandings; for ravens were they! And they flew away mocking our fathers and croaking coarse laughs!

And the other eggs held by those who had waited and by their father Yanauluha, became gorgeous macaws and were wafted by him with a toss of his wand to the far southward summer-land. As father, yet child of the macaw, he chose as the symbol and name of himself and as father of these his more deliberate children—those who had waited—the macaw and the kindred of the macaw, the *Mula-kwe;* whilst those who had chosen the ravens became the Raven-people, or the *Kaka-kwe.*

Thus first was our nation divided into the People of Winter and the People of Summer. Of the Winter those who chose the raven, who were many and strong; and of the Summer those who cherished the macaw, who were fewer and less lusty, yet of prudent understanding because more deliberate. Hence, Yanauluha their father, being wise, saw readily the light and ways of the Sun-father, and being made partaker of his breath, thus became among men as the Sun-father is among the little moons of the sky; and speaker to and of the Sun-father himself, keeper and dispenser of precious things and commandments, Earliest Priest of the Sun. He and his sisters became also the seed of all priests who pertain to the Midmost clan-line of the priest fathers of the people themselves, "masters of the house of houses." By him also, and his seed, were established and made good the priests-keepers of things.

The Twain Beloved and the priest fathers gathered in council for the naming and selection of man-groups and creature-kinds, spaces, and things. Thus determined they that the creatures and things of summer and the southern space pertained to the Southern people, or Children of the Producing Earth-mother; and those of winter and northern space, to the Winter people, or Children of the Forcing or Quickening Sky-father.

Of the Children of Summer, some loved and understood most the Sun, hence became the fathers of the Sun people. Some loved more the water, and became the Toad people, Turtle people, or Frog people, who so much love the water. Others, again loved the seeds of earth and became the People of Seed, such as those of the First-growing grass, and of the Tobacco. Yet still others loved the warmth and became the Fire or Badger people. According, then, to their natures and inclinations or their gifts from below or of the Masters of Life, they chose or were chosen for their totems.

Thus, too, it was with the People of Winter or the North. They chose, or were chosen and named, according to their resemblances or aptitudes; some as the Bear people, Coyote people, or Deer people; others as the Crane people, Turkey people, or Grouse people. In this wise it came to pass that the *Ashiwe* were divided of old in such wise as are their children today, into clans of brothers and sisters who may not marry one another, but from one to another of kin. Yea, and as the Earth-mother had increased and kept within herself all beings, cherishing them apart from their father even after they came forth, so were these our mothers and sisters made the keepers of the kin-names and of the seed thereof, nor may the children of each be cherished by any others of kin.

Now the Beloved Foremost Ones of these clans were prepared by instruction of the gods and the fathers of the house of houses and by being breathed of them, whereby they became *ashiwani* or priests also, but only the priests of possession, master keepers of sacred things and mysteries, each according to his nature of kinship. It was thus that the warmth-wanting Badger-people were given the great shell, the heart or navel of which is potent or sensitive of fire, as of the earthquake and the inner fire is the coiled navel of the Earth-mother. On the sunny sides of hills burrow the badgers, finding and dwelling amongst the dry roots whence is fire. Thus the "Two Badgers" were made keepers of the sacred heart-shell, makers and wardens of fire. So, too, were the Bear, Crane, and Grouse people given the *muetone,* or the contained seed-substance of hail, snow and new soil (for the bear sleeps, no longer guarding when winter comes, and with the returning crane, in the wake of the duck, comes winter in the trail of the white growing grouse). So, to the Toad and other water people, descended to them from Yanauluha the contained seed-substance of water; and to the All-seed-people, especially to the First-growing-grass people and the Tobacco people, was given of him also, the *chuetone,* or the contained seed-substance of corn grains.

Now when the foremost ones of more than one of these kin clans possessed a contained or sacred seed-substance, they banded together, forming a society for the better use and keeping of its medicine and its secret mysteries, and for the guidance and care thereby of their especial children. Thus, leading ones of the Bear people, Crane people, and Grouse people became the *Hleeta-kwe,* or Bearers of the Ice-wands as they are sometimes called, whose prayers and powers bring winter, yet ward off its evils to the flesh and fearsomeness to the soul. But at first, only four were the bands of priest-keepers of the mysteries: *Shiwana-kwe,* or the Priesthood of Priest people; *Saniakya-kwe,* or the Priesthood of the Hunt, who were of the Coyote, Eagle, and Deer kin, keepers of the seed-substance of Game; *Achiakya-kwe,* or the Great Knife people, makers and defenders of pathways for the people; and *Newe-kwe,* keepers of magic medicines and knowledge invincible of poison and other evil, whose first great father was Paiyatuma, God of Dew and the Dawn, himself. Out of these and of other clans were formed in later days by wisdom of the Father of Medicines and Rites (the great Poshaiyankya, when he returned, all as is told in other talk of our olden speech) all other societies. But when all was new, men did not know the meanings of their possessions, or even of the commandments; even as children know not the prayers. These they must first be taught, that in later days, when there is need therefor, they may know them and not be poor.

As it was with men and the creatures, so with the world; it was young and unripe. Unstable its surface was, like that of a marsh; dank, even the high places, like the floor of a cavern, so that seeds dropped on it sprang forth, and even the substance of offal became growing things.

Earthquakes shook the world and rent it. Beings of sorcery, demons and monsters of the under-world fled forth. Creatures turned fierce, becoming beasts of prey, wherefore others turned timid, becoming their quarry; wretchedness and hunger abounded, black magic, war, and contention entered when fear did into the hearts of men and the creatures. Yea, fear was everywhere among them, wherefore, everywhere the people, hugging in dread their precious possessions, became wanderers they, living on the seeds of grasses, eaters of dead and slain things! Yet still, they were guided by the Two Beloved, ever in the direction of the east, told and taught that they must seek, in the light and under the pathway of the Sun, the middle of the world, over which alone could they find the earth stable, or rest them and bide them in peace.

Zuni

PRAYER OF THE IMPERSONATORS OF THE MASKED GODS AT THE MONTHLY OFFERING OF PRAYER STICKS

And now indeed it is so.
At the New Year
Our fathers
Four times prepared their precious plume wands.
With their plume wands they took hold of me.

This many days
Anxiously we have awaited our time.
When the moon, who is our mother
Yonder in the west
As a small thing appeared,
Carrying our fathers' precious plume wand,
With our own poor plume wand
Fastened to our fathers' plume wand,

At the place called since the first beginning
Snow-hanging, or where snow hangs,
To our fathers,
Priests of the masked gods,
Culawitsi, pekwin priest,
Sayataca, bow priest,
Hututu, bow priest,
Yamuhaktu, bow priests,
To all the masked gods,
Our plume wands we gave.
Where they were to receive their plume wands,
All happily gathered together,
There we passed them on their roads.

This day
We shall give you plume wands.
Keeping your days,
Throughout the cycle of your months,
Throughout the summer,
Anxiously we shall await your time.
Our fathers,
Yonder toward the south
Wherever your roads come out,
We have given you plume wands.
When your springs were at an end,
Our fathers,
In their rain-filled room
Met together.
The flesh of their mother, cotton woman,
Four times counting up,
They gave their day counts human form.
Of our two fathers,
Sayataca, bow priest,
Molanhaktu, house chief,
They had need.

The two passed their fathers on their roads.
With the flesh of their mother,
Cotton woman,
Four times counted up, and given human form,
With this they took hold of them.

From where our fathers stay,
Carrying the day count
They made their roads go forth.
To their own houses
Their roads reached.

A little later
Carrying their fathers' day count
With their plume wands fastened together,
They made their roads go forth.
Yonder we took our way.
At the place called since the first beginning,
Aiyayaka.
Our fathers,
Rain makers,
Our fathers,
Priests of the masked gods,
Where they were all gathered together,
We passed them on their roads.
Giving them our fathers' plume wands,
Giving them their day count,
This many days
The days of their counting string,
Anxiously we have awaited our time.

When all their days were past,
When their day count was at an end
Again we prepared plume wands.
Carrying our plume wands
At the place called since the first beginning
Rock Face,
We passed our fathers on their roads.
Meeting our fathers,
We gave them plume wands.
Keeping their days
Anxiously waiting
We passed our days.

This many are the days.
And when their days were at an end,
Over there, following your springs,

We gave you plume wands.
When all your days are past,
Our fathers,
Priests of the masked gods,
Bow priests of the masked gods,
Culawitsi, pekwin priest,
Sayataca, bow priest,
Hututu, bow priest,
Yamuhaktu, bow priests,
Calako, bow priests,
All the masked gods
There from your home set with mountains,
Bringing your waters,
Bringing your seeds,
Bringing all your good fortune,
Our fathers,
You will make your roads come forth.

Yes, now every one of us will come forth.
Our fathers at Itiwana,
We shall pass on their roads.
Let no one be left behind.
All the men,
Those with snow upon their heads,
With moss upon their faces,
With bony knees,
No longer upright, but bent over canes,
Now all of us
Shall pass our fathers on their roads.
And the women,
With snow upon their heads,
Even those who are with child,
Carrying one on the back,
With another on the cradle board,
Leading one by the hand,
With yet another going before,
Even all of us
Shall pass you on your roads.
Indeed, it is so
The thoughts of our fathers,
Who at the New Year

With their precious plume wands
Appointed us,
Their thoughts we now fulfill.

This is all.
Thus with plain words we have passed you on your roads.
Now we fulfill the thoughts of our fathers.
Always with one thought
We shall live together.
This is all.
Thus with plain words we have passed you on your roads.
For whatever our fathers desired
When at the New Year
They sent forth their sacred words,
We have now fulfilled their thoughts.
To this end: My fathers,
My mothers,
My children,
Always with one thought
May we live together.
With your waters,
Your seeds,
Your riches,
Your power,
Your strong spirit,
All your good fortune,
With all this may you bless us.

Zuni

THE MIGRATION OF THE HOPI

This story begins in the conventional manner by stating that the Hopi people were living at Palatkwabi. There was considerable disorder—too much gambling, too much dancing—and the women were completely out of hand. Town Chief, after praying to the Sun for guidance, returned home and informed his son that on the morrow morning the boy must run all around the big mountain south of Palatkwabi. "Do your best," said Town Chief.

For three successive mornings the boy tried and failed. On the fourth morning, he succeeded. Town Chief congratulated him, and then told him that he must go out westward of the town and look for an antelope with two prongs. So, on the fifth morning, the boy did so. An antelope with two prongs fled away toward the big mountain, but the boy caught the animal and cut off the horn, returning with it to his father. "Tonight," said the father, "when the sun goes down, you come to me. I will be here all day, keeping that horn."

IN THE EVENING the boy went to his father's house, and his father had something by him. It was a mask, painted green. There were four masks lying there. The other three looked very ugly. When the boy came in, he began to tell him what he was to do. "You go out to the north from the village, then go to the west. I will go out by the south, and then west." They went by different directions, and then west, and they met and there his father fixed up the boy; he put an old antelope skin on his back. The good mask was at the bottom and the others on top, and then these four he put on his boy's head. "Now you go near the village, and the people will know about it," said the father. And he gave him some kind of fire. When he came close to the village somebody saw the fire coming, and it was coming closer, and the man got afraid and ran off. So the boy went around the village four times and then went off. So that man told them in the kiva that he had seen somebody with fire in his eyes and in his mouth. But the people did not believe it.

At night the boy came again, and that man and two others were standing outside the village and watching for him. They watched the fire coming closer, and then they all ran off, up to the house where some other men were watching. He was coming, but they were all frightened and ran away. When he got into the village, he went around four times again and they did not catch him. Next morning those men who saw him told about him. But the other men said, "We will go tonight and we will catch him." So at night they went into the empty house. The man who first saw him went with some others to watch for him. Soon he was coming, and they went and told the others in the house. They saw him and they all ran away, they did not catch him. He went round the village again.

Next morning they were all in the kiva talking about it, "Well, we have all to go and we will catch the boy," they said. Then the father said to the boy, "This will be the fourth night and they are going to catch you. Let them catch you. My son, I love you. You are supposed to be my leg and my hand and my heart. But I let you go and let the people kill you. We will all go after you. And I will not cry when they kill you. Nor do you cry when they kill you. I will tell them where to bury you." Then the father told his wife to make soap-weed suds and wash the boy's head. So in the evening the father put his beads around his neck and he told his boy, "Now you go a little earlier tonight." So he dressed himself and went.

All those men of that kiva went into the empty house, waiting for what was to come. They were watching for him. Then he came again. The other men who watched before were watching. "He is coming," they said to the men in the empty house. "Why did you not catch him?" they asked. "We were afraid of him."—"Well, let us be brave men," they said. When he went into the dance plaza they caught him and took him into the kiva. Then they made a big fire, for light. Then they took off the top mask and under it was another mask and they took it off and under it was another mask, and then they took off that third mask and there was that good mask, and that was *Soyal kachina,* Ahulani. He was dressed just as he is today, with a foxskin collar. Then they pulled it off, and there was that boy, Town Chief's son. And they felt pretty bad about him. "Well, you kill me!" said the boy. "Do as you wish. If you cut my head off, that will be all right," said the boy. Some of them did not want to kill him, but some said, "Why do we not kill him?" But the oldest man said, "Don't kill him, but just let him go." So they let him go; but they kept the mask in the kiva.

Well, the older men were crying because they knew something was going to happen. When they let him go, he went to his father's house and his father said, "Thank you, they did not kill you. But you have to go," said his father. At that time of night they were still practising in one of those kivas. Then the father gave him a smoke, and when he finished smoking then his father gave him something to eat. While he was eating, his mother came back, very happy. They had been having a good time. "Why did you not go?" — "Well, I did not want to go. Everybody was in there except you and your father," she said. "Just because we did not want to go, we did not go." She was tired from dancing, and went to sleep. But the father and son were sitting there.

Soon all the people went to sleep. "My son, take off your moccasins, all your leggings, also your shirt." Then he tied a prayer-feather on his son's head, and he tied two prayer-feathers on each horn. "Now let's go," he said. Then they went to the dance plaza, where was the shrine. He put his son inside of the shrine and he told his son, "You hold the horns down like this *(pointing them to the ground)*, and then you will go down into the earth," he said. The boy just pushed the horns down into the ground, and soon he was sinking into the ground. His father had said, "When all your head goes into the ground, hold up your hand and leave out four fingers and leave them all day. Next morning you put down one finger, next morning another finger, next morning another, fourth morning the last finger."

So the boy sank down and held up his hand with four fingers up. In the morning somebody was passing by and he saw the hand sticking out of the ground inside the shrine with four fingers up. He looked at it closely. He went into the kiva and he said he had seen something. They asked him what it was. He said in the shrine a hand was sticking out and four fingers were up. Then the older men went to the shrine and saw it. And when they came back into the kiva they were talking about it. And some of them said, "You know last night you caught somebody and brought him here and that is he," they said. Next morning they went to look at the hand. Only three fingers were up. They went into the kiva and talked about it. "Only three fingers are up; surely something is going to happen." The third morning only two fingers were up. The fourth morning only one finger was up.

The fifth morning the last finger was gone. This morning the water began to come up from all the fireplaces. In the afternoon the water was coming out everywhere. In the dance plaza something was making a big noise. They said they were going to have a flood. Before evening something was coming from that place where the hand had been. It was the Horned Water Snake. That boy had turned into the snake, Palulukon. Before night the people were transporting their things to a height on the east side of the village. In the morning when they woke up a big Horned Water Snake was coming out from the dance place. Some houses were falling, water was everywhere. There were two old men living close together. One old man went into the house of the other old man. They could not come down. The water kept on rising. They went to a corner of the house and up on the beam where people used to keep things. They got up there and sat there together.

In the morning Palulukon was growing bigger and bigger; water was everywhere.

One man said, "We have to give two children to that snake so he will go back. If we don't give the children, he will never go back," said the old man. "The boy will be the son of Crier Chief and the little girl, the daughter of War Chief." Then they all began to make prayer-sticks and put them in a flat basket. Then in the afternoon they gave the basket to the little boy and said to him, "Take these prayer-sticks and give them to Palulukon. When you meet him, don't be afraid, put your arms around him." These two little children were brave enough to go, they went into the water and reached the snake and put their basket of prayer-sticks close to him and their arms around him. Then Palulukon sank right down into the water; he was going back and with him the boy and girl.

Crier Chief told the people, "We can move from here to some other place. We were too crazy, that is why this happened. So we have to go off and leave our village." And so they started off towards Walpi. Well, they were going many days. Those old men sitting up on the house beam became turkeys and their tails were hanging down and the suds of the water touched their tails and they became white, and that is why the tips of turkey tails are white. After all the people went off, two little boys were left behind, and they were living way up in the fourth story, and while they were asleep, they were forgotten and left behind. Four days later the boys looked out and the water was going back into the hole the Horned Water Snake went into. Then the boys went down and around in all the houses and up in one house they went into, two turkeys were sitting. "Somebody has forgotten his turkeys," said the older boy; the younger was just beginning to walk.

While the boys were going about, the older carrying the other on his back, Palulukon said, "I guess I better come up and see where my people have gone." He came up and saw the people way off. They were by now far away. Those little boys were looking around and they went into the dance plaza and saw that big thing there. That big thing said, "Poor little boys, they left you." And they were very much afraid of him. Palulukon told them not to be afraid of him. "I am your uncle," he said, "Don't be afraid of me, I am your uncle. Two old men have been left and they have turned into turkeys. You go into that room and pull out some feathers from each of them." So they did. Then Palulukon said, "Go and follow the tracks of your people. They are far away, but you will overtake them some day."

So they took some food along, and the turkey feathers and followed the people. They went on many days. They found two men staying under a tree; one was lame and he could not walk, and one man had legs, but he was blind. The little boys were frightened. The man with eyes told him not to be afraid. "We are people," he said. "We will go all together." So the blind man carried the lame man, and the little boy carried his younger brother.

They came to the forest and a deer was standing close to them, and the lame man had a bow and arrow in his hand and he saw the deer standing close to them. He said to the blind man, "Wait!" he said. "Why?" — "There is a deer standing close to us. Let me shoot him. We have nothing to eat tonight." So the man with eyes shot the deer and killed him. And they stopped right there and made fire and skinned the deer and cooked the meat. That man said, "We will stop here all night and go on tomorrow morning."

At night they put the deer-head by the fire. The eyes exploded with a noise and scared them. The man who could not walk jumped up and ran off and the blind man was so scared he opened his eyes and could see. He said, "I am very glad my eyes are open and I can see," he said, and the other said, "I am very glad I can walk." The man who had been blind said, "I must not go to sleep, if I sleep I will get blind again," he said. "I must stay awake all night." And the man who had been lame said, "I must not go to sleep. If I sleep, I will get stiff again. I must walk about all night," he said. And so the blind man did not sleep, but kept his eyes open all night, and the other man walked all night. At sunrise the blind man said, "I guess I will not be blind again," and the lame man said, "I will walk always." Then after they ate their breakfast, each man took a boy on his back, and went on following their people.

It was a long time before they caught up with their people, at a place called Humulobi. Those people on their way from Palatkwabi took a rest every afternoon and before they rested they danced, they danced a harvest dance. They did that every day. At Humulobi they made a home and lived there a long time. But there were a lot of mosquitoes there and they were killing the babies. So they thought they would move again. So they started again, and every afternoon when they stopped, again they danced a harvest dance. That's the way they came to Walpi. That is why the *patki wungwe* clan owns the harvest dance called *lakunti*, and that is how they first got turkeys.

Tewa

5

THE VALLEY, THE PENINSULA
AND THE ISTHMUS

MOST PEOPLE, when they think of the Indians of Mexico, recall immediately the names "Maya" and "Aztec"; for in the popular imagination these words evoke a sense of mystery and grandeur—a vague picture of ruined cities lost in the jungles of Guatemala and Yucatan—a recollection of Cortez and the last stand of the Mexicans at Tenochtitlan. Possibly, the Aztec are best known, for they were the dominant tribe at the time of the Spanish conquest and the Spanish chroniclers have given them heroic stature.

There were many other Indian groups in the geographical area we call Mexico, however, which should be of interest to us. Out of the archaic culture in which clay figures were modeled, gingerbread fashion, rose the Huaxtec and Totonac, the Zapotec and Mixtec, the Toltec and Tarascan cultures. Most of these reached their height after the great Mayan civilization had declined; all were influenced by it in greater or less degree.

The Maya built their greatest cities in Honduras and Guatemala (as we call them today). After a time, they abandoned these cities for some reason of which we are ignorant, and moved north to the peninsula of Yucatan. All along their course, they have left us the material evidence to prove that they possessed the highest culture achieved in ancient America. They were the outstanding potters and sculptors. They built great, civic centers whose grandeur, proportion and majesty are a wonder to today's architects and planners. They were excellent astronomers. They were the first people, the world over, to develop a system of numeration based on a zero point. They invented a calendar more accurate than the one we presently use. They had a hieroglyphic writing in which they recorded their history and mythology.

Their artists and craftsmen, professionals as they were, have left us a remarkable record of the civilization which produced them; serving as they did an involved and highly ritualistic religion, they made permanent in stone all its elaborate symbolism and crowded their work with detail in tropical profusion.

After the move to Yucatan, the Mayan civilization declined; the Spanish conquest of Yucatan (1527 - 1546) was achieved against a broken, but still courageous people. Even though their material culture had fallen and their political dominion had long been forgotten, their ideas had influenced all Mexico and had spread far into both the North and South American continents.

Although the Mexican peoples we have already mentioned, Toltec, Aztec and so forth, derived most of their arts from the example of the Maya, many changes were wrought by time and distance in the practice of these arts. Any attempt to describe these changes in chronological fashion brings in questions and technical terms which would be out of place in this brief survey. Let us say, simply, that of the work done in the "Middle Civilizations"—those between the high point of the Mayan culture and modern times—the works of the Zapotec, Toltec and Mixtec are best known.

The Zapotec and Mixtec peoples did excellent goldwork, carving in wood and bone, pottery and manuscript-painting. Both Zapotec and Toltec were builders, and by no means mere slavish imitators of the Maya. The Toltec, (a pre-Aztec people of the highlands), were masterly engineers; they had the distinction of building bigger, if not better, civic constructions than the so-called "pyramids" of the Maya. The one-time Maya city of Chichen-Itzá in Yucatan was conquered by the Toltec and its architecture shows a mixed Mayan-Mexican style. The Toltec cities, like Chichen-Itzá, are literally crawling with representations of the "feathered serpent"—the symbol of the god, Quetzalcoatl, which recurs again and again in all the artistic efforts of these peoples. (See Plate 52 and *passim*.)

The Aztec, if their own histories can be believed, came from the "Seven Caves"—a mythical place of emergence from underground. (Compare with the Zuni myth on page 131.) In one of these caves, they found an idol of the war-god Huitzilopochtli *(Hummingbird Wizard)* which, having the gift of speech, advised them regarding their future courses. To make a long, rambling story short, they settled at last in the highlands of Mexico and built their Venice-like chief city, Tenochtitlan. For almost two hundred years, these fierce warriors exacted tribute from all the other tribes of the locality (See Plate 50) and extended their political sway from the Gulf of Mexico to the Pacific Ocean. These were the people overthrown by the Spaniards, who built Mexico City on the ruins of Tenochtitlan.

Aztec art, and Aztec culture generally, was influenced by the Toltec and other tribes previously domiciled in the valley of Mexico, just as these tribes had been influenced by the Maya. But to the forms of the earlier art, they added a *macabre*, blood-thirsty content of ideas all their own. As we know, the exactions of the Aztec and their constant draining of captives from the subject tribes for human sacrifice were extreme even by Indian standards, and caused the subject peoples to rally behind Cortez in the final stages of the Aztec empire. (See the second Hymn to Huitzilopochtli on page 162.)

The myths and stories which are given in illustration of the beliefs and customs of the Mayan and Mexican peoples are of peculiar interest. They are more sophisticated and possess a much higher artistic polish than any of the myths which have preceded them in this book. You will note that the mythology was sufficiently ancient and settled in the popular mind, so that the writer or singer could assume or take for granted that his function was not to teach but to embroider. The selection from the Quiché sacred book, the *Popol Vuh* (pages 151 to 161), is especially interesting for its revelation of the terrors that beset the Indian mind—the perils of the jungle, of disease, of mischance—all personified as deities, indeed the very figures commemorated on the buildings and temples. It explains as well the reason for the sacred character of the "ball-game" (See Plate 49, upper left), and the prevalence of the "twin" myth that is found in many North American Indian myth-cycles. The *Popol Vuh* alone survives of what must have been a richly imaginative literature.

The rest of this literature was either destroyed by the Spaniards as tending to keep alive a spirit of nationalism in their conquered Indians, or, like the so-called "Books of Chilam-Balam," was deliberately complicated by the Indians into a cabalistic gibberish which they could understand by oral tradition but which would mean nothing to the conquerors. A selection from one of these "books" is to be found on page 161. Note particularly how the symbolic significance of color is stressed in this passage. One of the Spanish missionaries, working in Yucatan during the early Seventeenth Century, wrote the following complaint to his ecclesiastical superiors: "Furthermore, it would be very advantageous if books were printed in the language of these Indians which would treat of Genesis and the creation of the world, because they have fables and histories which are very detrimental. Some of them have had them written down, and they keep them and read them in their assemblies. I had a copybook of this sort, which I took away from a choir-master named Cuytun from the town of Sucopo. He got away from me, and I never could get hold of him to learn the origin of this Genesis of his."

The symbolism of the Mexican poems on pages 162 to 166 (exquisitely, if not literally rendered into English) links very closely with the symbolism in the drawings and sculptures from Mexico. These poems are hymns to the gods, and songs composed for the accompaniment of a small drum *(teponaztli)*. The modern reader might very well be led astray in reading these hymns by the constant references to flowers and flower combats. It is the opinion of scholars that these flowery symbols refer to the bloodiest kind of battles and subsequent enslavement and ritual murder of the losers.

Southward of Mexico, and of Honduras and Guatemala, the peoples who dwelt on the land-link between North and South America present a complicated problem in arrangement. In the area between Honduras on the northwest and Colombia on the southeast, tribal designations are elusive. The artistic work of these people is classified as a rule by areas, and the areas are given their present-day geographical names. For example, the Coclé work takes its name from the province of Coclé in Panama, just southwest of the Canal. So it is with the names Chiriqui, Nicoya, Guetar and Chorotega. The work shown on Plates 61 to 64 is identified, therefore, by its place of origin and under modern political designations.

We know a little about some of the peoples—the San Blas, for instance, of Panama, and the Valiente, and the Mexican weavers of Saltillo. These last, by the way, are not part of the Central American complex, but all weaving has been grouped on Plate 60. The designs on the *appliquéd* blouses of the San Blas may have had some symbolic meaning in the far past, but the clue has been lost to us. The present San Blas are completely ignorant of their tribal history. They have a vague mythology, in which they explain the creation by God, and a subsequent destruction of the creation by fire, darkness and flood because of the sins of the people. After the flood, a great personage came to earth, borne on a golden plate, who taught the people the names of things and their use and some rules of conduct.

This personage was followed by a number of disciples who spread his teachings and who were, in turn, followed by ten great shamans. One of these was a woman. The shamans had great power over the elements. They investigated the underworld and the heavens, and they discovered many medicines. The exploits of the shamans shade into accounts of the deeds of legendary chiefs and heroes who led the people in their wars and supervised their migrations.

Along with these myths are a number of tales in which animals are involved. One of these recounts the felling of the World Tree at the behest of the principal culture hero. The people attempted to cut the tree down, but each time they left it a giant frog healed the cut overnight. After two such attempts, the culture hero instructed his brother to kill the frog. The tree was then successfully felled, and from its top flowed water, both fresh and salt, plants, reptiles, mammals, birds and fish. Other tales tell of conventional combats, won by that cunning which occupied so high a place among Indian virtues.

The interplay of ideas in Central America is illustrated, not only by the obvious resemblances between their myths and the myths of the northern groups, but graphically and especially on the plates. In Guatemala and Honduras, where the Maya had their old empire, the Maya influence is strong. The two pottery jars and the alabaster vase on Plate 64 are Mayan in design. The sculptured jar (whose design has been laid flat in order to show all sides) has been called the most beautiful example of earthenware ever executed in either North or South America. The design, carved before firing, consists of two serpents intertwined with heads in their own open jaws. (This is a style familiar in both Mexican and Mayan art, as may be seen on comparing this design with Plates 53 and 58.) The large head on the left, and the center figure represent the Mayan Sun God.

The feathered serpent worked his way southward, too; down through the Isthmus to Costa Rica and Panama, where he shares honors with alligator, jaguar, bird and bat gods, and other mysterious, symbolic monsters from South America. Further evidence of the northward influences from Colombia may be found on Plate 61, where Quimbaya region goldwork has clearly influenced the Coclé work. Since the Coclé region was a great trading center, it is clear that South American influences could easily have penetrated as far northward as trade extended.

SELECTIONS FROM *POPOL VUH*

Here is the story; here are the names of each of the Ahpú, for so are they named. Their parents were Ixpiyacoc and Ixmucané. Of them were born when there was neither sun nor moon, Hun-Hunahpú and Vucub-Hunahpú. They were born of Ixpiyacoc and Ixmucané.

Now Hun-Hunahpú begot and had two sons, and of these two sons the first was called Hunbatz and the second, Hunchouén.

The mother of these sons was called Ixbaquiyalo; this was the name of the wife of Hun-Hunahpú. And the other, Vucub-Hunahpú, had no wife.

These two sons by their nature were great sages; great was their wisdom. Here upon this earth they were wizards. Their habits were good, and their dispositions. Every art was taught to Hunbatz and Hunchouén, the sons of Hun-Hunahpú. They were flute players, singers, marksmen with the blowgun, painters, sculptors, jewellers, goldsmiths. Such were Hunbatz and Hunchouén.

Meanwhile, Hun-Hunahpú and Vucub-Hunahpú occupied themselves only in dice-playing and the ball game. Every day they contended in the ball game.

Thither came Voc, messenger of Huracán, of Chipi-Caculhá, of Raxa-Caculhá, that he might observe them. This Voc did not remain far from the earth or far from Xibalba, place of the demons; in an instant he could rise up to heaven, to the side of Huracán.

Then the mother of Hunbatz and Hunchouén died.

And Hun-Hunahpú and Vucub-Hunahpú having gone out to play ball, they trespassed on the road to Xibalba, on the road to the underworld. And the lords of that country heard them, Hun-Camé and Vucub-Camé, the lords of Xibalba.

"What are they doing up there on the earth? Who are they who make the earth tremble and make so much noise? Let them be called. Let them come here to play at the ball game with us, and we shall beat them. They have no respect for us; they do not know our power nor do they fear us. Over our very heads they contend—" so said the lords of the underworld.

And then they all took counsel. There were Hun-Camé and Vucub-Camé, the supreme judges. There were all the lords who served at Court, who were lords only by the grace of Hun-Camé and Vucub-Camé.

There were those lords whose names were Xiquiripat and Cuchumaquic, they who cause the shedding of man's blood. And Ahalpuh and Ahalganá, lords also whose office it is to make pus gush from the legs of men, and to turn faces yellow. This is what is called *chuganal*. And the lord Chamiabac and the lord Chamiaholom, keepers of the peace of the underworld, whose staffs were made of bone. It is they who make men so thin that only bones and skulls remain; it is they who stretch belly and bones until a man dies. And then they take him away. Such was the work of Chamiabac and Chamiaholom. So were they named.

Among the others were the lords named Ahalmez and Ahaltogob. They are the lords who cause misfortune to come to a man as he goes home, so that he is found wounded, or stretched out, mouth upward, on the ground and dead. This was the work of Ahalmez and Ahaltogob, as they are called.

And yet other lords came, among them Xic and Patán who bring death to men on the roads, that which is called sudden death or the vomit of blood. It is these lords who press down on the throats and chests of men, so that the blood rises in their throats and they die as they walk. This is the work of Xic and Patán.

Gathered all together in council, they planned the ways in which they would torment and punish Hun-Hunahpú and Vucub-Hunahpú. For the lords of Xibalba desired to have the instruments used by Hun-Hunahpú and Vucub-Hunahpú in their play — their shields of hide, their throat coverings, their gloves, the headdresses and masks they wore when they played in the ball game.

Now we shall tell how they departed for Xibalba and how they left behind them the sons of Hun-Hunahpú, Hunbatz and Hunchouén, whose mother had died. Afterwards we shall tell how Hunbatz and Hunchouén were overcome by Hunahpú and Ixbalanqué.

The messengers of Hun-Camé and Vucub-Camé arrived immediately. "Go," the lords of Xibalba said to them, "Go, summon Hun-Hunahpú and Vucub-Hunahpú. You will say to them, 'Come with us. The lords say you must come.' Let them come here to play ball with us, that our faces may be made happy by them, that they may make us admire them. Let them come." So said the lords. "And make them bring the instruments of the ball game, their headdresses, their gloves, and make them bring also the ball of rubber. 'Come quickly,' you will say to them." So did they instruct the messengers.

These messengers were owls—Chabi-Tucur, Huracán-Tucur, Caquix-Tucur and Holom-Tucur. So were the messengers of Xibalba named.

Chabi-Tucur was swift as an arrow; Huracán-Tucur had only one leg; Caquix-Tucur had a red shoulder; Holom-Tucur was only a flying head—he had no legs, but he had wings.

The four messengers had the dignity of chiefs. Coming up from Xibalba, they sped on their way, carrying their message to the courtyard where Hun-Hunahpú and Vucub-Hunahpú were playing the ball game which is called Nim-Xob Carchah. The messenger owls flew to the ball game and presented their message, precisely in the order in which it had been given them by Hun-Camé, Vucub-Camé, Ahalpuh, Ahalganá, Chamiabac, Chamiaholom, Xiquiripat, Cuchumaquic, Ahalmez, Ahaltogob, Xic and Patán.

"Have the lords Hun-Camé and Vucub-Camé really spoken in this manner? Is it true that they have commanded us to follow you?"

"You must bring all the equipment for the ball game. So have the lords said."

"Very well," said the young men. "Wait for us. We are only going to take leave of our mother."

And, having gone to their house, they said to their mother (for their father was already dead): "We must go, O mother, but our going will be in vain. The lords' messengers have come to get us. 'Make them come,' the lords have said. So have their envoys declared. But here our ball will remain as a pledge." Immediately, they went to hide the ball in the hole which was in the roof of the house. Then they said: "We shall some time return to play." And turning to Hunbatz and Hunchouén, they said: "Keep yourselves busy by playing the flute and by singing, by painting, by making images. Keep warm our house, and keep warm the heart of your grandmother."

While they were taking leave of their mother, she, Ixmucané, was moved and began to cry.

"Do not grieve," they told her, "We are going away but we have not yet died."

Then Hun-Hunahpú and Vucub-Hunahpú left, and the messengers led them along the road. And now they were going down the steep steps of the road to the underworld. They went down until they arrived at the bank of a river which ran rapidly between the cliffs called Nuzivancul and Cuzivan, and they passed between the cliffs. Then they passed over the river which runs between thorny gourd trees. The trees were numberless, but they passed through them without complaining.

Then they arrived at the banks of a river of blood, and they crossed it without drinking its waters; they only stood on the bank of the river, and so they were not yet overcome. They hurried on until they reached a place where four roads join, and there they were overcome, there at the crossing of the four roads. For, of these four roads, one was red, one was black, a third was white and the last was yellow. The black road spoke to them: "I am the road you must take, because I am the lords' road." So said the road. And there they were overcome. They were carried along the road to Xibalba, and when they arrived at the council chamber of the lords of Xibalba, they were already overcome.

Now those whom they saw seated there were only puppets, made of wood, and set up by the lords of Xibalba to deceive them.

"How are you, Hun-Camé," they said to the puppet. "How are you, Vucub-Camé," they said to the wooden man. But the puppets made no answer. And the great lords of Xibalba began to laugh, and all the other lords laughed noisily as well, because they thought them already defeated; they thought that Hun-Hunahpú and Vucub-Hunahpú were already overcome. And they kept on laughing.

Then spoke Hun-Camé and Vucub-Camé. "Very well," they said, "You have come. Tomorrow, make ready your masks, your headdresses and your gloves. Come, sit on our bench," they said. But the bench which they offered them was a burning stone, and on sitting there they were burned. They squirmed about on the bench, and had they not torn themselves loose their buttocks would have been burned off.

The lords of Xibalba laughed again; they were dying of laughter; they writhed with the pain their laughter caused in their bellies, in their blood and in their bones. All the lords of Xibalba laughed.

"Now go into that house," they said to Hun-Hunahpú and Vucub-Hunahpú, "There, someone will bring you your pine torch and your roll of tobacco, and there you will sleep."

And so they went into the House of Darkness. There was only blackness within that

House. Meanwhile, the lords of Xibalba spoke of what they were going to do. "Let us sacrifice them tomorrow. Let them die soon, soon; for we must have their equipment for the ball game." So said the lords of the underworld, one to another.

Now their pine torch was only a round, pointed flint-stone which men call zaquitoc. This is the sort of pine they used in Xibalba. Sharp-pointed, keen and shining-bright was the hard pine of Xibalba.

Hun-Hunahpú and Vucub-Hunahpú went into the House of Darkness. There they were given their torch, the single torch sent them by Hun-Camé and Vucub-Camé, together with a roll of tobacco for each one. And both the torch and the rolls of tobacco were lighted. These they sent them. These someone brought to Hun-Hunahpú and Vucub-Hunahpú.

They were squatting in the darkness when the bearers brought them the torch and the rolls of tobacco. As the bearers entered, the torch shone brilliantly. "Come to return these at dawn. Do not consume them. Return them whole. This is what the lords have commanded us to say to you." So was it said. And so were they overcome. The torch burned itself out. The rolls of tobacco which they had been given consumed themselves.

The punishments of Xibalba were many; there were punishments of many kinds.

The first was the House of Darkness, Quequma-ha, wherein was only blackness.

The second was the House where they shivered, Xuxulim-ha. It was very cold in that House. A cold and intolerable wind blew within it.

The third was the House of the Tigers, Balami-ha as it was called, in which were only tigers, pacing about, leaping on one another, growling and snarling. The tigers were locked within that House.

Zotzi-ha, the House of the Bats, was the name of the fourth place of punishment. Inside this House were only bats, which hooted, screeched and flew about. The bats also were locked in and could not escape.

The fifth place was called the House of the Knives, Chayim-ha, within which were only keen, cutting edges, lying quiet or grating against one another.

When Hun-Hunahpú and Vucub-Hunahpú came before Hun-Camé and Vucub-Camé, the lords said to them:

"Where are my rolls of tobacco? Where is the torch which they gave you last night?"

"They were consumed, lord."

"Very well, then. Today will be the end of your days. Now you will die. You will be destroyed. We shall make pieces of you, and your memory will be darkened. You will be sacrificed." So said Hun-Camé and Vucub-Camé.

Immediately, they sacrificed them, and they buried them in the place called Pucbal-Chah, or the place of sacrifice. But before burying them, they cut off Hun-Hunahpú's head. Then they buried the elder brother with the younger brother.

"Take the head and put it in that tree which stands in the road," said Hun-Camé and Vucub-Camé. And when they had put the head in the tree, immediately the tree was covered with fruit. Never before had that tree borne fruit, until the head of Hun-Hunahpú was placed among its branches. And today that kind of tree is called "the head of Hun-Hunahpú." So is it called.

Hun-Camé and Vucub-Camé looked up with wonder at the fruit of the tree. On all sides could be seen the round fruit, but no longer could they distinguish the head of Hun-Hunahpú. The head was one and the same thing with the fruit of the tree. So it seemed to all those of Xibalba who came to see.

To all of them the tree was wonderful, because of what had happened in an instant when the head of Hun-Hunahpú was placed among the branches. And the lords of Xibalba gave orders: "No one may pick this fruit. No one may come beneath this tree." So did they say; so did they forbid these things to all in Xibalba.

The succeeding sections tell of the adventures of the girl Ixquic; of her impregnation by the spittle of Hun-Hunahpú as she held out her hand to the fruit of the tree, of the doom pronounced on her by Hun-Camé and Vucub-Camé, and of the marvellous manner in which she persuaded her executioners to let her escape. She then finds her way to the place where the mother of Hun-Hunahpú and Vucub-Hunahpú is living with Hunbatz and Hunchouén. The old woman refuses at first to believe the girl's story that she is carrying the twin children of Hun-Hunahpú, but she is convinced after Ixquic, by the help of the god Chahal, guardian of corn fields, brings in a miraculous harvest of corn. The old woman says to her: "Those whom you bear will surely be wizards."

Now we shall tell of the birth of Hunahpú and Ixbalanqué. Here and now we shall tell the manner of their birth.

When the day of their birth arrived, the young woman named Ixquic was delivered but the old woman did not see the children as they were born. In an instant they were born, those two boys called Hunahpú and Ixbalanqué. There on the mountain they were born.

Then they came to their home, but they could not sleep. "Go, throw them out!" cried the old woman, because in truth they made a great deal of noise. Immediately they were placed on an ant-hill, and there they went peacefully to sleep. Then the twins were taken from that place and laid among thorns. What Hunbatz and Hunchouén hoped for was this—that the children should die right there on the ant-hill or that they should die among the thorns. They wanted this because of the hatred and envy they felt toward them.

So, in the beginning, they refused to receive their younger brothers in their house; they would not know them, and so they were nurtured in the fields.

Hunbatz and Hunchouén were great musicians and singers; they had grown up on hard work and they had been much in need; they had suffered many hardships but they had become very wise. They were flute players, singers, painters, and carvers. They knew how to do everything.

They knew of their birth; they knew that they were heirs to their fathers, those who had gone to Xibalba and there died. Very wise, also, were Hunbatz and Hunchouén, and within them they knew all about the birth of their younger brothers. But they did not let their knowledge be known, because of the envy they felt; their hearts were full of evil toward the twins, although Hunahpú and Ixbalanqué had given them no offense.

The children devoted themselves all day long to shooting with the blow-gun; they were not loved by their grandmother, nor by Hunbatz, nor by Hunchouén. They were given nothing to eat; only when the meal was over, and Hunbatz and Hunchouén had already eaten could they come in. But they did not become annoyed, nor did they become angry, and they suffered silently, because they knew their fate and they foresaw everything very clearly. Each day they brought the birds they had shot; Hunbatz and Hunchouén would eat them and give nothing to either of the two, to Hunahpú or Ixbalanqué.

The sole occupation of Hunbatz and Hunchouén was playing the flute and singing.

Then one time Hunahpú and Ixbalanqué arrived without bringing any birds. They came into the house, and the grandmother became very angry. "Why have you brought no birds?" she said to them, to Hunahpú and Ixbalanqué.

And they answered: "This is what has happened, grandmother. Our birds were caught in a tree, and we could not go up to get them, dear grandmother. Therefore, if our elder brothers want them, let them come with us and let them bring the birds down." So they said.

"That is good," said the elder brothers, answering, "We shall go with you at dawn."

Then the twins took counsel together how they would overcome Hunbatz and Hunchouén. "We shall change only their nature, their appearance; and in this way our word will be fulfilled. They have caused us much suffering. They wanted us to die; they wished that we, their younger brothers, should be lost. In their hearts they believed that we had come to be their servants. Because of all this, we shall overcome them and give them an example." So they said, one to another, as they went toward the foot of the tree called Canté, or yellow wood tree. Their elder brothers came with them.

They were shooting at birds with the blow-gun. It was not possible to count the birds that were singing in that tree, and the elder brothers were amazed to see so many birds. But not a single bird fell to the foot of the tree.

"Our birds do not fall to the ground. Go get them down," they said to the elder brothers.

"Very well," answered Hunbatz and Hunchouén. And immediately they began to climb the tree, but it increased in size and the trunk became wider and wider. Then the elder brothers wanted to get down, but they could no longer descend from the top of the tree. And then from aloft they began to cry out: "Brothers, what is happening to us! We are lost. Just looking down from this tree frightens us."

Hunahpú and Ixbalanqué answered them: "Take off your trousers and tie them under your bellies. Leave the ends loose and turn them about so that they hang behind you. In this way you will be able to walk easily." So did the younger brothers answer them.

"Very well," the elder brothers replied. They began to undo their sashes, and in an instant, the sashes turned into tails and the brothers took on the look of monkeys. They

156

bounded away, from branch to branch of the trees, over the crests of great mountains and small; deep in the forest they fled, making faces and swinging from the branches of the trees.

In this way were Hunbatz and Hunchouén overcome by Hunahpú and Ixbalanqué; only by magic were they able to do these things.

The younger brothers returned home, and on arriving they spoke to their grandmother and their mother, saying to them, "What could have happened to our elder brothers, O grandmother, that in an instant their faces turned into the faces of animals." So they said.

"If you have done any harm to your elder brothers, you have made me unhappy. You have filled me with grief. Surely you have not done such a thing to your brothers. Oh, my sons, my sons!" said the old woman to Hunahpú and Ixbalanqué. And they said to their grandmother, "Do not grieve. You will see again the face of our brothers; they will return, but it will be a hard trial for you, grandmother. You must take care not to laugh."

Then they began to play the flute, playing the song called Hunahpú-Qoy. Then they sang, playing the flute and drum also. Then they sat next to their grandmother, and they kept on playing and calling out with the music and song, singing the song called Hunahpú-Qoy.

Finally, Hunbatz and Hunchouén came up and began to dance; but when the old woman saw their ugly faces she began to laugh. She could not stop laughing, and they went off in an instant. She no longer saw their faces.

"You saw them, grandmother? They went off towards the woods. What have you done, O grandmother. Only four times may we make this test, and now only three chances remain. We are going to call them again with the flute and with the song, but you must not laugh. Let the test begin." So said Hunahpú and Ixbalanqué.

They began to play again. Hunbatz and Hunchouén came dancing back, and they arrived at the middle of the courtyard, grimacing and arousing laughter in their grandmother until once again she burst out. For they were most amusing with their monkey faces, their wide buttocks, their thin tails and their fat stomachs. All of this made the old woman laugh.

And again they fled off to the mountains. Hunahpú and Ixbalanqué said, "What shall we do now, little grandmother? Well, we shall try this third time."

Once more they played the flute. Once more the monkeys returned, dancing. The old woman stifled her laughter. But the monkeys' eyes shone with a red light, they opened wide their snouts and rubbed them, and it was wonderful to see the faces they made at each other.

When the old woman saw this, she burst into wild laughter. And because of the old woman's laughter, they saw the monkey faces no longer.

"And now we shall call them only this time, grandmother; they will come this fourth time only," said the boys. And they set about to play the flute again, but the elder brothers did not return the fourth time. They fled in a great hurry away through the forest.

The boys said to their grandmother: "We did everything possible, poor little grandmother. At first they came, and then we tried to call them again. But you must not grieve.

We are here, your grandsons. You must look after us, O mother, O grandmother, and keep in memory our elder brothers who were called Hunbatz and Hunchouén." So said Hunahpú and Ixbalanqué.

Hunbatz and Hunchouén were prayed to by the musicians and the singers and the people of old time. The painters and carvers in time past called on them for assistance. But they were turned into animals. They became monkeys because they grew proud and mistreated their brothers.

So did their hearts suffer; so were they lost. In this way did Hunbatz and Hunchouén become animals. They had stayed at home; they were musicians and singers; they had done great things while they lived with their grandmother and their mother.

Then began their labors, the work they must do to justify themselves before their grandmother and before their mother. The first of these was the making of a corn field.

"We are going to prepare the corn field," they said to their grandmother and their mother. "Do not grieve; here we are, your grandsons, we who are here in place of our brothers," said Hunahpú and Ixbalanqué.

Then they took their axes, their headdresses and their wooden hoes and went out, each one carrying on his shoulder his blowgun. On leaving the house, they asked their grandmother to bring them their food. "At noon, you will bring us our food, grandmother," they said.

"Very well, my grandsons," answered the old woman.

Soon they came to the place to be sown. When they plunged the hoe into the ground, it worked the earth; the hoe did the work by itself.

In the same way, when they drove the axe into the trunks of trees and into the branches, at once they would fall. All the trees and vines would remain stretched out on the earth. Swiftly would fall the trees, cut with a single blow of the axe.

The hoe had pulled out very much too. The brambles and thorns which the hoe had cut with a single blow could not be counted. It was not possible to say what had been pulled up and felled on all the mountains, great and small.

And choosing a creature called Ixmucur (the turtledove), they made it go up to the top of a tall tree. Hunahpú and Ixbalanqué said to it: "Keep watch when our grandmother comes to bring us our meal, and on the instant begin to sing. We shall then grab the hoe and the axe."

"Very well," replied the dove.

And so they began to shoot with the blowgun; certainly they were doing no farm work. A little later the dove sang and immediately one ran to pick up the hoe and the other to pick up the axe. And wrapping up his head, one covered his hands with dirt and dirtied his face like a real workman, and the other purposely threw chips of wood on his head as if he had really been cutting trees.

So were they seen by the grandmother. Immediately they ate; but in fact they had not done any farm work and they had their dinner without earning it. They returned to their house.

The next day they came back and on arriving at the field they found that all the trees and vines had risen again and all the brambles and thorns had joined and enlaced again.

"Who played this trick on us?" they said. "No doubt all the animals great and small have done it; the lion, the tiger, the deer, the rabbit, the wildcat, the coyote, the wild boar, the little birds, the big birds; these were the ones who did it and in one night they accomplished it."

Again they set about to prepare the field and to level the earth and hew the trees. Then they talked about what they should do with the cut timber and the underbrush which had been pulled up.

"We shall keep a watch over our corn field. Perhaps we can surprise whoever comes to do all this damage," they said one to the other. And so talking, they returned home.

"What do you think, grandmother? Someone has tricked us. Our tilled field has turned into a field covered with tall grass and dense forest. So we found it when we arrived a short while ago, grandmother," they said to their grandmother and mother. "But we shall return there and keep watch because it isn't right that such things should happen to us," they said.

Then they dressed and went immediately to their field of hewn trees, and there they hid themselves, concealing themselves in the shade.

Then all the animals got together, one of each species out of all animals, small and great. And it was exactly mid-night when they arrived, saying each in his language, "Arise, trees! Arise, vines!"

They were saying this as they arrived and they gathered beneath the trees and beneath the vines and they came on until they showed themselves before the eyes of Hunahpú and Ixbalanqué.

The lion and the tiger were the first and the brothers wanted to seize them, but the animals did not let themselves be caught. Then they approached the deer and the rabbit and they managed to seize their tails, only they pulled them away. The tails remained in their hands and for this reason the deer and the rabbit have short tails.

The wild cat, the coyote, the wild boar, all the animals passed in front of Hunahpú and Ixbalanqué, whose hearts were burning with rage because they could not catch them.

Then, at last, a newcomer bounded in, and this one, who was Mouse, they caught, and they wrapped him in a cloth. And when they caught him, they squeezed his head and they were going to choke him, and they burned his tail in the fire, whence it comes about that the mouse's tail has no hair. The two boys, Hunahpú and Ixbalanqué also wanted to punch him in the eyes.

Mouse said: "I mustn't die at your hands. And neither is it your business to sow a corn field."

"What are you telling us, now?" said the boys to the mouse.

"Unloosen me a little, because in my heart I have something to tell you and I will tell you immediately. Only, first give me something to eat," said the mouse.

"Afterwards we will give you your meal, but speak first," they answered him.

"Very well. Know then that the possessions of your fathers Hun-Hunahpú and Vucub-Hunahpú, so called, they who died in Xibalba, the very things with which they used to play the ball game are there hanging in the roof of the house—the collar, the gloves and the ball. Your grandmother does not want to show them to you because on their account your fathers died."

"Do you know it surely?" said the boys to the mouse. Their hearts grew very happy when they heard the news of the rubber ball. And as the mouse had spoken, they pointed out his food to him.

"This will be your meal: corn, red pepper, seeds, kidney beans, cacao: all this is yours, and if there should be something which is kept in the storehouse or forgotten, it will also be yours. Eat it!" Hunahpú and Ixbalanqué told Mouse.

"Wonderful!" the mouse said, "but what will I say to your grandmother if she sees me?"

"Have no fear, because we are here and we shall know what to say to our grandmother. Now let us go quickly to the house. Let us go quickly to where these things are hung. Search in the garret of the house while we pretend to eat our meal," they said to the mouse.

Then, having so decided and settled matters, Hunahpú and Ixbalanqué arrived home at noon. They brought the mouse with them, but they did not let him be seen; one of them went directly into the house and the other approached the corner and from there made the mouse climb up immediately.

They asked their grandmother for food. "Prepare our food; we want a sauce of chile peppers, grandmother," they said. And immediately the food was prepared for them and a plate of broth was put before them.

But this was only to trick their grandmother and their mother. They drank up the water which was in the large earthenware jar. "We are dying of thirst; go get us something to drink," they said to their grandmother.

"Very well," she answered and went away. Then they began to eat, but in fact they were not hungry; what they were doing was only a deception. In their plate of pepper sauce, they saw the reflection of the mouse as he climbed rapidly toward the ball which hung from the roof of the house. They sent a certain Xan, the animal called Xan, which is like a mosquito, to the river to drill through the side of their grandmother's pitcher. Although she tried to keep the water from running out, she could not close the hole made in the pitcher.

"What is our grandmother doing? Our mouths are dry for lack of water, we are dying of thirst," they said to their mother. They sent her out to get water. The mouse then cut the rope which held up the ball, and it fell into the garret of the house along with the collar, the gloves and the other things. The boys took them up at once and ran to hide them on the pathway which led to the ball court.

Then they walked to the river, to join their grandmother and their mother, who were very busy trying to plug the hole in the pitcher. And as each one came up with his blowgun, he said when he arrived at the river: "What are you doing? We tired of waiting and we came."

"Look here at the hole in my pitcher. It cannot be plugged," said the grandmother. But they plugged it at once and they returned home together, they marching before their grandmother.

So was accomplished the finding of the ball.

The legend then tells how Hunahpú and Ixbalanqué were playing ball when word was brought them that the lords of Xibalba had summoned them to trial, just as their fathers had been summoned. They come through most of the ordeal successfully; in the House of the Bats, however, a great Camazotz (vampire-bat) cuts off Hunahpú's head and the lords of Xibalba hang it up in the ball court as a trophy. Ixbalanqué deceives the lords and recovers Hunahpú's head. In the long run, the lords of Xibalba are defeated in a trial of magic power.

Maya (Quiché)

THE RITUAL OF THE FOUR WORLD-QUARTERS

THE LORD OF THE PEOPLE of the South is the first of the men of the Noh family. Ix-Kan-tacay is the name of the first of the men of the Puch family. They guard nine rivers. They watch over the place of the nine mountains.

The red flint stone is the stone of the red Bee God. The red *ceiba* tree, the tree of abundance, is his arbor which is set in the east. The red bullet-tree is their tree also, as is the red zapote . . . the red vine. Reddish are their yellow turkeys. Red toasted corn is their corn.

The white flint stone is their stone in the north. The white *ceiba* tree is the arbor of the white Bee God. White-breasted are their turkeys. White lima beans are their lima beans. White corn is their corn.

The black flint stone is their stone in the west. The black *ceiba* tree of abundance is their arbor. Black speckled corn is their corn. Black wild pigeons are their turkeys. Black maize is their green-corn. Black beans are their beans. Black lima beans are their lima beans.

The yellow flint stone is the stone of the south. The *ceiba* tree, the yellow *ceiba* tree of abundance is their arbor. The yellow bullet-tree is their tree. Colored like the yellow bullet-tree are the wild pigeons which are their turkeys. Yellow green-corn is their green-corn. Yellow-backed are their beans.

Eleven ahau was the *Katun* when they carried burdens on their backs. Then came the men who measured, the land-surveyors who marked out the leagues with their sticks of the brazil tree. Then it was that they came to the place of the city, laid out the roads, cleared and cleaned and built.

Then a spokesman was established to sit at the head of the council-mat. In the east Ix Noh Uc presides, and Ox Tocoy-Moo and Ox Pauah Ek and Ah Miz.

Batun presides to the north, and Ah Puch and Balam-na and Ake.

Iban presides to the west, and Ah Chab and Ah Tucuch.

Ah Yamas presides to the south and Ah Puch and Cauich and Ah Couoh.

The red wild bees are in the east. A large red blossom is their cup. The red *plumeria* is their flower.

The white wild bees are in the north. The white day-flower is their flower. A large white blossom is their cup.

The black wild bees are in the west. The black laurel is their flower. A large black blossom is their cup.

The yellow wild bees are in the south. A large yellow blossom is their cup.

Then they swarmed at Cozumel in great numbers among the *magueys* of that land, the calabash trees of that land, the *ceiba* trees of that land. The Wind God of the south was their priest. He commanded the great army which kept watch over the temple of the archer at Tantum, and the temples of the green turtle and of the deified fathers of cities.

Maya

TWO HYMNS TO HUITZILOPOCHTLI

HUITZILOPOCHTLI is first in rank, no one, no one is like unto him: not vainly do I sing his praises, coming forth in the garb of our ancestors; I shine; I glitter.

He is a terror to the Mixteca; he alone destroyed the Picha-Huasteca, he conquered them.

The Dart-Hurler is an example to the city, as he sets to work. He who commands in battle is called the representative of my God.

When he shouts aloud he inspires great terror, the divine hurler, the god turning himself in the combat, the divine hurler, the god turning himself in the combat.

Amanteca, gather yourselves together with me in the house of war against your enemies, gather yourselves together with me.

Pipiteca, gather yourselves together with me in the house of war against your enemies, gather yourselves together with me.

Aztec

Huitzilopochtli,
Only a subject,
Only a mortal was.

A magician,
A terror,
A stirrer of strife,
A deceiver,
A maker of war,
An arranger of battles,
A lord of battles;
And of him it was said
That he hurled
His flaming serpent,
His fire stick;
Which means war,
Blood and burning;
And when his festival was celebrated,
Captives were slain,
Washed slaves were slain,
The merchants washed them.
And thus he was arrayed:
With headdress of green feathers,
Holding his serpent torch,
Girded with a belt,
Bracelets upon his arms,
Wearing turquoises,
As a master of messengers.

Aztec

THE HYMN OF TLALOC

IN MEXICO the god appears; thy banner is unfolded in all directions, and no one weeps.

I, the god, have returned again, I have turned again to the place of abundance of blood-sacrifices; there when the day grows old, I am beheld as a god.

Thy work is that of a noble magician; truly thou hast made thyself to be of our flesh; thou hast made thyself, and who dare affront thee?

Truly he who affronts me does not find himself well with me; my fathers took by the head the tigers and the serpents.

In Tlalocan, in the verdant house, they play at ball, they cast the reeds.

Go forth, go forth to where the clouds are spread abundantly, where the thick mist makes the cloudy house of Tlaloc.

There with strong voice I rise up and cry aloud.

Go ye forth to seek me, seek for the words which I have said, as I rise, a terrible one, and cry aloud.

After four years they shall go forth, not to be known, not to be numbered, they shall descend to the beautiful house, to unite together and know the doctrine.

Go forth, go forth to where the clouds are spread abundantly, where the thick mist makes the cloudy house of Tlaloc.

Aztec

HYMN TO CIHUACOATL

Quilaztli, plumed with eagle feathers, with the crest of eagles, painted with serpents' blood, comes with her hoe, beating her drum, from Colhuacan.

She alone, who is our flesh, goddess of the fields and shrubs, is strong to support us.

With the hoe, with the hoe, with hands full, with the hoe, with hands full, the goddess of the fields is strong to support us.

With a broom in her hands the goddess of the fields strongly supports us.

Our mother is as twelve eagles, goddess of drum-beating, filling the fields of tzioac and maguey like our lord Mixcoatl.

She is our mother, a goddess of war, our mother, a goddess of war, an example and a companion from the home of our ancestors, Colhuacan.

She comes forth, she appears when war is waged, she protects us in war that we shall not be destroyed, an example and companion from the home of our ancestors.

She comes adorned in the ancient manner with the eagle crest, in the ancient manner with the eagle crest.

Aztec

HYMN OF THE HIGH PRIEST OF XIPE TOTEC

The nightly drinking, why should I oppose it? Go forth and array yourselves in the golden garments, clothe yourselves in the glittering vestments.

My god descended upon the water, into the beautiful glistening surface; he was as a lovely water cypress, as a beauteous green serpent; now I have left behind me my suffering.

I go forth, I go forth about to destroy, I, Yoatzin; my soul is in the cerulean water; I am seen in the golden water; I shall appear unto mortals; I shall strengthen them for the words of war!

My god appears as a mortal; O Yoatzin, thou art seen upon the mountains; I shall appear unto mortals; I shall strengthen them for the words of war.

Aztec

164

A PLAIN SONG OF THE MEXICANS

I alone will clothe thee with flowers, mine alone is the song which casts down our grief before God in thy house.

True it is that my possessions shall perish, my friendships, their home and their house; thus I, O Yoyontzin, pour forth songs to the Giver of Life.

Let the green quechol birds, let the tzinitzcan twine flowers for us, only dying and withered flowers, that we may clothe thee with flowers, thou ruler, thou Nezahual coyotl.

Ye youths and ye braves, skilled in wisdom, may you alone be our friends, while for a moment here we shall enjoy this house.

For thy fame shall perish, Nopiltzin, and thou, Tezozomoc, where are thy songs? No more do I cry aloud, but rest tranquil that ye have gone to your homes.

Ye whom I bewailed, I know nevermore, never again; I am sad here on earth that ye have gone to your homes.

Nahua

A SONG OF HUEXOTZINCO

Only sad flowers, sad songs, are here in Mexico, in Tlatilolco, in this place these alone are known, alas.

It is well to know these, if only we may please the Giver of Life, lest we be destroyed, we his subjects, alas.

We have angered Him, we are only wretched beings, slaves by blood; we have seen and known affliction, alas.

We are disturbed, we are embittered, thy servants here in Tlatilolco, deprived of food, made acquainted with affliction, we are fatigued with labor, O Giver of Life, alas.

Weeping is with us, tears fall like rain, here in Tlatilolco; as the Mexican women go down to the water, we beg of them for ourselves and our friends, alas.

Even as the smoke, rising, lies in a cloud over Mount Atloyan, in Mexico, so does it happen unto us, O Giver of Life, alas.

And you Mexicans, may you remember concerning us when you descend and suffer before the majesty of God, when there you shall howl like wolves.

There, there will be only weeping as your greeting when you come, there you will be accursed, all of you, workers in filth, slaves, rulers or warriors, and thus Tenochtitlan will be deserted.

Oh friends, do not weep, but know that sometime we shall have left behind us the things of Mexico, and then their water shall be made bitter and their food shall be made bitter, here in Tlatilolco, as never before, by the Giver of Life.

The disdained and the slaves shall go forth with song; but in a little while their oppressors shall be seen in the fire, amid the howling of wolves.

Nahua

165

TWO SONGS FOR THE TEPONAZTLI

(Tico, tico, toco, toto, and as the song approaches the end, tiqui, titi, tito, titi)

At Tollan there stood the house of beams, there yet stands the house of plumed serpents left by Nacxitl Topiltzin; going forth weeping, our nobles went to where he was to perish, down there at Tlapallan.

We went forth from Cholula by way of Poyauhtecatl, and ye went forth weeping down by the water toward Acallan.

I come from Nonohualco as if I carried quechol birds to the place of the nobles; I grieve that my lord has gone, garlanded with feathers; I am wretched like the last flower.

With the falling down of mountains I wept, with the lifting up of sands I was wretched, that my lord had gone.

At Tlapallan he was waited for, it was commanded that there he should sleep, thus being alone.

In our battles my lord was garlanded with feathers; we were commanded to go alone to Xicalanco.

Alas! and alas! who will be in thy house to attire thee? Who will be the ruler in thy house, left desolate here in Tollan, in Nonohualco?

After he was drunk, the ruler wept; we glorified ourselves to be in thy dwelling.

Misfortune and misery were written against us there in Tollan, that our leader Nacxitl Topiltzin was to be destroyed and thy subjects made to weep.

We have left the turquoise houses, the serpent houses there in Tollan, where ruled our leader Nacxitl Topiltzin.

Nahua

(Tico, toco, tocoto, and then it ends, ticoto, ticoto)

The sweet voiced quechol there, ruling the earth, has intoxicated my soul.

I am like the quetzal bird, I am created in the house of the one only God; I sing sweet songs among the flowers; I chant songs and rejoice in my heart.

The fuming dew-drops from the flowers in the field intoxicate my soul.

I grieve to myself that ever this dwelling on earth should end.

I foresaw, being a Mexican, that our rule began to be destroyed, I went forth weeping that it was to bow down and be destroyed.

Let me not be angry that the grandeur of Mexico is to be destroyed.

The smoking stars gather together against it; the one who cares for flowers is about to be destroyed.

He who cared for books wept, he wept for the beginning of the destruction.

Nahua

PLATES 33-64

MOUNTAIN AND MESA

THE VALLEY, THE PENINSULA

AND THE ISTHMUS

YUROK

SHASTA

MISSION

BASKETRY

MAIDU

MAIDU

KAROK

BASKET-CAP, MODOC

YUROK

HUPA

POMO

HUPA

MISSION

MISSION

LIGHTNING

REPRESENTATIVE UNITS AND SYMBOLS

BIRDS

CLOUDS AND RAIN

BIRDS

CLOUD

BUTTERFLY

RAINBOW

CLOUDS

CLOUD SERPENTS

BIRD HANGING
FROM SKY BAND

THUNDER-BIRD

SUN

PLUMED SERPENT

ALTAR WITH FEATHERS

RAIN SERPENT

SUN   FLOWER

DEER

BIRDS

EXIT TRAIL OF LIFE

WORM (ON BASKET)

TURTLE   LION

COUGAR AND CARDINAL POINTS

CORN

CLIFF-DWELLINGS AND PUEBLO POTTERY

COCHITI

PUEBLO   CASAS GRANDES   POTTERY

SAN JUAN

HAWIKUH

CASAS GRANDES

HAWIKUH

SANTA ANA

CASAS GRANDES

SAN ILDEFONSO

SIA

ACOMA

ZUNI

MIMBRES   POTTERY

MOTIVE FROM LAGUNA JAR

MOTIVE FROM LAGUNA JAR

ACOMA

SAN ILDEFONSO

ZUNI

PUEBLO

ZUNI

POTTERY

ZUNI

ZUNI

MOTIVE FROM ZUNI JAR

ZUNI

MOTIVE FROM ZUNI JAR

PUEBLO POTTERY

ACOMA

SANTO DOMINGO

SAN ILDEFONSO

ACOMA

SANTO DOMINGO

LAGUNA

ZUNI

SIA

SIA

ACOMA

BASKETS

AND TRAYS

WHITE MOUNTAIN APACHE

HOPI POTTERY

WHITE MOUNTAIN APACHE

PIMA

HOPI

PIMA

JICARILLA APACHE

MESCALERO APACHE

HAVASUPAI

PIMA

SILVER AND TURQUOISE   ZUNI

HOPI KACHINA

(AFTER WATERCOLOR
PAINTING BY FRED KABOTI)

HOPI KACHINA

NAVAHO

TRAY, HOPI

KACHINA TRAY
HOPI

BEADWORK

MESCALERO
APACHE

HIDE MASK, ZUNI

TURQUOISE AND
SHELL MOSAIC
ARIZONA

HIDE MASK, ZUNI

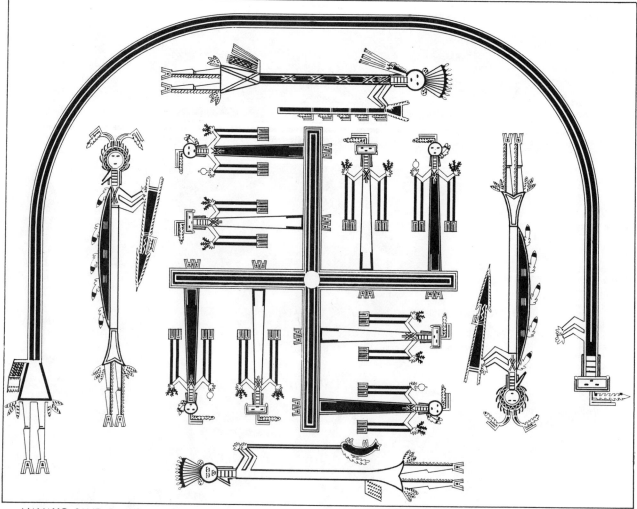

NAVAHO SAND PAINTING

Black cross-bars represent pine logs; the circle water. Figures of gods with their wives (goddesses) sit upon the logs. Round heads denote male; rectangular heads, female. Rattles and piñon sprigs bring male and female rains which bring forth vegetation. Arching over all is the rainbow goddess upon which the gods travel. (After Stevenson)

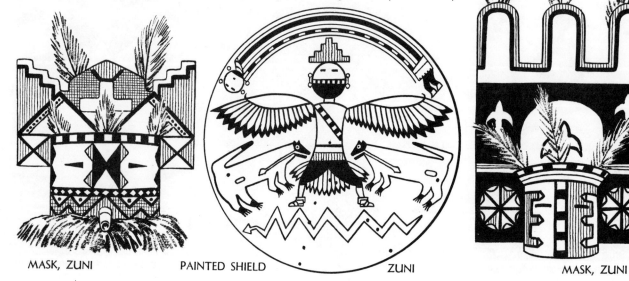

MASK, ZUNI   PAINTED SHIELD   ZUNI   MASK, ZUNI

HOPI CEREMONIAL BLANKET

WOMAN'S DRESS, ACOMA

WOMAN'S DRESS, ACOMA

HOPI WEDDING SHAWL

NAVAHO BLANKET

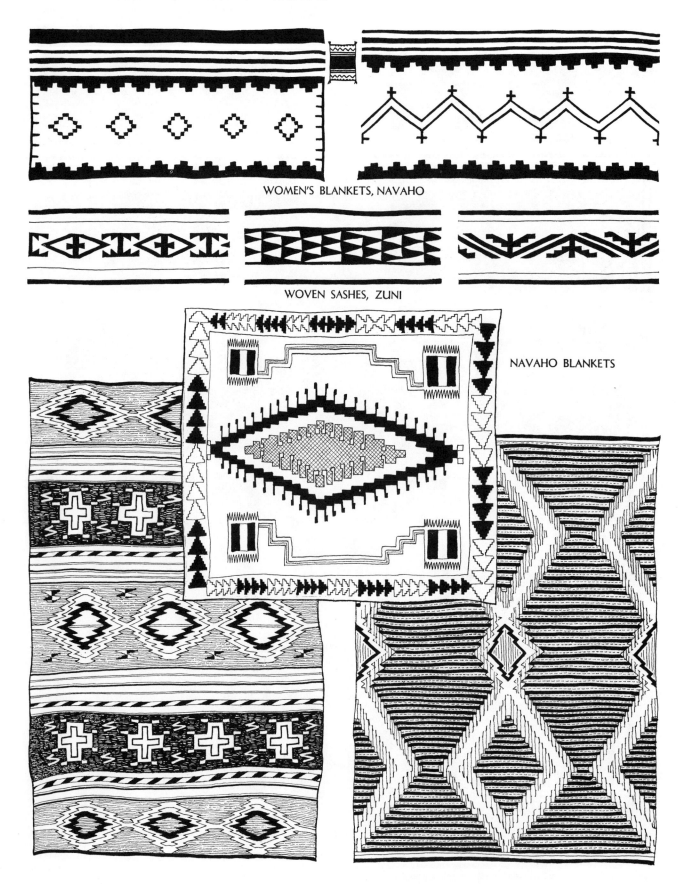

WOMEN'S BLANKETS, NAVAHO

WOVEN SASHES, ZUNI

NAVAHO BLANKETS

"CHIEF" BLANKET, NAVAHO

WOMAN'S DRESS, NAVAHO

NAVAHO BLANKET

CEREMONIAL BLANKET, HOPI

WOMAN'S DRESS, HOPI

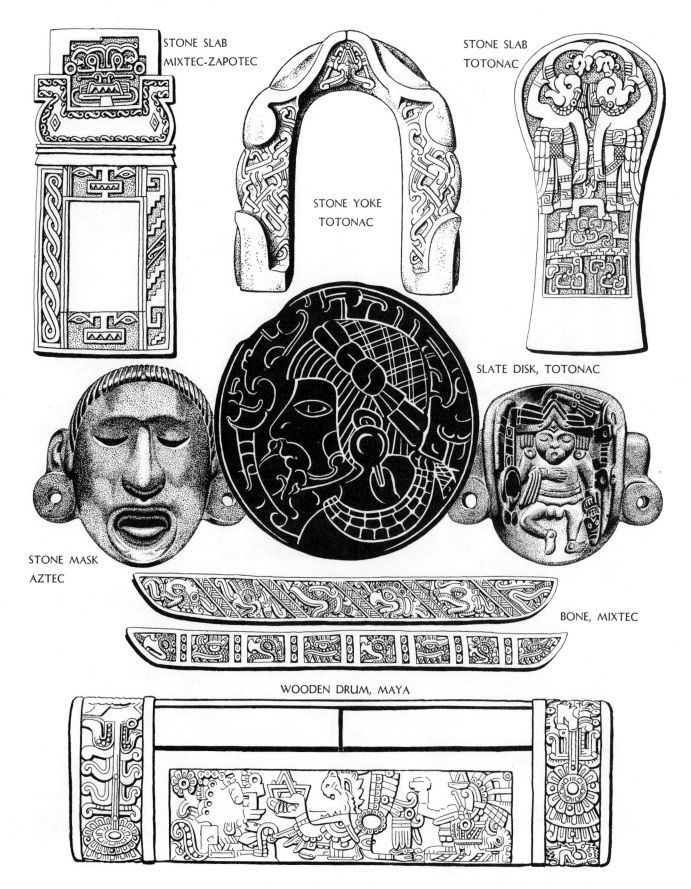

STONE SLAB
MIXTEC-ZAPOTEC

STONE SLAB
TOTONAC

STONE YOKE
TOTONAC

SLATE DISK, TOTONAC

STONE MASK
AZTEC

BONE, MIXTEC

WOODEN DRUM, MAYA

FUNERARY URN, ZAPOTEC

CLAY, TOTONAC

STONE, AZTEC

CLAY INCENSE   BURNER, AZTEC

CLAY FIGURE, HUAXTEC

CLAY FIGURE, TARASCAN

POTTERY STAMP, AZTEC

FUNERARY URN, ZAPOTEC

POTTERY DESIGNS, TOLTEC

PRE-AZTEC AND AZTEC POTTERY

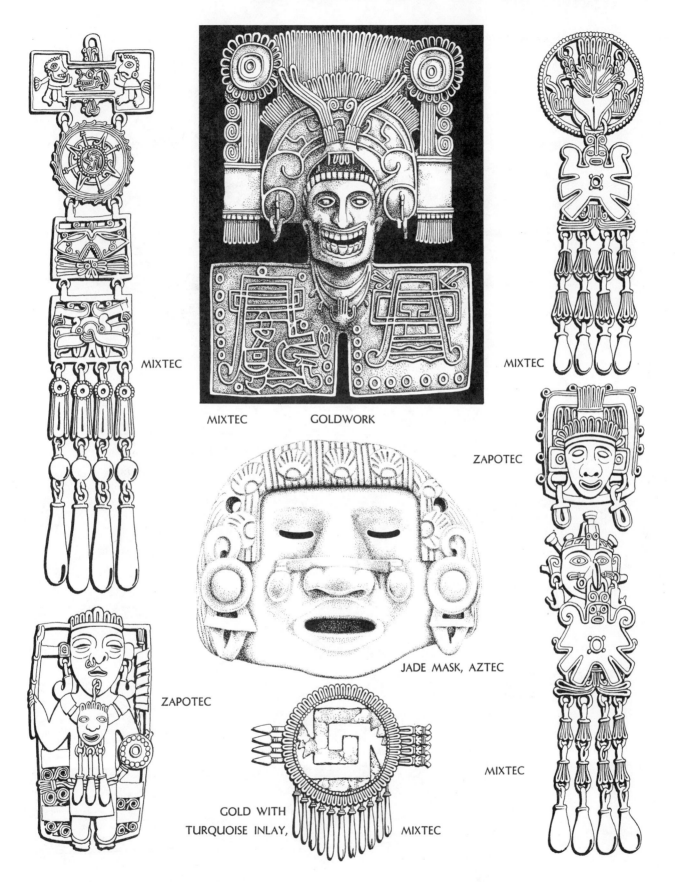

MIXTEC

MIXTEC

MIXTEC   GOLDWORK

MIXTEC

ZAPOTEC

JADE MASK, AZTEC

ZAPOTEC

GOLD WITH
TURQUOISE INLAY,   MIXTEC

MIXTEC

PAINTING FROM CODEX, MIXTEC-ZAPOTEC (AFTER JOYCE)

CODEX, AZTEC

PORTION OF MAYA MURAL (AFTER MORRIS)

MAYA   POTTERY

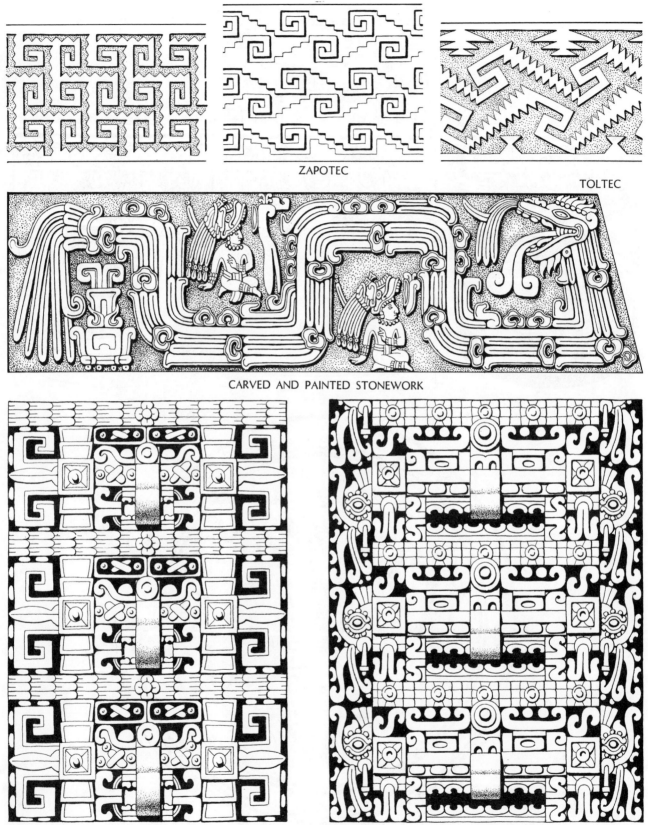

ZAPOTEC

TOLTEC

CARVED AND PAINTED STONEWORK

MAYA

MAYA

AZTEC CALENDAR STONE

MAYA HIEROGLYPHS

(CARVED ON STONE STELA)

CARVED STONE
PANEL, MAYA

CARVED AND PAINTED WALL, (DETAIL) MAYA

STELA, MAYA

TEMPLE OF QUETZALCÓATL

EXAMPLES OF THE USE OF THE FEATHERED
SERPENT QUETZALCÓATL, THE ANCIENT
MEXICAN SERPENT GOD

STONE LINTEL, MAYA

PAINTED VASE, MAYA

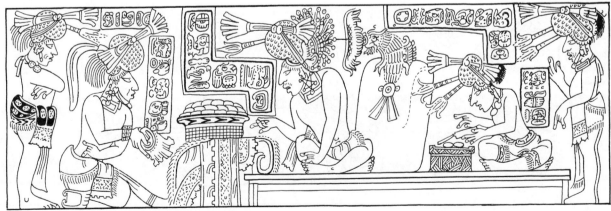

WOODEN LINTEL, MAYA

STONE LINTEL, MAYA

STELA

STELA

LINTEL

STELA

STELA

CARVED STONE, MAYA

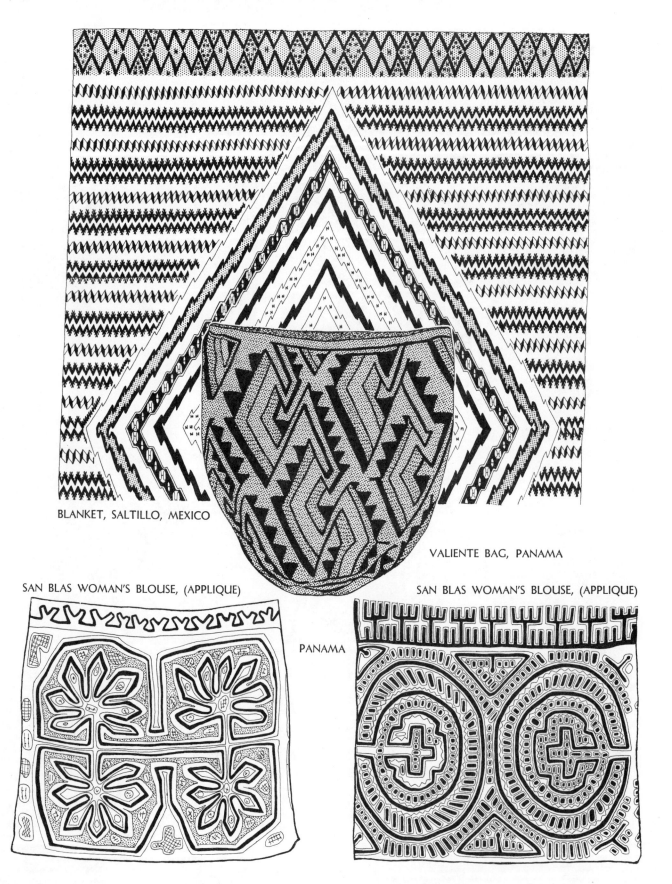

BLANKET, SALTILLO, MEXICO

VALIENTE BAG, PANAMA

SAN BLAS WOMAN'S BLOUSE, (APPLIQUE)

PANAMA

SAN BLAS WOMAN'S BLOUSE, (APPLIQUE)

GOLDWORK

PANAMA

PANAMA

COLOMBIA

COSTA RICA

COLOMBIA

PANAMA

COSTA RICA

COLOMBIA

PANAMA

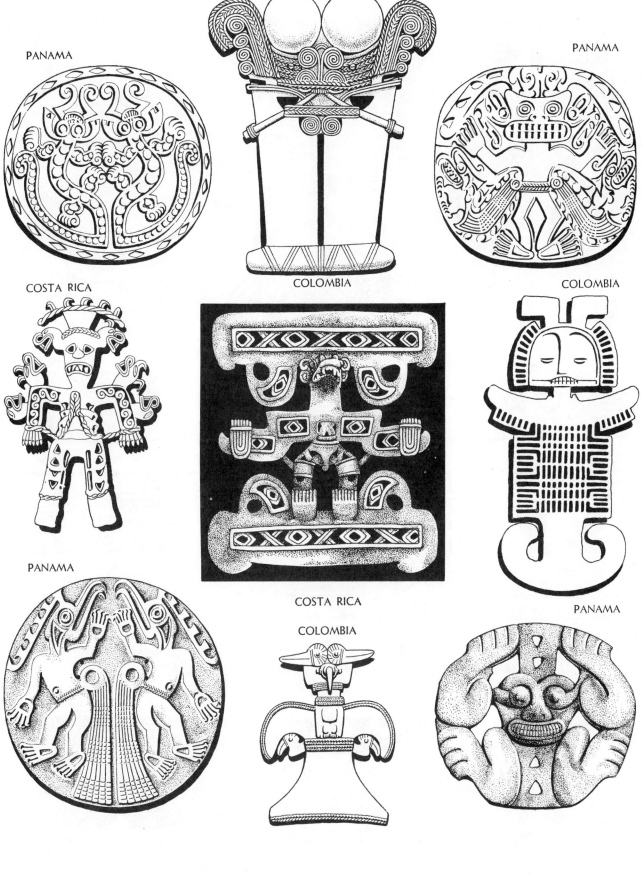

EL SALVADOR

POTTERY

COSTA RICA

COSTA RICA

PANAMA

COSTA RICA

COSTA RICA

COSTA RICA

NICARAGUA

COSTA RICA

COSTA RICA

COSTA RICA

STONE METATE, GUATEMALA

STONE METATE, PANAMA

POTTERY PLATE, PANAMA

POTTERY VASE, PANAMA

STONE STOOL, PANAMA

POTTERY PLATE, COSTA RICA

POTTERY JAR, PANAMA

POTTERY VASE, PANAMA

POTTERY JAR, PANAMA

POTTERY JAR, HONDURAS

POTTERY JAR, PANAMA

POTTERY JAR, EL SALVADOR

POTTERY JAR, GUATEMALA

(AFTER SAVILLE)

POTTERY JAR, COLOMBIA

ALABASTER VASE, HONDURAS

POTTERY JAR, PANAMA

6

THE COAST AND THE
MOUNTAINS

O NCE THE ISTHMUS has been crossed and we stand in South America, we find ourselves in a vast area whose surface, in the archaeological sense, has only been scratched. One region, the Andean, has been studied extensively; therein also, some of the traditional history of pre-Conquest times survives. But in all the rest of the continent, the evidence must be dug literally out of dump heaps and graves, organized, studied and an outline of cultures deduced from bits of pottery, fragments of textiles, gold work and stone implements. In order to avoid involvement in terminology (to say nothing of scholars' disputes), the artistic efforts selected for display have been chosen on the basis of two, broad classifications—the work of the Andean peoples, to be found in this chapter, and the work of the rest of the continent, which will be treated in the following chapter.

It is generally agreed that South America was peopled by tribes moving southward from Mexico and Central America, although this generalization is disputed by specialists. From these unknown progenitors, there arose in what we call Peru a mountain or highland culture known as Tiahuanaco, and two coastal cultures—called Chimu in the north, and Nazca in the south. These terms are geographical. The people whose cultures are so classified were from many tribes, strictly so called.

From some unknown date before Christ, these cultures rose and fell and rose again over a span of some fourteen hundred years—a period corresponding roughly in time to the rise and fall of the Mayan empires. At about the time the Toltec and Aztec were taking over in Mexico, the Incas were building their imperial system in Peru. In 1521 A.D., Cortez ended the aboriginal cultures of Mexico with the capture of Tenochtitlan; in 1532, Pizarro took Cuzco, the capital and holy city of the Incas.

Although the Incas have left an impress on the popular mind comparable to that of the Aztec, and most artistic achievements of the Andean peoples are credited to them as a people, this is not the truth. The Incas had something to add to the cultures they absorbed as we shall see, but the full creative force of Indian art in the Andean region had been exercised before the Incas came to power. One of the most important archaeological sites in South America is Tiahuanaco, a ruin in the Bolivian highlands near Lake Titicaca from which the name of the entire culture is derived. The famous monolithic gateway, a detail of which is shown on Plate 72, is the essence of Tiahuanaco art; it is associated with the worship of the creator-god Viracocha, whose story will be found in an Inca version on page 206. The carving of this gateway shows a wonder of detail, with conventionalized representations of the human figure, the condor and the puma. These design motives will be found repeated in the textiles shown on Plates 66, 67 and 68, and in the large pottery jars on Plate 73. The carving of the greenish granite monolith on Plate 72 is also Viracocha, minus his tears and with a wealth of design elements added that betray a decadent art. This is a good example of what happens when ideas descend from the originating group and mingle with some other. Here, the transition has been from Tiahuanaco to Chimu.

The Chimu were architects and town-planners on a grand scale. They were also skilled craftsmen in weaving, pottery and gold work. Their art is predominantly realistic, though formalism is not absent. Their paintings, or rather drawings, for the emphasis is on line and form rather than color, have been of great value in reconstructing their culture by reason of their realistic treatment of costumes and everyday activity. The portraits in pottery (See Plate 74) are their finest work.

For color work, we must turn to the Nazca peoples; their textiles were unsurpassed. In contrast to that of the Chimu, Nazca art is stylized and loaded with symbolism. The Nazca pantheon included the Spotted Cat, the Bird-Demon, the Multiple-Headed God, the Centipede God and the Puma God; all of these may be found on Plates 65, 66 and 73. They are a weird and hostile-looking group indeed, with their protruding tongues and mouth masks. In contrast to these, the monkeys on Plate 67 are amusing creatures, and the fish on Plate 66 seem content to chase one another's tails in complete lack of self-consciousness.

The Incas, as we have observed, were the conquerors and cultural heirs of their predecessors; they were not originators. They built an empire which stretched at its height from northern Ecuador, down the Pacific side of South America to northern Chile and Argentina. At the time Pizarro conquered them, the Incas were engaged in a family row which divided their forces against the invader.

The reader is referred again to the story of Viracocha on page 206. The story relates on the authority of Sarmiento De Gamboa, an obedient henchman of the Spanish crown, that the founders of the Inca dynasty were sons of Viracocha, who created them to be lords. Garcilaso de la Vega, "El Inca", tells a different story of the Inca origin which will be found on page 221. The facts are these: the Incas, a small, highland tribe, swept out on an imperialistic adventure which established them as the dominant power in Peru. They were bold rulers, despotic but benevolent so long as they were unchallenged. This kind of paternalism broke the spirit of the subject Peruvians and they became no longer creators and originators in art and techniques but obedient subjects and servants of the ruling class —craftsmen but no longer artists. Inca art itself is rather timid. Inca designs tended to be geometric (See Plates 69, 70, 72 and 74); they were always in good taste and technically excellent, but lacking the imaginative qualities of the earlier work.

The Incas were excellent farmers, engineers, architects and builders of fortresses, bridges and roads; they were a practical people. The fortress of Sacsahuaman, for instance, has been called the most unbelievable achievement of ancient man in the Americas. But as artists they derived from those who preceded them in the Andean region. Their goldsmiths and silversmiths did superior work, indeed some of the best. The miniature figures, such as the llama and the alpaca on Plate 71 are highly successful in expressing both form and texture. The finest Inca weaving was done by the Virgins of the Sun for the Inca's personal use.

Just as in Central America, the aboriginal literature of South America comes to us in dilute form. Sarmiento De Gamboa and Garcilaso de la Vega, though chroniclers, were close enough to the originals and to the people to carry over in their work much of the Peruvian spirit. Garcilaso's mother was an Inca. The hymns on page 233 and the little fairy-story immediately below, are included on very good authority and may be taken as typical of Inca feeling with very little influence from the Spanish conquerors.

THE SHEPHERD AND THE DAUGHTER OF THE SUN

IN THE SNOW-CLAD CORDILLERA above the valley of Yucay, called Pitu-siray, a shepherd watched the flock of white llamas intended for the Inca to sacrifice to the Sun. He was a native of Laris, named Acoya-napa, a very well disposed and gentle youth. He strolled behind his flock, and presently began to play upon his flute very softly and sweetly, neither feeling anything of the amorous desires of youth, nor knowing anything of them.

He was carelessly playing his flute one day when two daughters of the Sun came to him. They could wander in all directions over the green meadows, and never failed to find one of their houses at night, where the guards and porters looked out that nothing came that could do them harm. Well! the two girls came to the place where the shepherd rested quite at his ease, and they asked him about his llamas.

The shepherd, who had not seen them until they spoke, was surprised, and fell on his knees, thinking that they were the embodiments of two out of the four crystalline fountains which were very famous in those parts. So he did not dare to answer them. They repeated their question about the flock, and told him not to be afraid, for they were children of the Sun, who was lord of all the land, and to give him confidence they took him by the arm. Then the shepherd stood up and kissed their hands. After talking together for some time the shepherd said that it was time for him to collect his flock, and asked their permission. The elder princess, named Chuqui-llantu, had been struck by the grace and good disposition of the shepherd. She asked him his name and of what place he was a native. He replied that his home was at Laris and that his name was Acoya-napa. While he was speaking Chuqui-llantu cast her eyes upon a plate of silver which the shepherd wore over his forehead, and which shone and glittered very prettily. Looking closer she saw on it two figures, very subtilely contrived, who were eating a heart. Chuqui-llantu asked the shepherd the name of that silver ornament, and he said it was called *utusi*. The princess returned it to the shepherd, and took leave of him, carrying well in her memory the name of the ornament and the figures, thinking with what delicacy they were drawn, almost seeming to her to be alive. She talked about it with her sister until they came to their palace. On entering, the doorkeepers looked to see if they brought with them anything that would do harm, because it was often found that women had brought with them, hidden in their clothes, such things as fillets and necklaces. After having looked well, the porters let them pass, and they found the women of the Sun cooking and preparing food. Chuqui-llantu said that she was very tired with her walk, and that she did not want any supper. All the rest supped with her sister, who thought that Acoya-napa was not one who could cause inquietude. But Chuqui-llantu was unable to rest owing to the great love she felt for the shepherd Acoya-napa, and she regretted that she had not shown him what was in her breast. But at last she went to sleep.

In the palace there were many richly furnished apartments in which the women of the Sun dwelt. These virgins were brought from all the four provinces which were subject to the Inca, namely Chincha-suyu, Cunti-suyu, Anti-suyu and Colla-suyu. Within, there were four fountains which flowed towards the four provinces, and in which the women bathed, each in the fountain of the province where she was born. They named the fountains in this way. That of Chincha-suyu was called *Chuclla-puquio,* that of Cunti-suyu was known as *Ocoruro-puquio, Siclla-puquio* was the fountain of Anti-suyu, and *Llulucha-puquio* of Colla-suyu. The most beautiful child of the Sun, Chuqui-llantu, was wrapped in profound sleep. She had a dream. She thought she saw a bird flying from one tree to another, and singing very softly and sweetly. After having sung for some time, the bird came down and regarded the princess, saying that she should feel no sorrow, for all would be well. The princess said that she mourned for something for which there could be no remedy. The singing bird replied that it would find a remedy, and asked the princess to tell her the cause of her sorrow. At last Chuqui-llantu told the bird of the great love she felt for the shepherd boy named Acoya-napa, who guarded the white flock. Her death seemed inevitable. She could have no cure but to go to him whom she so dearly loved, and if she did her father the Sun would order her to be killed. The answer of the singing bird, by name *Checollo,* was that she should arise and sit between the four fountains. There she was to sing what she had most in her memory. If the fountains repeated her words, she might then safely do what she wanted. Saying this the bird flew away, and the princess awoke. She was terrified. But she dressed very quickly and put herself between the four fountains. She began to

repeat what she remembered to have seen of the two figures on the silver plate, singing:
"*Micuc isutu cuyuc utusi cucim.*"
Presently all the fountains began to sing the same verse.

Seeing that all the fountains were very favourable, the princess went to repose for a little while, for all night she had been conversing with the *checollo* in her dream.

When the shepherd boy went to his home he called to mind the great beauty of Chuqui-llantu. She had aroused his love, but he was saddened by the thought that it must be love without hope. He took up his flute and played such heart-breaking music that it made him shed many tears, and he lamented, saying: "Ay! ay! ay! for the unlucky and sorrowful shepherd, abandoned and without hope, now approaching the day of your death, for there can be no remedy and no hope." Saying this, he also went to sleep.

The shepherd's mother lived in Laris, and she knew, by her power of divination, the cause of the extreme grief into which her son was plunged, and that he must die unless she took order for providing a remedy. So she set out for the mountains, and arrived at the shepherd's hut at sunrise. She looked in and saw her son almost moribund, with his face covered with tears. She went in and awoke him. When he saw who it was he began to tell her the cause of his grief, and she did what she could to console him. She told him not to be downhearted, because she would find a remedy within a few days. Saying this she departed and, going among the rocks, she gathered certain herbs which are believed to be cures for grief. Having collected a great quantity she began to cook them, and the cooking was not finished before the two princesses appeared at the entrance of the hut. For Chuqui-llantu, when she was rested, had set out with her sister for a walk on the green slopes of the mountains, taking the direction of the hut. Her tender heart prevented her from going in any other direction. When they arrived they were tired, and sat down by the entrance. Seeing an old dame inside they saluted her, and asked her if she could give them anything to eat. The mother went down on her knees and said she had nothing but a dish of herbs. She brought it to them, and they began to eat with excellent appetites. Chuqui-llantu then walked round the hut without finding what she sought, for the shepherd's mother had made Acoya-napa lie down inside the hut, under a cloak. So the princess thought that he had gone after his flock. Then she saw the cloak and told the mother that it was a very pretty cloak, asking where it came from. The old woman told her that it was a cloak which, in ancient times, belonged to a woman beloved by Pachacamac, a deity very celebrated in the valleys on the coast. She said it had come to her by inheritance; but the princess, with many endearments, begged for it until at last the mother consented. When Chuqui-llantu took it into her hands she liked it better than before and, after staying a short time longer in the hut, she took leave of the old woman, and walked along the meadows looking about in hopes of seeing him whom she longed for.

We do not treat further of the sister, as she now drops out of the story, but only of Chuqui-llantu. She was very sad and pensive when she could see no signs of her beloved shepherd on her way back to the palace. She was in great sorrow at not having seen him, and when, as was usual, the guards looked at what she brought, they saw nothing but the cloak. A splendid supper was provided, and when every one went to bed the princess took the cloak and placed it at her bedside. As soon as she was alone she began to weep, thinking of the shepherd. She fell asleep at last, but it was not long before the cloak was changed into the being it had been before. It began to call Chuqui-llantu by her own name. She was terribly frightened, got out of bed, and beheld the shepherd on his knees before her, shedding many tears. She was satisfied on seeing him, and inquired how he had got inside the palace. He replied that the cloak which she carried had arranged about that. Then Chuqui-llantu embraced him, and put her finely worked *lipi* mantles on him, and they slept together. When they wanted to get up in the morning, the shepherd again became the cloak. As soon as the sun rose, the princess left the palace of her father with the cloak, and when she reached a ravine in the mountains, she found herself again with her beloved shepherd, who had been changed into himself. But one of the guards had followed them, and when he saw what had happened he gave the alarm with loud shouts. The lovers fled into the mountains which are near the town of Calca. Being tired after a long journey, they climbed to the top of a rock and went to sleep. They heard a great noise in their sleep, so they arose. The princess took one shoe in her hand and kept the other on her foot. Then looking towards the town of Calca both were turned into stone. To this day the two statues may be seen between Calca and Huayllapampa.

Inca

VIRACOCHA AND THE COMING OF THE INCAS

THE NATIVES OF THIS LAND affirm that in the beginning, and before this world was created, there was a being called Viracocha. He created a dark world without sun, moon or stars. Owing to this creation he was named Viracocha Pachayachachi, which means "Creator of all things." And when he had created the world he formed a race of giants of disproportioned greatness painted and sculptured, to see whether it would be well to make real men of that size. He then created men in his likeness as they are now; and they lived in darkness.

Viracocha ordered these people that they should live without quarrelling, and that they should know and serve him. He gave them a certain precept which they were to observe on pain of being confounded if they should break it. They kept this precept for some time, but it is not mentioned what it was. But as there arose among them the vices of pride and covetousness, they transgressed the precept of Viracocha Pachayachachi and falling, through this sin, under his indignation, he confounded and cursed them. Then some were turned into stones, others into other things, some were swallowed up by the earth, others by the sea, and over all there came a general flood which they call *uñu pachacuti*, which means "water that overturns the land." They say that it rained 60 days and nights, that it drowned all created things, and that there alone remained some vestiges of those who were turned into stones, as a memorial of the event, and as an example to posterity, in the edifices of Pucara, which are 60 leagues from Cuzco.

Some of the nations, besides the Cuzcos, also say that a few were saved from this flood to leave descendants for a future age. Each nation has its special fable which is told by its people, of how their first ancestors were saved from the waters of the deluge. That the ideas they had in their blindness may be understood, I will insert only one, told by the nation of the Cañaris, a land of Quito and Tumibamba, 400 leagues from Cuzco and more.

They say that in the time of the deluge called *uñu pachacuti* there was a mountain named Guasano in the province of Quito and near a town called Tumipampa. The natives still point it out. Up this mountain went two of the Cañaris named Ataorupagui and Cusicayo. As the waters increased the mountain kept rising and keeping above them in such a way that it was never covered by the waters of the flood. In this way the two Cañaris escaped. These two, who were brothers, when the waters abated after the flood, began to sow. One day when they had been at work, on returning to their hut, they found in it some small loaves of bread, and a jar of chicha, which is the beverage used in this country in place of wine, made of boiled maize. They did not know who had brought it, but they gave thanks to the Creator, eating and drinking of that provision. Next day the same thing happened. As they marvelled at this mystery, they were anxious to find out who brought the meals. So one day they hid themselves, to spy out the bringers of their food. While they were watching they saw two Cañari women preparing the victuals and putting them in the accustomed place. When about to depart the men tried to seize them, but they evaded their would-be captors and escaped. The Cañaris, seeing the mistake they had made in molesting those who had done them so much good, became sad and prayed to Viracocha for pardon for their sins, entreating him to let the women come back and give them the accustomed meals. The Creator granted their petition. The women came back and said to the Cañaris— "The Creator has thought it well that we should return to you, lest you should die of hunger." They brought them food. Then there was friendship between the women and the Cañari brothers, and one of the Cañari brothers had connexion with one of the women. Then, as the elder brother was drowned in a lake which was near, the survivor married one of the women, and had the other as a concubine. By them he had ten sons who formed two lineages of five each, and increasing in numbers they called one Hanansaya which is the same as to say the upper party, and the other Hurinsaya, or the lower party. From these all the Cañaris that now exist are descended.

In the same way the other nations have fables of how some of their people were saved, from whom they trace their origin and descent. But the Incas and most of those of Cuzco, those among them who are believed to know most, do not say that anyone escaped from the flood, but that Viracocha began to create men afresh, as will be related further on. One thing is believed among all the nations of these parts, for they all speak generally and as well known of the general flood which they call *uñu pachacuti*. From this we may clearly understand that if, in these parts they have a tradition of the great flood, this great mass of the floating islands which they afterwards called the Atlanticas, and now the Indies of Castille, or America, must have begun to receive a population immediately after the flood, although, by their account, the details are different from those which the true

Scriptures teach us. This must have been done by divine Providence, through the first people coming over the land of the Atlantic Island, which was joined to this, as has been already said. For as the natives, though barbarous, give reasons for their very ancient settlement, by recording the flood, there is no necessity for setting aside the Scriptures by quoting authorities to establish this origin. We now come to those who relate the events of the second age after the flood, which is the subject of the next chapter.

FABLE OF THE SECOND AGE, AND CREATION OF THE BARBAROUS INDIANS ACCORDING TO THEIR ACCOUNT

IT IS RELATED that everything was destroyed in the flood called *uñu pachacuti*. It must now be known that Viracocha Pachayachachi, when he destroyed that land as has been already recounted, preserved three men, one of them named Taguapaca, that they might serve and help him in the creation of new people who had to be made in the second age after the deluge, which was done in this manner. The flood being passed and the land dry, Viracocha determined to people it a second time, and, to make it more perfect, he decided upon creating luminaries to give it light. With this object he went, with his servants, to a great lake in the Collao, in which there is an island called Titicaca, the meaning being "the rock of lead," of which we shall treat in the first part. Viracocha went to this island, and presently ordered that the sun, moon, and stars should come forth, and be set in the heavens to give light to the world, and it was so. They say that the moon was created brighter than the sun, which made the sun jealous at the time when they rose into the sky. So the sun threw over the moon's face a handful of ashes, which gave it the shaded colour it now presents. This frontier lake of Chucuito, in the territory of the Collao, is 57 leagues to the south of Cuzco. Viracocha gave various orders to his servants, but Taguapaca disobeyed the commands of Viracocha. So Viracocha was enraged against Taguapaca, and ordered the other two servants to take him, tie him hands and feet, and launch him in a *balsa* on the lake. This was done. Taguapaca was blaspheming against Viracocha for the way he was treated, and threatening that he would return and take vengeance, when he was carried by the water down the drain of the same lake, and was not seen again for a long time. This done, Viracocha made a sacred idol in that place, as a place for worship and as a sign of what he had there created.

Leaving the island, he passed by the lake to the main land, taking with him the two servants who survived. He went to a place now called Tiahuanacu in the province of Collasuyu, and in this place he sculptured and designed on a great piece of stone, all the nations that he intended to create. This done, he ordered his two servants to charge their memories with the names of all tribes that he had depicted, and of the valleys and provinces where they were to come forth, which were those of the whole land. He ordered that each one should go by a different road, naming the tribes, and ordering them all to go forth and people the country. His servants, obeying the command of Viracocha, set out on their journey and work. One went by the mountain range or chain which they call the heights over the plains on the South Sea. The other went by the heights which overlook the wonderful mountain ranges which we call the Andes, situated to the east of the said sea. By these roads they went, saying with a loud voice "Oh you tribes and nations, hear and obey the order of Ticci Viracocha Pachayachachi, which commands you to go forth, and multiply and settle the land." Viracocha himself did the same along the road between those taken by his two servants, naming all the tribes and places by which he passed. At the sound of his voice every place obeyed, and people came forth, some from lakes, others from fountains, valleys, caves, trees, rocks and hills, spreading over the land and multiplying to form the nations which are to-day in Peru.

Others affirm that this creation of Viracocha was made from the Titicaca site where, having originally formed some shapes of large strong men which seemed to him out of proportion, he made them again of his stature which was, as they say, the average height of men, and being made he gave them life. Thence they set out to people the land. As they spoke one language previous to starting, they built those edifices, the ruins of which may still be seen, before they set out. This was for the residence of Viracocha, their maker. After departing they varied their languages, noting the cries of wild beasts, insomuch that, coming across each other afterwards, those could not understand who had before been relations and neighbours.

Whether it was in one way or the other, all agree that Viracocha was the creator of these people. They have the tradition that he was a man of medium height, white and dressed in a white robe like an alb secured round the waist, and that he carried a staff and a book in his hands.

Besides this they tell of a strange event; how that Viracocha, after he had created all people, went on his road and came to a place where many men of his creation had congregated. This place is now called Cacha. When Viracocha arrived there, the inhabitants were estranged owing to his dress and bearing. They murmured at it and proposed to kill him from a hill that was near. They took their weapons there, and gathered together with evil intentions against Viracocha. He, falling on his knees on some plain ground, with his hands clasped, fire from above came down upon those on the hill, and covered all the place, burning up the earth and stones like straw. Those bad men were terrified at the fearful fire. They came down from the hill, and sought pardon from Viracocha for their sin. Viracocha was moved by compassion. He went to the flames and put them out with his staff. But the hill remained quite parched up, the stones being rendered so light by the burning that a very large stone which could not have been carried on a cart, could be raised easily by one man. This may be seen at this day, and it is a wonderful sight to behold this hill, which is a quarter of a league in extent, all burnt up. It is in the Collao.

After this Viracocha continued his journey and arrived at a place called Urcos, 6 leagues to the south of Cuzco. Remaining there some days he was well served by the natives of that neighborhood. At the time of his departure, he made them a celebrated *huaca* or statue, for them to offer gifts to and worship; to which statue the Incas, in after times, offered many rich gifts of gold and other metals, and above all a golden bench. When the Spaniards entered Cuzco they found it, and appropriated it to themselves. It was worth $17,000. The Marquis Don Francisco Pizarro took it himself, as the share of the General.

Returning to the subject of the fable, Viracocha continued his journey, working his miracles and instructing his created beings. In this way he reached the territory on the equinoctial line, where are now Puerto Viejo and Manta. Here he was joined by his servants. Intending to leave the land of Peru, he made a speech to those he had created, apprising them of the things that would happen. He told them that people would come, who would say that they were Viracocha their creator, and that they were not to believe them; but that in the time to come he would send his messengers who would protect and teach them. Having said this he went to sea with his two servants, and went travelling over the water as if it was land, without sinking. For they appeared like foam over the water, and the people, therefore, gave them the name of Viracocha which is the same as to say the grease or foam of the sea. At the end of some years after Viracocha departed, they say that Taguapaca, whom Viracocha ordered to be thrown into the lake of Titicaca in the Collao, as has already been related, came back and began, with others, to preach that he was Viracocha. Although at first the people were doubtful, they finally saw that it was false, and ridiculed them.

This absurd fable of their creation is held by these barbarians and they affirm and believe it as if they had really seen it to happen and come to pass.

THE ANCIENT FREEDOMS OF THESE KINGDOMS OF PERU AND THEIR PROVINCES

It is important to note that these barbarians could tell nothing more respecting what happened from the second creation by Viracocha down to the time of the Incas. But it may be assumed that, although the land was peopled and full of inhabitants before the Incas, it had no regular government, nor did it have natural lords elected by common consent to govern and rule, and who were respected by the people, so that they were obeyed and received tribute. On the contrary all the people were scattered and disorganized, living in complete liberty, and each man being sole lord of his house and estate. In each tribe there were two divisions. One was called Hanansaya, which means the upper division, and the other Hurinsaya, which is the lower division, a custom which continues to this day. These divisions do not mean anything more than a way to count each other, for their satisfaction; though afterwards it served a more useful purpose, as will be seen in its place.

As there were dissensions among them, a certain kind of militia was organized for defence, in the following way. When it became known to the people of one district that some from other parts were coming to make war, they chose one who was a native, or he might be a stranger, who was known to be a valiant warrior. Often such a man offered himself to aid and to fight for them against their enemies. Such a man was followed and his orders were obeyed during the war. When the war was over he became a private man as he had been before, like the rest of the people, nor did they pay him tribute either before or afterwards, nor any manner of tax whatever. To such a man they gave and still give the name of *Sinchi* which means valiant. They call such men "Sinchi-cuna" which means "valiant now" as who should say—"now during the time the war lasts you shall be our valiant man, and afterwards no": or another meaning would be simply "valiant men," for "cuna" is an adverb of time, and also denotes the plural. In whichever meaning, it is very applicable to these temporary captains in the days of general liberty. So that from the general flood of which they have a tradition to the time when the Incas began to reign, which was 3519 years, all the natives of these kingdoms lived on their properties without acknowledging either a natural or an elected lord. They succeeded in preserving, as it is said, a simple state of liberty, living in huts or caves or humble little houses. This name of *Sinchi* for those who held sway only during war, lasted throughout the land until the time of Tupac Inca Yupanqui, the tenth Inca, who instituted *Curacas* and other officials in the order which will be fully described in the life of that Inca. Even at the present time they continue this use and custom in the provinces of Chile and in other parts of the forests of Peru to the east of Quito and Chachapoyas, where they only obey a chief during war time, not any special one, but he who is known to be most valiant, enterprising and daring in the wars. The reader should note that all the land was private property with reference to any dominion of chiefs, yet they had natural chiefs with special rights in each province, as for instance among the natives of the valley of Cuzco and in other parts, as we shall relate of each part in its place.

THE FIRST SETTLERS IN THE VALLEY OF CUZCO

I have explained how the people of these lands preserved their inheritances and lived on them in ancient times, and that their proper and natural countries were known. There were many of these which I shall notice in their places, treating specially at present of the original settlers of the valley where stands the present city of Cuzco. For from there we have to trace the origin of the tyranny of the Incas, who always had their chief seat in the valley of Cuzco.

Before all things it must be understood that the valley of Cuzco is in 13° 15′ from the equator on the side of the south pole. In this valley, owing to its being fertile for cultivation, there were three tribes settled from most ancient times, the first called Sauaseras, the second Antasayas, the third Huallas. They settled near each other, although their lands for sowing were distinct, which is the property they valued most in those days and even now. These natives of the valley lived there in peace for many years, cultivating their farms.

Some time before the arrival of the Incas, three *Sinchis,* strangers to this valley, the first named Alcabisa, the second Copalimayta, and the third Culunchima, collected certain companies and came to the valley of Cuzco, where, by consent of the natives, they settled and became brothers and companions of the original inhabitants. So they lived for a long time. There was concord between these six tribes, three native and three immigrant. They relate that the immigrants came out to where the Incas then resided, as we shall relate presently, and called them relations. This is an important point with reference to what happened afterwards.

Before entering upon the history of the Incas I wish to make known or, speaking more accurately, to answer a difficulty which may occur to those who have not been in these parts. Some may say that this history cannot be accepted as authentic being taken from the narratives of these barbarians, because, having no letters, they could not preserve such details as they give from so remote an antiquity. The answer is that, to supply the want of letters, these barbarians had a curious invention which was very good and accurate. This was that from one to the other, from fathers to sons, they handed down past events, repeating the story of them many times, just as lessons are repeated from a professor's chair, making the hearers say these historical lessons over and over again until they were fixed in the memory. Thus each one of the descendants continued to communicate the annals in the order described with a view to preserve their histories and deeds, their ancient traditions, the numbers of their tribes, towns, provinces, their days, months and years, their battles, deaths, destructions, fortresses and *Sinchis*. Finally they recorded, and they still record, the most notable things which may be expressed in numbers (or statistics), on certain cords called *quipu*, which is the same as to say reasoner or accountant. On these cords they make certain knots by which, and by differences of colour, they distinguish and record each thing as by letters. It is a thing to be admired to see what details may be recorded on these cords, for which there are masters like our writing masters.

Besides this they had, and still have, special historians in these nations, an hereditary office descending from father to son. The collection of these annals is due to the great diligence of Pachacuti Inca Yupanqui, the ninth Inca, who sent out a general summons to all the old historians in all the provinces he had subjugated, and even to many others throughout those kingdoms. He had them in Cuzco for a long time, examining them concerning their antiquities, origin, and the most notable events in their history. These were painted on great boards, and deposited in the temple of the Sun, in a great hall. There such boards, adorned with gold, were kept as in our libraries, and learned persons were appointed, who were well versed in the art of understanding and declaring their contents. No one was allowed to enter where these boards were kept, except the Inca and the historians, without a special order of the Inca.

In this way they took care to have all their past history investigated, and to have records respecting all kinds of people, so that at this day the Indians generally know and agree respecting details and important events, though, in some things, they hold different opinions on special points. By examining the oldest and most prudent among them, in all ranks of life, who had most credit, I collected and compiled the present history, referring the sayings and declarations of one party to their antagonists of another party, for they are divided into parties, and seeking from each one a memorial of its lineage and of that of the opposing party. These memorials, which are all in my possession, were compared and corrected, and ultimately verified in public, in presence of representatives of all the parties and lineages, under oaths in presence of a judge, and with expert and very faithful interpreters also on oath, and I thus finished what is now written. Such great diligence has been observed, because the facts which will be obvious on the true completion of such a great work—the establishment of the tyranny of the cruel Incas of this land—will make all the nations of the world understand the judicial and more than legitimate right that the King of Castille has to these Indies and to other lands adjacent, especially to these kingdoms of Peru. As all the histories of past events have been verified by proof, which in this case has been done so carefully and faithfully by order and owing to the industry of the most excellent Viceroy Don Francisco de Toledo, no one can doubt that everything in this volume is most sufficiently established and verified without any room being left for reply or contradiction. I have been desirous of making this digression because, in writing the history, I have heard that many entertain the doubts I have above referred to, and it seemed well to satisfy them once for all.

HOW THE INCAS BEGAN TO TYRANNIZE OVER THE LANDS AND INHERITANCES

Having explained that, in ancient times, all this land was owned by the people, it is necessary to state how the Incas began their tyranny. Although the tribes all lived in simple liberty without recognising any lord, there were always some ambitious men among them, aspiring for mastery. They committed violence among their countrymen and among strangers to subject them and bring them to obedience under their command, so that they might serve them and pay tribute. Thus bands of men belonging to one region went to others to make war and to rob and kill, usurping the lands of others.

As these movements took place in many parts by many tribes, each one trying to subjugate his neighbour, it happened that 6 leagues from the valley of Cuzco, at a place called Paccari-tampu, there were four men with their four sisters, of fierce courage and evil intentions, although with lofty aims. These, being more able than the others, understood the pusillanimity of the natives of those districts and the ease with which they could be made to believe anything that was propounded with authority or with any force. So they conceived among themselves the idea of being able to subjugate many lands by force and deception. Thus all the eight brethren, four men and four women, consulted together how they could tyrannize over other tribes beyond the place where they lived, and they proposed to do this by violence. Considering that most of the natives were ignorant and could easily be made to believe what was said to them, particularly if they were addressed with some roughness, rigour and authority, against which they could make neither reply nor resistance because they are timid by nature, they sent abroad certain fables respecting their origin, that they might be respected and feared. They said that they were the sons of

Viracocha Pachayachachi, the Creator, and that they had come forth out of certain windows to rule the rest of the people. As they were fierce, they made the people believe and fear them, and hold them to be more than men, even worshipping them as gods. Thus they introduced the religion that suited them. The order of the fable they told of their origin was as follows.

THE FABLE OF THE ORIGIN OF THE INCAS OF CUZCO

All the native Indians of this land relate and affirm that the Incas Ccapac originated in this way. Six leagues S.S.W. of Cuzco by the road which the Incas made, there is a place called Paccari-tampu, at which there is a hill called Tampu-tocco, meaning "the house of windows." It is certain that in this hill there are three windows, one called "Maras-tocco," the other "Sutic-tocco," while that which is in the middle, between these two, was known as "Ccapac-tocco," which means "the rich window," because they say that it was ornamented with gold and other treasures. From the window called "Maras-tocco" came forth, without parentage, a tribe of Indians called Maras. There are still some of them in Cuzco. From the "Sutic-tocco" came Indians called Tampus, who settled round the same hill, and there are also men of this lineage still in Cuzco. From the chief window of "Ccapac-tocco," came four men and four women, called brethren. These knew no father nor mother, beyond the story they told that they were created and came out of the said window by order of Ticci Viracocha, and they declared that Viracocha created them to be lords. For this reason they took the name of Inca, which is the same as lord. They took "Ccapac" as an additional name because they came out of the window "Ccapac-tocco," which means "rich," although afterwards they used this term to denote the chief lord over many.

The names of the eight brethren were as follows: The eldest of the men, and the one with the most authority was named Manco Ccapac, the second Ayar Auca, the third Ayar Cachi, the fourth Ayar Uchu. Of the women the eldest was called Mama Occlo, the second Mama Huaco, the third Mama Ipacura, or, as others say, Mama Cura, the fourth Mama Raua.

The eight brethren, called Incas, said—"We are born strong and wise, and with the people who will here join us, we shall be powerful. We will go forth from this place to seek fertile lands and when we find them we will subjugate the people and take the lands, making war on all those who do not receive us as their lords." This, as they relate, was said by Mama Huaco, one of the women, who was fierce and cruel. Manco Ccapac, her brother, was also cruel and atrocious. This being agreed upon between the eight, they began to move the people who lived near the hill, putting it to them that their reward would be to become rich and to receive the lands and estates of those who were conquered and subjugated. For these objects they moved ten tribes or *ayllus*, which means among these barbarians "lineages" or "parties"; the names of which are as follows:

I. Chauin Cuzco Ayllu of the lineage of Ayar Cachi, of which there are still some in Cuzco, the chiefs being Martin Chucumbi, and Don Diego Huaman Paucar.

II. Arayraca Ayllu Cuzco-Callan. At present there are of this *ayllu* Juan Pizarro Yupanqui, Don Francisco Quispi, Alonso Tarma Yupanqui of the lineage of Ayar Uchu.

III. Tarpuntay Ayllu. Of this there are now some in Cuzco.

IV. Huacaytaqui Ayllu. Some still living in Cuzco.

V. Sañoc Ayllu. Some still in Cuzco.

The above five lineages are Hanan-Cuzco, which means the party of Upper Cuzco.

VI. Sutic-Tocco Ayllu is the lineage which came out of one of the windows called "Sutic-Tocco," as has been before explained. Of these there are still some in Cuzco, the chiefs being Don Francisco Avca Micho Avri Sutic, and Don Alonso Hualpa.

VII. Maras Ayllu. These are of the men who came forth from the window "Maras-Tocco." There are some of these now in Cuzco, the chiefs being Don Alonso Llama Oca, and Don Gonzalo Ampura Llama Oca.

VIII. Cuycusa Ayllu. Of these there are still some in Cuzco, the chief being Cristoval Acllari.

IX. Masca Ayllu. Of this there is in Cuzco, Juan Quispi.

X. Oro Ayllu. Of this lineage is Don Pedro Yucay.

I say that all these *ayllus* have preserved their records in such a way that the memory of them has not been lost. There are more of them than are given above, for I only insert the chiefs who are the protectors and heads of the lineages, under whose guidance they are preserved. Each chief has the duty and obligation to protect the rest, and to know the history of his ancestors. Although I say that these live in Cuzco, the truth is that they are in a suburb of the city which the Indians call Cayocache and which is known to us as Belem, from the church of that parish which is that of our Lady of Belem.

Returning to our subject, all these followers above-mentioned marched with Manco Ccapac and the other brethren to seek for land (*and to tyrannize over those who did no harm to them, nor gave them any excuse for war, and without any right or title beyond what has been stated*). To be prepared for war they chose for their leaders Manco Ccapac and Mama Huaco, and with this arrangement the companies of the hill of Tampu-tocco set out, to put their design into execution.

THE ROAD WHICH THESE COMPANIES OF THE INCAS TOOK TO THE VALLEY OF CUZCO, AND OF THE FABLES WHICH ARE MIXED WITH THEIR HISTORY

The Incas and the rest of the companies or *ayllus* set out from their homes at Tampu-tocco, taking with them their property and arms, in sufficient numbers to form a good squadron, having for their chiefs the said Manco Ccapac and Mama Huaco.

Manco Ccapac took with him a bird like a falcon, called *indi,* which they all worshipped and feared as a sacred, or, as some say, an enchanted thing, for they thought that this bird made Manco Ccapac their lord and obliged the people to follow him. It was thus that Manco Ccapac gave them to understand, and it was always kept in a covered hamper of straw, like a box, with much care. He left it as an heirloom to his son, and the Incas had it down to the time of Inca Yupanqui. In his hand he carried with him a staff of gold, to test the lands which they would come to.

Marching together they came to a place called Huanacancha, four leagues from the valley of Cuzco, where they remained for some time, sowing and seeking for fertile land. Here Manco Ccapac had connection with his sister Mama Occlo, and she became pregnant by him. As this place did not appear able to sustain them, being barren, they advanced to another place called Tampu-quiro, where Mama Occlo begot a son named Sinchi Rocca. Having celebrated the natal feasts of the infant, they set out in search of fertile land, and came to another place called Pallata, which is almost contiguous to Tampu-quiro, and there they remained for some years.

Not content with this land, they came to another called Hays-quisro, a quarter of a league further on. Here they consulted together over what ought to be done respecting their journey, and over the best way of getting rid of Ayar Cachi, one of the four brothers. Ayar Cachi was fierce and strong, and very dexterous with the sling. He committed great cruelties and was oppressive both among the natives of the places they passed, and among his own people. The other brothers were afraid that the conduct of Ayar Cachi would cause their companies to disband and desert, and that they would be left alone. As Manco Ccapac was prudent, he concurred with the opinion of the others that they should secure their object by deceit. They called Ayar Cachi and said to him, "Brother! Know that in Ccapac-tocco we have forgotten the golden vases called *tupac-cusi,* and certain seeds, and the *napa,* which is our principal ensign of sovereignty." The *napa* is a sheep of the country, the colour white, with a red body cloth, on the top ear-rings of gold, and on the breast a plate with red badges such as was worn by rich Incas when they went abroad; carried in front of all on a pole with a cross of plumes of feathers. This was called *suntur-paucar.* They said that it would be for the good of all, if he would go back and fetch them. When Ayar Cachi refused to return, his sister Mama Huaco, raising her foot, rebuked him with furious words, saying, "How is it that there should be such cowardice in so strong a youth as you are? Get ready for the journey, and do not fail to go to Tampu-tocco, and do what you are ordered." Ayar Cachi was shamed by these words. He obeyed and started to carry out his orders. They gave him, as a companion, one of those who had come with them, named Tampu-chacay, to whom they gave secret orders to kill Ayar Cachi at Tampu-tocco, and not to return with him. With these orders they both arrived at Tampu-tocco. They had scarcely arrived when Ayar Cachi entered through the window Ccapac-tocco, to get the things for which he had been sent. He was no sooner inside than Tampu-chacay, with great celerity, put a rock against the opening of the window and sat upon it, that Ayar Cachi might remain inside and die there. When Ayar Cachi turned to the opening and found it closed he understood the treason of which the traitor Tampu-chacay had been guilty, and determined to get out if it was possible, to take vengeance. To force an opening he used such force and shouted so loud that he made the mountain tremble. With a loud voice he spoke these words to Tampu-chacay, "Thou traitor! thou who hast done me so much harm, thinkest thou to convey the news of my mortal imprisonment? That shall never happen. For thy treason thou shalt remain outside, turned into a stone." So it was done, and to this day they show the stone on one side of the window Ccapac-tocco. Turn we now to the seven brethren who had remained at Hays-quisro. The death of Ayar Cachi being known, they were very sorry for what they had done, for, as he was valiant, they regretted much to be without him when the time came to make war on any one. So they mourned for him. This Ayar Cachi was so dexterous with a sling and so strong that with each shot he pulled down a mountain and filled up a ravine. They say that the ravines, which we now see on their line of march, were made by Ayar Cachi in hurling stones.

The seven Incas and their companions left this place, and came to another called Quirirmanta at the foot of a hill which was afterwards called Huanacauri. In this place they consulted together how they should divide the duties of the enterprise amongst themselves, so that there should be distinctions between them. They agreed that as Manco Ccapac had had a child by his sister, they should be married and have children to continue the lineage, and that he should be the leader. Ayar Uchu was to remain as a *huaca* for the sake of religion. Ayar Auca, from the position they should select, was to take possession of the land set apart for him to people.

Leaving this place they came to a hill at a distance of two leagues, a little more or less, from Cuzco. Ascending the hill they saw a rainbow, which the natives call *huanacauri*. Holding it to be a fortunate sign, Manco Ccapac said: "Take this for a sign that the world will not be destroyed by water. We shall arrive and from hence we shall select where we shall found our city." Then, first casting lots, they saw that the signs were good for doing so, and for exploring the land from that point and becoming lords of it. Before they got to the height where the rainbow was, they saw a *huaca* which was a place of worship in human shape, near the rainbow. They determined among themselves to seize it and take it away from there. Ayar Uchu offered himself to go to it, for they said that he was very like it. When Ayar Uchu came to the statue or *huaca*, with great courage he sat upon it, asking it what it did there. At these words the *huaca* turned its head to see who spoke, but, owing to the weight upon it, it could not see. Presently, when Ayar Uchu wanted to get off he was not able, for he found that the soles of his feet were fastened to the shoulders of the *huaca*. The six brethren, seeing that he was a prisoner, came to succour him. But Ayar Uchu, finding himself thus transformed, and that his brethren could not release him, said to them— "O Brothers, an evil work you have wrought for me. It was for your sakes that I came where I must remain for ever, apart from your company. Go! go! happy brethren. I announce to you that you will be great lords. I, therefore, pray that in recognition of the desire I have always had to please you, you will honour and venerate me in all your festivals and ceremonies, and that I shall be the first to whom you make offerings. For I remain here for your sakes. When you celebrate the *huarachico* (which is the arming of the sons as knights) you shall adore me as their father, for I shall remain here for ever." Manco Ccapac answered that he would do so, for that it was his will and that it should be so ordered. Ayar Uchu promised for the youths that he would bestow on them the gifts of valour, nobility, and knighthood, and with these last words he remained, turned into stone. They constituted him the *huaca* of the Incas, giving it the name of Ayar Uchu Huanacauri. And so it always was, until the arrival of the Spaniards, the most venerated *huaca*, and the one that received the most offerings of any in the kingdom. Here the Incas went to arm the young knights until about twenty years ago, when the Christians abolished this ceremony. It was religiously done, because there were many abuses and idolatrous practices, offensive and contrary to the ordinances of God our Lord.

ENTRY OF THE INCAS INTO THE VALLEY OF CUZCO, AND THE FABLES THEY RELATE CONCERNING IT

The six brethren were sad at the loss of Ayar Uchu, and at the loss of Ayar Cachi; and, owing to the death of Ayar Cachi, those of the lineage of the Incas, from that time to this day, always fear to go to Tampu-tocco, lest they should have to remain there like Ayar Cachi.

They went down to the foot of the hill, whence they began their entry into the valley of Cuzco, arriving at a place called Matahua, where they stopped and built huts, intending to remain there some time. Here they armed as knight the son of Manco Ccapac and of Mama Occlo, named Sinchi Rocca, and they bored his ears, a ceremony which is called *huarachico*, being the insignia of his knighthood and nobility, like the custom known among ourselves. On this occasion they indulged in great rejoicings, drinking for many days, and at intervals mourning for the loss of their brother Ayar Uchu. It was here that they invented the mourning sound for the dead, like the cooing of a dove. Then they performed the dance called *Ccapac Raymi,* a ceremony of the royal or great lords. It is danced, in long purple robes, at the ceremonies they call *quicochico,* which is when girls come to maturity, and the *huarachico,* when they pierce the ears of the Incas, and the *rutuchico,* when the Inca's hair is cut the first time, and the *ayuscay,* which is when a child is born, and they drink continuously for four or five days.

After this they were in Matahua for two years, waiting to pass on to the upper valley to seek good and fertile land. Mama Huaco, who was very strong and dexterous, took two wands of gold and hurled them towards the north. One fell, at two shots of an arquebus, into a ploughed field called Colcapampa and did not drive in well, the soil being loose and not terraced. By this they knew that the soil was not fertile. The other went further, to near Cuzco, and fixed well in the territory called Huanay-pata, where they knew the land to be fertile. Others say that this proof was made by Manco Ccapac with the staff of gold which he carried himself, and that thus they knew of the fertility of the land, when the staff sunk in the land called Huanay-pata, two shots of an arquebus from Cuzco. They knew the crust of the soil to be rich and close, so that it could only be broken by using much force.

Let it be by one way or the other, for all agree that they went trying the land with a pole or staff until they arrived at this Huanay-pata, when they were satisfied. They were sure of its fertility, because after sowing perpetually, it always yielded abundantly, giving more the more it was sown. They determined to usurp that land by force, in spite of the natural owners, and to do with it as they chose. So they returned to Matahua.

From that place Manco Ccapac saw a heap of stones near the site of the present monastery of Santo Domingo at Cuzco. Pointing it out to his brother Ayar Auca, he said, "Brother! you remember how it was arranged between us, that you should go to take possession of the land where we are to settle. Well! look at that stone." Pointing out the stone he continued, "Go thither flying," for they say that Ayar Auca had developed some wings, "and seating yourself there, take possession of land seen from that heap of stones. We will presently come to settle and reside." When Ayar Auca heard the words of his brother, he opened his wings and flew to that place which Manco Ccapac had pointed out. Seating himself there, he was presently turned into stone, and was made the stone of possession. In the ancient language of this valley the heap was called *cozco*, whence that site has had the name of Cuzco to this day. From this circumstance the Incas had a proverb which said, "Ayar Auca cuzco huanca," or, "Ayar Auca a heap of marble." Others say that Manco Ccapac gave the name of Cuzco because he wept in that place where he buried his brother Ayar Cachi. Owing to his sorrow and to the fertility, he gave that name which in the ancient language of that time signified sad as well as fertile. The first version must be the correct one because Ayar Cachi was not buried at Cuzco, having died at Ccapac-tocco as has been narrated before. And this is generally affirmed by Incas and natives.

Five brethren only remaining, namely Manco Ccapac, and the four sisters, and Manco Ccapac being the only surviving brother out of four, they presently resolved to advance to where Ayar Auca had taken possession. Manco Ccapac first gave to his son Sinchi Rocca a wife named Mama Cuca, of the lineage of Sañu, daughter of a Sinchi named Sitic-huaman, by whom he afterwards had a son named Sapaca. He also instituted the sacrifice called *capa cocha*, which is the immolation of two male and two female infants before the idol Huanacauri, at the time when the Incas were armed as knights. These things being arranged, he ordered the companies to follow him to the place where Ayar Auca was.

Arriving on the land of Huanay-pata, which is near where now stands the *Arco de la plata* leading to the Charcas road, he found settled there a nation of Indians named Huallas, already mentioned. Manco Ccapac and Mama Occlo began to settle and to take possession of the land and water, against the will of the Huallas. In this business they did many violent and unjust things. As the Huallas attempted to defend their lives and properties, many cruelties were committed by Manco Ccapac and Mama Occlo. They relate that Mama Occlo was so fierce that, having killed one of the Hualla Indians, she cut him up, took out the inside, carried the heart and lungs in her mouth, and with an *ayuinto*, which is a stone fastened to a rope, in her hand, she attacked the Huallas with diabolical resolution. When the Huallas beheld this horrible and inhuman spectacle, they feared that the same things would be done to them, being simple and timid, and they fled and abandoned their rights. Mama Occlo reflecting on her cruelty, and fearing that for it they would be branded as tyrants, resolved not to spare any Huallas, believing that the affair would thus be forgotten. So they killed all they could lay their hands upon, dragging infants from their mothers' wombs, that no memory might be left of these miserable Huallas.

Having done this Manco Ccapac advanced, and came within a mile of Cuzco to the S. E., where a *Sinchi* named Copalimayta came out to oppose him. We have mentioned this chief before and that, although he was a late comer, he settled with the consent of the natives of the valley, and had been incorporated in the nation of Sauaseray Panaca, natives of the site of Santo Domingo at Cuzco. Having seen the strangers invading their lands and tyrannizing over them, and knowing the cruelties inflicted on the Huallas, they had chosen Copalimayta as their *Sinchi*. He came forth to resist the invasion, saying that the strangers should not enter his lands or those of the natives. His resistance was such that Manco Ccapac and his companions were obliged to turn their backs. They returned to Huanaypata, the land they had usurped from the Huallas. From the sowing they had made they derived a fine crop of maize, and for this reason they gave the place a name which means something precious.

After some months they returned to the attack on the natives of the valley, to tyrannize over them. They assaulted the settlement of the Sauaseras, and were so rapid in their attack that they captured Copalimayta, slaughtering many of the Sauaseras with great cruelty. Copalimayta, finding himself a prisoner and fearing death, fled out of desperation, leaving his estates, and was never seen again after he escaped. Mama Huaco and Manco Ccapac usurped his houses, lands and people. In this way Manco Ccapac, Mama Huaco, Sinchi Rocca, and Manco Sapaca settled on the site between the two rivers, and erected the House of the Sun, which they called Ynti-cancha. They divided all that position, from Santo Domingo to the junction of the rivers into four neighbourhoods or quarters which they call *cancha*. They called one Quinti-cancha, the second Chumpi-cancha, the third Sayri-cancha, and the fourth Yarampuy-cancha. They divided the sites among themselves, and thus the city was peopled, and, from the heap of stones of Ayar Auca it was called Cuzco.

Inca

DEATH OF PACHACUTI INCA YUPANQUI

BEING IN THE HIGHEST PROSPERITY and sovereignty of his life, he fell ill of a grave infirmity, and, feeling that he was at the point of death, he sent for all his sons who were then in the city. In their presence he first divided all his jewels and contents of his wardrobe. Next he made them plough furrows in token that they were vassals of their brother, and that they had to eat by the sweat of their hands. He also gave them arms in token that they were to fight for their brother. He then dismissed them.

He next sent for the Incas *orejones* of Cuzco, his relations, and for Tupac Inca his son to whom he spoke, with a few words, in this manner: "Son! you now see how many great nations I leave to you, and you know what labour they have cost me. Mind that you are the man to keep and augment them. No one must raise his two eyes against you and live, even if he be your own brother. I leave you these our relations that they may be your councillors. Care for them and they shall serve you. When I am dead, take care of my body, and put it in my houses at Patallacta. Have my golden image in the House of the Sun, and make my subjects, in all the provinces, offer up solemn sacrifice, after which keep the feast of *purucaya,* that I may go to rest with my father the Sun." Having finished his speech they say that he began to sing in a low and sad voice with words of his own language. They are as follows:

> "I was born as a flower of the field,
> As a flower I was cherished in my youth,
> I came to my full age, I grew old,
> Now I am withered and die."

Having uttered these words, he laid his head upon a pillow and expired, giving his soul to the devil, having lived a hundred and twenty-five years. For he succeeded, or rather he took the Incaship into his hands when he was twenty-two, and he was sovereign one hundred and three years.

Inca

THE FESTIVAL OF THE SUN

THE WORD *RAYMI* is equivalent to our word Easter. Among the four festivals which the Kings celebrated in the city of Cuzco, the most solemn was that in honour of the Sun, during the month of June. It was called *Yntip Raymi,* which means the "Solemn Feast of the Sun." They called this feast especially *Raymi,* and though the word was also used for other festivals, this was *the* Raymi, and took place in the June solstice.

They celebrated this festival of the Sun in acknowledgment that they held and adored Him as the sole and universal God who, by his light and power, creates and sustains all things on earth; and that He was the natural father of the first Ynca Manco Ccapac and of his wife Mama Ocllo Huaco, and of all their descendants, who were sent to this earth for the benefit of all people. For these reasons, as they themselves say, this was their most solemn feast.

There were present at it all the chief captains not then employed in war, and all the Curacas, lords of vassals, from all parts of the empire, not because they were ordered to be present, but because they rejoiced to take part in the solemnities of so great a festival. For, as the ceremonies included the worship of the Sun God and of the Ynca their king, there was no one who did not desire to take part in it. When the Curacas were prevented, by old age or sickness, from being present, or by the public service or the long distance, they sent their sons and brothers, accompanied by the noblest of their kindred, to be at the festival in their place. The Ynca was there in person, if not prevented by absence at the wars or while inspecting the provinces.

The opening ceremonies were performed by the king himself as High Priest; for, although there was always a High Priest of the blood royal, who was legitimate uncle or brother of the Ynca, yet the Ynca himself officiated at this great festival, as first-born of the Sun.

The Curacas came in all the splendour they could afford. Some wore dresses adorned with bezants of gold and silver, and with the same fastened as a circlet round their headdresses. Others came in a costume neither more nor less than that in which Hercules is painted, wrapped in the skins of lions, with the heads fixed over their own. These were the Indians who claimed descent from a lion. Others came attired in the fashion that they paint angels, with great wings of the bird called *Cuntur*. These wings are black and white, and so long that the Spaniards have often killed birds measuring fourteen feet between the tips of the wings. These are the Indians who declare that they are descended from a *Cuntur*. The Yuncas came attired in the most hideous masks that can be imagined, and they appeared at the feasts making all sorts of grimaces, like fools and simpletons; and for this purpose they brought instruments in their hands, such as badly-made flutes and tambourines, and pieces of skin, to assist them in their fooleries. Other Curacas wore various costumes to distinguish them, and each different tribe came with the arms with which they fought in war. Some had bows and arrows; others lances, darts, javelins, clubs, slings, axes with short handles, and two-handed axes with long handles.

They brought with them paintings of the deeds they had performed in the service of the Sun and of the Yncas, and also great drums and trumpets, with many musicians to play them. In short, they all came in the best attire they could procure, and attended by the grandest and most imposing retinue their means would admit of.

All prepared themselves for the *Raymi* of the Sun by a rigorous fast; for, in three days they ate nothing but a little unripe maize, and a few herbs called *Chucam*, with plain water. During this time no fire was lighted throughout the city, and all men abstained from sleeping with their wives.

After the fast, in the evening before the festival, the Ynca sacrificial Priests prepared the sheep and lambs for sacrifice, and got ready the other offerings of food and drink that were to be offered to the Sun. All these offerings had been provided by the people who came to the feast, not only the Curacas and envoys, but also all their relations, vassals, and servants.

The Women of the Sun were engaged, during the night, in preparing an immense quantity of maize pudding called *Canca*. This was made up into small round cakes, about the size of an apple. It must be understood that the Indians never ate their corn kneaded and made into bread, except at this feast and at another called *Situa,* and they did not eat this bread during the whole meal, but only two or three mouthfuls of it at the beginning. Their usual food, in place of bread, was maize toasted or boiled in the grain.

The flour for this bread, especially for what was intended for the Ynca and those of the blood royal, was ground by the chosen virgins of the Sun, who cooked all the other food for this feast; that it might appear to be given rather by the Sun to his children than by his sons to him; and it was therefore prepared by the virgins, as women of the Sun.

Another vast assemblage of women ground the corn and cooked the food for the common people. And though the bread was intended for the people, it was yet prepared with care, because this bread was looked upon as sacred, and was only allowed to be eaten once during the year, on occasion of this feast, which was, among the people, the festival of their festivals.

The necessary preparations having been made, the Ynca came forth at dawn, on the day of the festival, accompanied by all his relations, marching according to their age and dignity. They proceeded to the great square, which was called *Huacay-pata.* Here they waited for sunrise, all of them being barefooted, and all watching the east with great attention. As soon as the sun appeared, they all bent down resting on their elbows (which, among these Indians, is the same as going down on the knees), with the arms apart and the hands raised. Thus they worshipped, and kissed the air (which with them is the equivalent to kissing the hand or the dress of a Prince in Spain); and they adored with much fervour and devotion, looking upon the Sun as their god and natural father.

The Curacas, not being of the blood royal, assembled in an adjoining square, called the *Casi-pata,* where they used the same forms of adoration as the Yncas.

Presently the King rose to his feet, the rest being still prostrate, and took two great cups of gold, called *aquilla,* full of the beverage that they drink. He performed this ceremony as the first-born, in the name of his father, the Sun, and, with the cup in his right hand, invited all his relations to drink. This custom of inviting each other to drink was the usual mode by which superiors showed favour and complacency to inferiors, and by which one friend saluted another.

Having given the invitation to drink, the Ynca emptied the vase in his right hand, which was dedicated to the Sun, into a jar of gold, whence the liquor flowed down a stone conduit of very beautiful masonry from the great square to the temple of the Sun, thus being looked upon as drunk by the deity. From the vase in his left hand the Ynca himself drank, that being his share, and then divided what remained among the other Yncas, pouring it into smaller cups of gold and silver. Gradually the principal vase, which the Ynca held, was emptied; and the partakers thus received such virtue from it as was imparted by its having been sanctified by the Sun or the Ynca, or rather by both together. Each member of the blood royal drank of this liquor. The Curacas in the other square received drinks of the beverage made by the chosen virgins, but not that which had also been sanctified by the Ynca.

This ceremony having been performed, which was but a foretaste of what would have to be drunk afterwards, all went in procession to the temple of the Sun. All took off their shoes, except the King, at two hundred paces before reaching the doors; but the King remained with his shoes on, until he came to the doors. The Ynca and his relations then entered the temple as legitimate children of the deity, and there worshipped the image of the Sun. But the Curacas, being unworthy of so great an honour, remained outside in a large square before the temple doors.

The Ynca offered to the Sun the golden vases with which he had performed the ceremony, and the other members of his family gave their cups to the Ynca priests, who were set apart for that office; for persons who were not priests, even if they were of the royal blood, were not allowed to perform the priestly office. Having offered up the cups of the Yncas, the priests came to the doors to receive those of the Curacas, who took their places according to their seniority as vassals, and presented the gold and silver articles which they had brought from their provinces as offerings to the Sun. These offerings were in the form of sheep, lambs, lizards, toads, serpents, foxes, tigers, lions, and many sorts of birds, in short, of all the animals in the provinces, each imitated from nature in gold and silver, though the size of each article was not great.

As soon as the offerings were made, the chiefs returned to their places in procession; and presently the priests came out with many lambs, ewes, and rams of all colours, for the native sheep of that country are of different colours, like the horses in Spain. All this flock was the property of the Sun. They took a black lamb, for among the Indians this colour was preferred for the sacrifices, as more sacred. For they said that a black beast was black all over, while a white one, though its body might be white, always had a black nose, which was a defect, and caused it to be less perfect than a black beast. For this reason also, the Kings generally dressed in black, and their mourning was the natural colour of the wool, which they call grey.

This first sacrifice of a black lamb was made to prognosticate the omens of the festival. For they almost always sacrificed a lamb before undertaking any act either of peace or war, in order to see, by examining the heart and lungs, whether it was acceptable to the Sun, that is to say, whether it would be successful or the reverse. In order to seek an omen to tell them whether a harvest would be good; for some crops they used a lamb, for others a ram, for others a sterile ewe; but they never killed a fruitful sheep even to eat, until it was past bearing.

They took the lamb or sheep, and placed it with the head towards the east. They did not tie its feet, but three or four Indians held it, and it was cut open on the left side while still alive. They then forced their hands in, and pulled out the heart with the lungs and gullet up to the mouth, and the whole had to be taken out entire, without being cut.

If the lungs were palpitating, or had not ceased to live as they call it, the augury was looked upon as most fortunate. If this omen appeared, they took no note of others that might appear of an opposite character. For they said that the excellence of this lucky omen would overcome the evil of all contrary signs. They then took the entrails, blew air into them, and fastened up the mouth, or held it tight with their hands. Presently they began to watch the ways by which the air entered and distended the veins and arteries. If they were very full of air, it was looked upon as a good omen. They had other ways of seeking auguries of which I took no note, but I remember having seen these two methods practised on two occasions when I was a child. I went into a yard on one occasion, where some old unbaptised Indians were performing a sacrifice, not of the Raymi, for that festival had been abolished before I was born, but for some special purpose, in order to watch the omens. With this object they sacrificed lambs and sheep, as on the feast of Raymi, for their special sacrifices were performed in imitation of those at the great festivals.

It was considered a very bad omen if the beast rose on its feet while they were opening its side, in spite of those who held it; or if the entrails broke and did not come out whole. It was also an evil sign if the lungs or heart were torn or bruised in being pulled out; and there were other signs which, as I have said, I neither inquired about nor took note of. I remember this because I heard the Indians, who made the sacrifice, asking each other concerning the bad or evil omens, and they did not mind me because I was but a child.

To return to the solemnities of the Raymi. If the sacrifice of the lamb did not furnish good auguries, they made another sacrifice of a sheep, and if this was also unpropitious they offered up another. But, even if the third sacrifice was unlucky, they did not desist from celebrating the festival, though they did so with inward sorrow and misgiving, believing that their father, the Sun, was enraged against them for some fault or negligence that they must have unintentionally committed against his service.

They feared that cruel wars, failure of crops, diseases in their flocks, and other misfortunes might befall them. But when the omens were propitious, their joy was very great with which they celebrated the festival, as they looked forward to future good fortune.

After the sacrifice of the lamb, they brought a great quantity of lambs and sheep for a general sacrifice, and they did not cut these open while they were alive, but beheaded them first. The blood and hearts of all these, as well as of the first lamb, were preserved and offered to the Sun, and the bodies were burnt until they were converted to ashes.

It was necessary that the fire for the sacrifice should be new, and given by the hand of the Sun, as they expressed it. For this purpose they took a large bracelet, called *chipana* (like those they usually wear on the left thumb). This was held by the high priest. It was larger than usual, and had on it a highly polished concave plate, about the diameter of an orange. They put this towards the Sun, at an angle, so that the reflected rays might concentrate on one point, where they had placed a little cotton well pulled out, for they did not know how to make tinder; but the cotton was soon lighted in the natural way. With this fire, thus obtained from the hands of the Sun, they consumed the sacrifice, and roasted all the meat on that day. Portions of the fire were then conveyed to the temple of the Sun, and to the convent of virgins, where they were kept in all the year, and it was an evil omen if they were allowed to go out. If on the eve of the festival, which was the time when they made the preparations for the sacrifice, there was no sun wherewith to light the new fire, they obtained it by means of two thin cylindrical sticks, about the girth of a man's finger, and half a *vara* long, which they rubbed together. They give the name of *Vyaca* both to the sticks and to the act of obtaining fire from them, the same word serving both for a noun and a verb. The Indians use these sticks instead of flint and steel, and they travel with them, so as to have the means of making a fire at their sleeping places, when in an uninhabited region. I have often seen this when I have made a journey with the Indians, and the shepherds make use of sticks for the same purpose.

They looked upon it as a bad omen to light the fire for the festival in this way, saying that, as the Sun refused to kindle the flame with his own hand, he must be angry with them. All the meat for the feast was roasted in public, in the two squares, and it was distributed amongst all those who were present at the feast, whether Yncas, Curacas, or common people. And each received a piece of the bread called *Canca* with the meat. This was the first dish in their grand and solemn banquet. Afterwards they received a great quantity of eatables, which were eaten without drinking; for it was the universal custom of the Indians of Peru not to drink while they were eating.

From what has been related, the assertion made by some Spaniards may have arisen that the Yncas and their vassals communicated like Christians. We have described the custom of the Indians, and each reader can make out the similitude as he pleases.

After the eating was over, they brought liquor in great quantity, for this was one of the most prevalent vices among the Indians. But at the present day, through the mercy of God and the good example which has been set them in this particular by the Spaniards, no Indian can get drunk without being despised and reviled by his fellows. If the Spaniards had set a like example as regards other vices, they would have been apostolic preachers of the gospel.

The Ynca, seated in his golden chair, which was placed on a platform of the same metal, sent to the members of the tribes called Hanan Cuzco and Hurin Cuzco, desiring them to drink, in his name, with the most distinguished Indians belonging to other nations. First, they invited the captains who had shown valour in war, who, even when they were not lords of vassals, were for their bravery preferred to Curacas. But if a Curaca, besides being a lord of vassals, was also a captain in the wars, they did him honour both on the one account and on the other. Next the Ynca ordered the Curacas living in the vicinity of Cuzco, to be invited to drink, being those whose ancestors the first Ynca Manco Ccapac had reduced to his service. These chiefs, owing to the great privilege of bearing the name of Ynca, which that Prince had granted them, were looked upon as nobles of the highest rank next to the Yncas of the blood royal, and before all the chiefs of other tribes. For those kings never thought of diminishing in the smallest degree any privilege or favour that their ancestors had granted to any of their vassals, but on the contrary confirmed and increased them.

In these drinking bouts that the Indians had with each other, it must be understood that they all held their cups touching each other, two and two, and whether large or small, they were always of the same size and shape, and of the same metal, whether gold, silver or wood. This custom was enforced that each might drink the same quantity. He who gave an invitation to drink carried the two cups in his hands, and if the invited person was of lower rank he was given the cup in the left hand, if of equal or higher rank, the cup in the right; and with more or less ceremony according to the position in life of one and the other. Then they both drank together, and, the person inviting to drink, having received back his cup, returned to his place. On these occasions the first invitation was from a superior to his inferior, in token of favour and kindness. Afterwards the inferior invited his superior, as an acknowledgment of his vassalage and duty.

In observing this custom, the Ynca first sent an invitation to his vassals, in each nation preferring the captains before those who were not warriors. The Ynca who took the invitation said to the invited person:—"The sole Ynca sends me to invite you to drink, and I come to drink with you in his name." The captain or Curaca then took the cup with much reverence, raised his eyes to the Sun, as though he would give thanks for so undeserved a favour conferred by his son, and having drunk, he returned the cup to the Ynca without another word, only making signs of adoration with his hands and kissing the air with his lips.

And it must be understood that the Ynca did not send invitations to drink to all the Curacas (though he did so to all captains) but only to a select number, who were most worthy and who were most devoted to the public good. For this was the mark at which they all shot, as well the Ynca as the Curacas and the ministers of peace and war. The rest of the Curacas were invited to drink by the same Yncas who brought the cups, but in their own names and not in that of the Ynca, which satisfied them, because the invitation came from one who was a child of the Sun, like their king.

After the first invitation to drink, the captains and Curacas of all the nations returned the challenges in the order that they had received them, some to the Ynca himself, and the others to his relations, according as the first invitation had been received. The Ynca was approached without a word, and merely with the signs of adoration I have already described. He received them with much condescension, and took the cups they presented, but as he could not, nor was it lawful for him to drink of them all, he merely put them to his lips, drinking a little from all of them, from some more, from others less, according to the favour he wished to show to their owners, which was regulated by their rank and merit. And he ordered the attendants, who were all Yncas by privilege, to drink for him with those captains and Curacas; who having done so, returned the cups.

The Curacas held these cups in great veneration as sacred things, because the sole Ynca had touched them with his hands and lips. They never drank out of them again, nor touched them, but looked upon them as idols fit to be worshipped, in memory of their having been touched by the Ynca. Certainly nothing can show more than this how great was the love and veneration, both internal and outward, that these Indians felt for their kings.

The invitation and the return challenge to drink having been observed, all returned to their places. Presently the dances and songs began, in different fashions, and with the several insignia, masks, and dresses used by each nation. While the singing and dancing continued they did not leave off drinking, the Yncas and Curacas inviting each other, according to their special friendships, or to the nearness of their places of residence.

The celebration of the feast of Raymi lasted for nine days, during which time there was abundance of eating and drinking, and such rejoicing as each person could show. But the sacrifices for observing omens were only made on the first day. As soon as the nine days were over the Curacas returned to their lands with the permission of the King, very joyful and contented at having celebrated the principal feast of their god the Sun. When the King was occupied in war or in visiting his dominions, he celebrated the feast in the place where he happened to be, but not with so much solemnity as when he was at Cuzco; while the Ynca governor, the High Priest, and others of the blood royal who remained behind, took care to celebrate it in the capital. On those occasions the Curacas assembled in the provinces, each one going to the feast which was held nearest to the place of his abode.

Inca

PACHACUTEC

THE YNCA PACHACUTEC, being now old, resolved to rest and not to make further conquests; for he had increased his empire until it was more than one hundred and thirty leagues from north to south, and in width from the snowy chain of the Andes to the sea, being sixty leagues from east to west in some places, and seventy in others, more or less. He now devoted himself to the confirmation of the laws of his ancestors, and to the enactment of new laws for the common good.

He founded many towns in those lands which by industry and by means of the numerous irrigation channels he caused to be made, were converted from sterile and uncultivated wilds into fruitful and rich districts.

He built many temples of the Sun in imitation of that of Cuzco, and many convents of virgins. He ordered many store-houses on the royal roads to be repaired, and houses to be built where the Yncas might lodge when travelling.

He also caused store-houses to be built in all villages, large or small, where supplies might be kept for succouring the people in time of scarcity, and he ordered these depots to be filled from the crops of the Ynca and of the Sun. In short, it may be said that he completely reformed the empire, as well as regards their vain religion, which he provided with new rites and ceremonies, destroying the numerous idols of his vassals, as by enacting new laws and regulations for the daily and moral life of the people, forbidding the abuses and barbarous customs to which the Indians were addicted before they were brought under his rule.

He also reformed the army in such fashion as proved him to be as great a captain as he was a king and a ruler; and he increased the honours and favours shown to those who distinguished themselves in war. He especially favoured and enlarged the great city of

Cuzco, enriching it with new edifices and a larger population. He ordered a palace to be built for himself near the schools founded by his great grandfather Ynca Rocca. On account of these deeds, as well as for his amiable disposition and benignant government, he was loved and worshipped as another Jupiter. He reigned, according to the accounts of the Indians, more than fifty years, and some say more than sixty years. He lived in much peace and tranquillity, being alike beloved and obeyed, and at the end of this long time he died. He was universally lamented by all his vassals, and was placed among the number of their gods, as were the other Kings Yncas, his ancestors. He was embalmed, according to their custom, and the mourning, sacrifices and burial ceremonies lasted for a year.

He left as his heir the Ynca Yupanqui, who was his son by the Ccoya Anahuarque, his legitimate wife and sister. He left more than three hundred other sons and daughters, and some even say that, judging from his long life and the number of his wives, he must have had four hundred either legitimate or illegitimate children; and though this is a great many, the Indians say that it was few for such a father.

The Spanish historians confuse these two Kings, father and son, giving the names of both to one. The father was named Pachacutec. The name Ynca was common to all, for it was their title from the days of the first Ynca, called Manco Ccapac. In our account of the life of Lloque Yupanqui we described the meaning of the word Yupanqui, which word was also the name of this King, and combining the two names, they formed Ynca Yupanqui, which title was applied to all the Kings Yncas, so that Yupanqui ceased to be a special name. These two names are equivalent to the names Caesar Augustus, given to all the Emperors. Thus the Indians, in recounting the deeds of their Kings, and calling them by their names, would say, Pachacutec Ynca Yupanqui. The Spaniards understood that this was one King, and they do not admit the son and successor of Pachacutec, who was called Ynca Yupanqui, taking the two titles as his special name, and giving the same name to his own eldest son. But the Indians, to distinguish him from his father, called the latter Tupac (which means 'He who shines') Ynca Yupanqui. He was father of Huayna Ccapac Ynca Yupanqui, and grandfather of Huascar Ynca Yupanqui; and so all the other Yncas may be called by these titles. I have said this much to enable those who read this history to avoid confusion.

The Father Blas Valera, speaking of this Ynca, says as follows: "The Ynca Huira-ccocha being dead and worshipped among the Indians as a god, his son, the great Titu, with surname of Manco Ccapac, succeeded him. This was his name until his father gave him that of Pachacutec, which means 'Reformer of the World.' That title was confirmed after-wards by his distinguished acts and sayings, insomuch that his first name was entirely for-gotten. He governed his empire with so much industry, prudence and resolution, as well in peace as in war, that not only did he increase the boundaries of all the four quarters, called *Ttahua-ntin suyu,* but also he enacted many laws, all which have been confirmed by our Catholic Kings, except those relating to idolatry and to forbidden degrees of marriage. This Ynca above all things ennobled and increased, with great privileges, the schools that were founded in Cuzco by the King Ynca Rocca. He added to the number of the masters, and ordered that all the lords of vassals and captains and their sons, and all the Indians who held any office, should speak the language of Cuzco; and that no one should receive any office or lordship who was not well acquainted with it. In order that this useful law might have full effect, he appointed very learned masters for the sons of the princes and nobles, not only for those in Cuzco, but also for those throughout the provinces, in which he stationed masters that they might teach the language of Cuzco to all who were employed in the service of the state. Thus it was that in the whole empire of Peru one language was spoken, although now (owing to negligence) many provinces, where it was understood, have entirely lost it, not without great injury to the preaching of the gospel. All the Indians who, by obeying this law, still retain a knowledge of the language of Cuzco, are more civilised and more intelligent than the others.

"This Pachacutec prohibited any one, except princes and their sons, from wearing gold, silver, precious stones, plumes of feathers of different colours, nor the wool of the vicuña, which they weave with admirable skill. He permitted the people to be moderately ornamented on the first days of the month, and on some other festivals. The tributary Indians still observe this law, and content themselves with ordinary clothes, by which they avoid much vice which gay clothing is apt to cause. But the Indians, who are servants to Spaniards, and those who live in Spanish cities, are very extravagant in this particular, and do much harm alike to their pockets and consciences. This Ynca also ordered that great frugality should be observed in eating, although in drinking more freedom was allowed, both among the princes and the common people. He ordained that there should be special judges to try the idle, and desired that all should be engaged in work of some kind, either in serving their parents or masters, or in the service of the state; so much so, that even boys and girls of from five to seven years of age were given something to do suitable to their years. The blind, lame, and dumb, who could use their hands, were employed in some kind of work, and the aged were sent to scare the birds from the crops, and were supplied with food and clothing from the public store-houses. In order that labour might not be so continuous as to become oppressive, the Ynca ordained that there should be three holidays every month, in which the people should divert themselves with various games. He also commanded that there should be three fairs every month, when the labourers in the field should come to the market and hear anything that the Ynca or his Council might have ordained. They called these assemblies *Catu,* and they took place on the holidays.

"The Ynca also made a law that every province should have a fixed boundary enclosing the forests, pastures, rivers, lakes, mountains, and lands for tillage; all which should belong to that province and be within its jurisdiction in perpetuity. No Governor or Curaca could diminish or divide or appropriate to his own use any portion; but the land was divided according to a fixed rule which was defined by the same law for the common good, and the special benefit of the inhabitants of the province. The royal estates and those of the Sun were set apart, and the Indians had to plough, sow, and reap the crops, as well on their own lands as on those of the State. Hence it will be seen that it is false, what many have asserted, that the Indians had no proprietary right in the land. For this division was not made with reference to proprietary right, but for the common and special work to be expended upon the land. It was a very ancient custom among the Indians to work together not only on public lands, but also on their own, and with this view they measured the land, that each might complete such portion as he was able. The whole population assembled, and first worked their own lands in common, each one helping his neighbours, and then they began upon the royal estates; and the same practice was followed in sowing and in reaping. Almost in the same way they built their houses. The Indian who required a house went to the Council to appoint a day when it should be built, the inhabitants with one accord assembled to assist their neighbour, and thus the house was completed. The Ynca approved of this custom, and confirmed it by law. To this day many villages of Indians observe this law, and help each other with Christian charity; but avaricious men, who think only of themselves, do themselves harm and their neighbours no good.

"In fine, this King, with the advice of his Council, made many laws, rules, ordinances, and customs for the good of the people in numerous provinces. He also abolished many others which were detrimental either to the public peace or to his sovereignty. He also enacted many statutes against blasphemy, patricide, fratricide, homicide, treason, adultery, child-stealing, seduction, theft, arson; as well as regulations for the ceremonies of the temple. He confirmed many more that had been enacted by the Yncas his ancestors; such as that sons should obey and serve their fathers until they reached the age of twenty-five, that none should marry without the consent of the parents, and of the parents of the girl; that a marriage without this consent was invalid and the children illegitimate; but that if the consent was obtained afterwards the children then became legitimate. This Ynca also confirmed the laws of inheritance to lordships according to the ancient customs of each province; and he forbade the judges from receiving bribes from litigants. This Ynca made many other laws of less importance, which I omit, to avoid prolixity. Further on I shall relate what laws he made for the guidance of judges, for the contracting of marriages, for making wills, and for the army, as well as for reckoning the years. In our time the Viceroy, Don Francisco de Toledo, changed or revoked many laws and regulations made by this Ynca; and the Indians, admiring his absolute power, called him the second Pachacutec, for they said he was the Reformer of the first Reformer. Their reverence and veneration for this Ynca was so great that to this day they cannot forget him."

Down to this point is from what I found amongst the torn papers of Father Blas Valera. That which he promises to write further on, touching the judges, marriages, wills, the army, and the reckoning of the year, is lost, which is a great pity. On another leaf I found part of the sententious sayings of this Ynca Pachacutec, which are as follows:—

"When subjects, captains and Curacas, cordially obey the King, then the kingdom enjoys perfect peace and quiet.

"Envy is a worm that gnaws and consumes the entrails of the envious.

231

"He that envies and is envied, has a double torment.

"It is better that others should envy you for being good, than that you should envy others, you yourself being evil.

"He that envies another, injures himself.

"He that envies the good, draws evil from them for himself, as does the spider in taking poison from flowers.

"Drunkenness, anger and madness go together; only the first two are voluntary and to be removed, while the last is perpetual.

"He that kills another without authority or just cause, condemns himself to death.

"He that kills his neighbour must of necessity die; and for this reason the ancient Kings, our ancestors, ordained that all homicides should be punished by a violent death, a law which we confirm afresh.

"Under no circumstances should thieves be tolerated, who, being able to gain a livelihood by honest labour and to possess it by a just right, wish to have more by robbing and stealing. It is very just that he who is a thief should be put to death.

"Adulterers, who destroy the peace and happiness of others, ought to be declared thieves, and condemned to death without mercy.

"The noble and generous man is known by the patience he shows in adversity.

"Impatience is the sign of a vile and base mind, badly taught and worse accustomed.

"When subjects do their best to obey without any hesitation, kings and governors ought to treat them with liberality and kindness; but when they act otherwise, with rigour and strict justice, though always with prudence.

"Judges who secretly receive gifts from suitors ought to be looked upon as thieves, and punished with death as such.

"Governors ought to attend to two things with much attention. The first is, that they and their subjects keep and comply exactly with the laws of their king. The second, that they consult with much vigilance and care, touching the common and special affairs of their provinces. The man who knows not how to govern his house and family, will know much less how to rule the state. Such a man should not be preferred above others.

"The physician herbalist that is ignorant of the virtues of herbs, or who, knowing the uses of some, has not attained a knowledge of all, understands little or nothing. He ought to work until he knows all, as well the useful as the injurious plants, in order to deserve the name he pretends to.

"He who attempts to count the stars, not even knowing how to count the marks and knots of the 'quipus,' ought to be held in derision."

These are the sayings of Ynca Pachacutec. He speaks of the marks and knots of the accounts because, as they had neither letters for writing nor figures for ciphering, they kept their accounts by means of marks and knots.

Inca

232

THREE INCA PRAYERS

TO VIRACOCHA

Viracocha, Lord of the Universe!
Whether male or female,
at any rate commander of heat and reproduction,
being one who,
even with His spittle, can work sorcery,
Where art Thou?
Would that Thou wert not hidden from this son of Thine!
He may be above;
He may be below;
or, perchance, abroad in space.
Where is his mighty judgment-seat?
Hear me!
He may be spread abroad among the upper waters;
or, among the lower waters and their sands
He may be dwelling.
Creator of the world,
Creator of man,
great among my ancestors,
before Thee
my eyes fail me,
though I long to see Thee;
for, seeing Thee,
knowing Thee,
learning from Thee,
understanding Thee,
I shall be seen by Thee,
and Thou wilt know me.
The Sun—the Moon;
The Day—the Night;
Summer—Winter;
not in vain,
in orderly succession,
do they march
to their destined place,
to their goal.
They arrive
wherever

Thy royal staff
Thou bearest.
Oh! Harken to me,
listen to me,
let it not befall
that I grow weary
and die.

TO VIRACOCHA

O conquering Viracocha!
Ever-present Viracocha!
Thou who art without equal upon the earth!
Thou who art from the beginnings of the world until its end!
Thou gavest life and valour to men, saying,
"Let this be a man."
And to woman, saying,
"Let this be a woman."
Thou madest them and gavest them being.
Watch over them, that they may live in health and in peace.
Thou who art in the highest heavens,
and among the clouds of the tempest,
grant them long life,
and accept this our sacrifice,
O Creator.

TO PACHACAMAC

O Pachacamac!
Thou who hast existed from the beginning,
Thou who shalt exist until the end,
powerful but merciful,
Who didst create man by saying,
"Let man be,"
Who defendest us from evil,
and preservest our life and our health,
art Thou in the sky or upon the earth?
In the clouds or in the deeps?
Hear the voice of him who implores Thee,
and grant him his petitions.
Give us life everlasting,
preserve us, and accept this our sacrifice.

Inca

7

PAMPAS, JUNGLES AND ISLANDS

BEYOND THE HIGH CIVILIZATIONS of Peru, we find ourselves among peoples who are even yet in a fairly primitive state—peoples of the pampas or plains of South America who developed a horse culture as did their analogues in North America, and peoples who dwell in the great forests and jungles of the back country. There is much yet to be learned of the ethnology of these peoples, of their origins and even of their physical characteristics.

Basketry was practiced in South America except in limited areas where fibers were lacking. There are many methods and styles, and the decoration is usually structural, i.e., a result of the weaving technique employed. Color designs were made by dyeing, or by using materials whose natural colors were appropriate. The Indians of the Guianas did excellent basketry, using for design motives the deer, the monkey, the beetle and frog. They used the same designs in their beadwork. (See Plate 78.)

Many South American groups practiced weaving, but the work does not compare with the Peruvian textiles. In non-weaving areas, designs were painted on hides; a typical design is shown on Plate 75.

Except for the southern tip of the continent and the northwest tip of the island of Cuba, pottery was made throughout South America and the West Indies. Plates 75 to 77 show many styles of this work. There are crude jars from Chile and Argentina on Plate 75; a florid vase from Brazil on Plate 77; a well-modeled vase from Colombia on Plate 76 and ware from the island of Marajo, Brazil.

The opening words of the Preface of this book were taken from Columbus's log and are the entry he made after landing on what we believe was Watling Island. The natives he met were Arawak, one of the groups who lived at that time on the West Indian islands. Other groups were the Ciboney, who may have come originally from Florida, and the Carib who, like the Arawak, had emigrated from the South American continent. The native cultures of all these peoples were wiped out in a few years, but from the records of the Spanish missionaries and from a few legends gathered in our own time from the South American descendants of these native groups we have some idea of what they did and thought. Plate 79 illustrates some of their crafts—pottery and stonework. The three-pointed stones are called *zemis* and were very important in the daily life of the Indians. They were physical homes in which friendly spirits might reside and remain near the owner, and into which unfriendly spirits might be enticed and rendered harmless.

The skillfully carved stone collar recalls the Mexican yoke on Plate 46. The use of these stone collars or yokes is not known, but was without doubt of ritual significance. Pottery from the islands is crude but ambitious—like the work of a clever child working in clay without manual skill.

Just as the artistic work of the peoples beyond Peru is sparse by reason of lack of evidence and investigation, so it is with their expression of ideas and beliefs. From the myths and legends here collected, it will be seen that the peoples of the Guianas, the Brazilian backwoods and the islands have, in their range of ideas and their cosmogony, no very elevated plane of thought. Living as they do on a bare existence level, they do not aspire nor can we blame them. There is greater art in the stories from the Chaco, however, and a very remarkable quality in the little Araucanian songs which follow this note. How much of this quality is owing to European influences, it would be hard to say.

ARAUCANIAN SONGS

SONG OF THE GREAT CHIEF

He wears over his body
his great, embroidered mantle
and his *chiripa*
and his sash of authority.
He is like to the sun which is rising—
his golden *trarilonco*
rests on his brow,
on his haughty head.
Like the lion
he has strength.

His face is clear
and without a beard
and his smooth hair
is black.
This is the look
of a great chief,
mamita, mamita.

SONG OF CAUPOLICAN

A man he was,
a man he was,
our first chief.
Great Caupolican,
great Caupolican
was he named, oh my friend.
By his death, his death.
only then did we know what a man
was Caupolican.

SONG OF THE SPIRIT OF CAUPOLICAN

Who is this
who comes like the tiger—
on the wind passes
with his ghostly body?
When the strong ones see him,
even they
speak softly:
"It is he, brothers,
"Caupolican."

GOD

How are you, God?
For you
I am good.
From all evil things
spare me, good friend.
All good things
bring forth in my soul,
good friend, God.
Through you

we have the sun,
and for you
we live well.
Now we hold the *fiesta*
and we drink happily,
good God.

THE WEEPER

If I had only
one son who would cry for me,
immediately
my weeping would cease.

FOR MY LOVE

Looking at you, I loved you—
little darling,
my heart is dying
for the thought of you, lost.
If God should wish
to take away your heart,
little sister, in every country
I would cry for my lost one.

FOR HER

Because they called you a good woman
I came for you,
little sister. I galloped
four days, aye,
little companion,
because of your good, shining face.

Araucanian

CARANCHO TEACHES MEN HOW TO MAKE FIRE

ANOTHER CHIEF came to visit these people. He asked, "Haven't you any fire?" "No, but we would like to have some because we have to eat our meat raw." "Why don't you ask Carancho (*the Hawk*)?" "We cannot, we are surrounded by water." "Well, but I succeeded in getting here." "Yes, but the water does not allow us to pass through. The water is armed with clubs to kill us. Why don't you go and speak to Carancho? Have you fire?" "Yes, but I did not bring it with me because I thought you had it. Carancho will come. When he is here, you must obey him or he will put out your fire." The chief left, and crossed the water without any trouble.

The first chief said, "Now we must wait for Carancho, who will come soon." Others said, "We'd better look for honey." "No, it is better to wait here. Carancho won't be long," said the chief.

The second chief went to speak to Carancho, "Listen, Carancho, there are people over there who have no fire. They need it badly because they have to eat their food raw." Carancho said, "I shall go there tomorrow." "You and I have equal power," said Fox, "I'll fly over there." "Have you wings?" "Yes I have, and I shall fly high into the sky." Fox flew higher and higher, but his feathers (fixed with wax) were falling out. The people said, "Look at this poor fox, he is losing his feathers." Carancho said, "This fellow will soon fall. Let him." The people called, "Fox, come back!" Fox was high in the sky. He heard the people, but answered, "These are not my feathers, these are my hairs." He lost all his feathers, fell down, and broke his neck. Carancho said, "I foresaw it. I am the only one who can help people, and nobody else. Tomorrow I shall go to see these people."

At dawn Carancho left to visit these people. He said to himself, "I shall teach these people and bring them here." He walked until he found the water. "Water, why do you behave like this? Why do you put out the fire?" The water explained, "This is the order I received. We have a master, it is Wien (a water serpent)." Carancho said, "I came in behalf of these people for whom I feel sorry because they eat their meat raw. I shall kill you and your master too." "You can kill us only if you bring fire, otherwise we shall kill you."

Carancho came near the village and saw the people who were eating raw meat. They said, "Who is coming? Who is this man?" "I am Carancho." An unmarried girl cried to Carancho, "Carancho, come into my hut and I shall tell you everything that has happened here." "I shall come, but first tell me if you have a husband. Anyway, I cannot get to your house because I cannot cross the water. Tell me something about this water and its master and what I have to do." The girl replied, "Give me fire. There is plenty of water here, but no fire, and we cannot cook our food. Help us. I can still speak, but the others have lost their speech because they are about to be transformed, since they have no fire." "If you obey me, I shall do something for you. Do as I say," said Carancho. "Yes." "Bring as many fish as you can," ordered Carancho. Carancho was nice to everybody. They brought the fish. "Now," said Carancho, "bring me branches of the pi'taladik and of the kuwak'á" (*wood which the Toba use for making their fire drill*). The people came back with the wood. Carancho was busy; he bored a small hole in the middle of a stick, inserted another one into the shaft of an arrow (*moé*). He twirled this stick rapidly, and after a while the wood smoked and glowed. He took some caraguatá tinder and built a big fire. He heated the heads of his spear and arrows, and plunged them into the water. The water dried up. The Master of the Water died and the people could make fire. Carancho stayed in the village. They made more fires and grilled their fish. Carancho stayed with these people.   *Toba and Pilaga*

THE GRATEFUL WATER SERPENT
MAKES GAME ANIMALS TAME BUT
CARANCHO MAKES THEM ELUSIVE AGAIN

THERE WAS A SERPENT NAMED LIK as large as a table. A man was walking in the bush and met him. At first he was very much afraid. The serpent asked, "Where is there water, Grandson?" "The water is far away, Grandfather, but if you wish we can go there." "Yes, I want to go there." "Follow me," said the man. The serpent asked, "Won't you carry me?" "How can I? You are very heavy." "No, I am light." "But you are so large," countered the man. "Yes, I am large, but light." "But you are full of fish." (It is true, Lik is full of fish. The fish are under his tail and when he moves he carries them with him.) The serpent went on, "If you carry me I shall give you all the fish I have inside me." The man lifted him and found him very light. He carried him to the place where there was water. He said, "The water is over there." The serpent encouraged him, "Hurry up, you can rest when we get there." When they arrived the man put him down. The serpent promised him that he would give him all the fish he wanted. "You just come back here and ask me." The man said, "Yes, I shall come back here, but do as you promised. A bad man wouldn't have carried you." The serpent entered the water, and the man went home.

The man said to Carancho, "Over there I met a water serpent; I put him down in our lagoon. He is loaded with fish, which are in his tail." Carancho ordered, "Tomorrow you take me over there." The man thought it was a good idea for Carancho to talk to the serpent. The following day they arrived at the lagoon. They called the serpent. "Carancho wants to get acquainted with you," said the man. They talked together. "What do you want?" asked the serpent. "I told the man to come alone and he has brought you. Why did he do that?" "I am hungry," said Carancho. "Look at all these people. Give me what they want. I am not here to do you any harm; I respect you." "That's good. I shall increase the water and multiply the fish. But don't throw the fish away. Take good care of this fish so you will always have some. If you don't take care of the fish, you will suffer. Such is my will. If you are obedient, you will live. You are Carancho, the killer of the monsters and of the man eaters. You may help me. I will take pity on all of you. If you want to eat some animals just imitate their cries and they will come."

Formerly, if you wanted ducks, ostriches, or deer, you had only to cry like them and the serpent would give them to you. Carancho was delighted to have food for nothing. If a person was hungry, the food came to him by itself.

Later on, Carancho disapproved of this because the men killed too many animals. Carancho said that he no longer wanted the food to be procured without work. He wanted the people to have to look for it. "May the animals be wild," he said. Carancho caused animals not to come by themselves.

Toba and Pilaga

FIRE

A MAN found an arara nest with two young birds in a cave in a high and vertical cliff. He took his little brother-in-law along, chopped down a tree, leaned it against the wall of rock, and bade the boy climb up to the nest and catch the young ones. The boy went up, but as soon as he stretched out his hand toward the young araras, the parent birds rushed at him with fierce screams, so that he got frightened and did not dare to grasp them. Then the man got angry, knocked the tree aside, and left.

The boy, unable to descend without the tree, remained sitting by the nest for five days. He nearly died of thirst and hunger. From time to time he would softly sing: *"He, piednyo padko!"* (Oh, brother-in-law, give me some drink!). He was completely covered by the droppings of the araras and swallows that flew above him.

Then a jaguar came past the foot of the cliff. He saw the boy's shadow moving and rushed up to seize it, but only caught the air. He waited till the boy again moved and again tried to seize his shadow, but in vain. Then the boy spat down, and now the jaguar raised his head and saw him. "What are you doing up there?" he asked. The boy told about how his brother-in-law had left him. "What is in the hole?" asked the jaguar. "Young araras," answered the boy. "Then throw them down!" ordered the jaguar. The boy threw down one of them, which the jaguar immediately devoured. "Was there only one young one?" he then asked. "No," was the answer, "there is a second one." "Then, throw it down, too," commanded the jaguar again, and when the boy had obeyed he ate up the second one, too.

Then the jaguar brought the tree there, placed it against the rock, and asked the boy to step down. He began to climb down the trunk, but when quite close to the ground he got scared: *"Dydmã kod-kab id-kre"* (You are going to eat me up), he cried and hurriedly climbed up again. "No," the jaguar quieted him, "come down, I'll give you water to drink." Three times the boy almost got down, and three times his fear of the jaguar drove him back. At last, however, he climbed down all the way.

The jaguar took him on his back and carried him to a creek. The boy drank till he remained lying there and fell asleep. At last the jaguar pinched his arm and awakened him. He washed the dirt off him and said that, having no children, he would take him home as his son.

In the jaguar's house a long jatobá trunk was lying, which was burning at one end. While the Indians of that time ate only flesh dried in the sun, the jaguar had quantities of roast game. "What is smoking there?" asked the boy. "That is fire," answered the jaguar. "What is fire?" asked the boy. "You will find out at night when it warms you," the jaguar explained. Then he gave roast meat to the boy, who ate till he fell asleep. He slept till midnight; then he woke up, ate again, and then again fell asleep.

Before daybreak the jaguar went hunting. The boy followed him some distance, then climbed a tree on the road, where he waited for the jaguar to return. But toward noon he got hungry, returned to the jaguar's house, and begged his wife for food. "What?" she shouted, turning round toward the boy and, pointing at her teeth, "Look here!" The boy cried out from fear and ran back to the tree, where he waited for the jaguar, to whom he told about the occurrence. The jaguar took him back home and scolded his wife: "I told you not to frighten my son!" His wife excused herself, saying she had been merely jesting.

The next morning the jaguar made a bow and arrow for the boy. He took him outside and told him to shoot at a termite nest. He did, and the arrow pierced the nest. Then the jaguar ordered him to kill his wife with the arrow if she threatened him again, but to make sure of his aim. Then he again went hunting.

At noon the boy got hungry again, went home, and asked the jaguar's wife for a piece of roast flesh. But instead of answering, she threatened him with her claws and teeth. Then he aimed at her, and now she in alarm cried, "Hold on! I'll give you to eat!" But the boy shot the arrow at her side so that it came out on the other. Then he ran off, while she sank down with a roar. For awhile he heard her roaring, then nothing was to be heard.

He met the jaguar and told him he had killed his wife. "That does not matter," answered he. At home he gave the boy a lot of roast meat in addition and told him to follow along the creek, then he would be sure to reach his tribe. But he was to be on guard: if a rock or the aroeira tree called him, he should answer; but he was to keep still if he heard the gentle call of a rotten tree. In two days he was to return and fetch the fire.

The boy moved along the brook. After a while he heard the rock shout and answered. Then he heard the call of the aroeira and again answered. Then a rotten tree cried out, and the boy, forgetting the jaguar's warning, answered it too. That is why men are shortlived; if he had answered only the first two, they would enjoy as long life as the rocks and the aroeira trees.

After a while the boy again heard a cry and answered. It was Megalō-kamdu're (soul of the dead). He came up and asked the boy, "Whom are you calling?" "I am calling my father," answered he. "Am not I your father?" "No, my father looks quite differently, he has long hair." Then after a while Megalō-kamdu're went away and returned after a while with long hair, pretending he was the boy's father. But the boy refused to recognize him because his father had big ear-plugs. Again Megalō-kamdu're went away and soon after returned with what had been missing, but the boy still insisted he did not look like his father. "Are you not by chance Megalō-kamdu're?" he asked. Then the man seized him and wrestled with him till he was quite worn out, whereupon he put the boy into his big carrying-basket and went home with his burden.

On the way Megalō-kamdu're noticed on a tree a flock of coatis. He set down his basket, shook the coatis down, killed them, and packed them all on top of the boy in the basket. Then he took this on his back again by means of a tump-line. Then the boy, who had somewhat recovered in the meantime, called to him to make a trail through the woods first so he could carry the load better. Megalō-kamdu're accepted the suggestion, set down his basket, and cleared the road. In the meantime the boy slipped out, laid a heavy stone on the bottom, packed the coatis on top, and hurried away.

Megalō-kamdu're, having finished his job, came back to his basket and picked it up, but found it still very heavy. But at last he got home with his burden. He set the basket down and said to his numerous children, "There I have brought a nice little bird!" Then one child took out a coati, raised it and asked, "Is it this?" "No," answered Megalō-kamdu're. The child took out another, "This?" "No." Then he took out all of them, one by one, and got to the stone. "Now there is only a stone here!" "Then I must have lost it on the way," said Megalō-kamdu're and went back to look for it. But he found nothing, for the boy had long made his escape.

Back in his village, he told about his adventures with the jaguar and Megalō-kamdu're. "Now let us all fetch the fire so we need not eat raw food any more!" he concluded. Then various animals came to offer their help: first the jaho', but they sent him away because he was too weak; he was to run in the rear and extinguish what blaze fell off. The jacu' was also spurned; but the tapir was considered strong enough to carry the tree.

When the Indians, led by the boy, got to the jaguar's house, he gave them the fire. "I have adopted your son," he said to the boy's father. Then the tapir carried the burning log to the village. The jacu', running after him with the jaho', swallowed a live coal that had dropped and thus got his red throat.

Apinayé (North Brazil)

STAR-WOMAN

A YOUNG MAN'S WIFE had died. He allowed his hair to grow long and slept in the bushes behind his mother's house. As he was lying there, he noticed a pretty little star above. He thought to himself how nice it would be if this star came down to him. But when he looked up again after a while the star had disappeared. Then a frog came hopping to his bed and jumped on his body. He threw it aside, but it returned and leaped at him. He hurled it far away into the bush; then he fell asleep. When the frog noticed this, he assumed the form of a girl and lay down beside him. The man awoke and asked, "Where have you come from?" "From there," answered the girl; "what has been the matter with you?" "A frog twice jumped on my body." "That was I! Did you not see the star directly above you?" "Yes, but now it is gone." "That was I, too. I am Kandyekwe'i (Star-woman)." They remained together all night, and before daybreak she returned to the sky.

The following night she came again, bringing a bowl full of sweet-potatoes and yams, which she ate together with her mate, to whom these plants were as yet unknown, for the Indians then had no cultivation, but ate rotten wood with their meat.

At daybreak the man hid Star-woman in a big lidded gourd, which he carefully tied up. When his comrades later called him to a log-race, he first opened the vessel again and looked in, and Star-woman smiled at him. He fastened the cover on carefully and joined the others. His younger brother, however, observed him. In his absence he opened the lid and saw the girl, who lowered her head for shame when she saw that it was not her mate. The brother hurriedly closed the cover. When the man returned from the race, he at once opened the lid of the bottle, but Star-woman kept her head down and would not look at him. So he took her out and now publicly lived with her. She was very beautiful and light-skinned.

Star-woman went bathing with her mother-in-law. When they got to the water she transformed herself into a little opossum and jumped on the old woman's shoulder, but was thrown aside. She jumped a second time and was again pushed away by the old woman. Then she jumped up a third time, saying she wanted to tell the old woman something. She called her attention to a thick tree on the bank of the creek, which bore all manner of maize cobs, and explained that the Indians were to eat this maize instead of rotten wood. As an opossum she climbed up and threw down quantities of cobs. Then she reassumed human shape, packed the cobs together, and carried them into the village. There she showed her mother-in-law how to make maize cakes. They ate of the new dish, also giving some to a boy. When he came eating across the plaza, where the men sat in assembly, they called him to ask what he was eating. The boy gave them some of his cake, and all liked it extremely well.

Then the men resolved to chop down the maize tree. They went to work with a stone axe and had got the tree near the point of falling when they got tired and sat down to rest. But when about to go to work again they discovered in alarm that the notch they had cut had got closed again.

They sent two boys to the village for a better axe. On the way the two discovered a steppe opossum, which they killed and immediately roasted and consumed, though this animal is taboo to boys. Hardly had they finished their meal when they turned into senile, stooping old men. Thus another messenger found them who had been sent after them in search of the stone axe. He led the two into the village, where an old magician-doctor undertook their rejuvenation. He washed them and poured water over them till they were all but suffocated. Then they turned back into the boys they had been.

When the men had finally felled the tree with great difficulty, Star-woman advised them to make a clearing and plant maize. The Indians did so, and since then they have had their cultivated plots.

Star-woman, however, later returned to the sky after her husband's death.

Apinayé (North Brazil)

THE DELUGE

THE BIG SNAKE Kane-roti came up from the sea and made the Rio Tocantins and the Rio Araguaya. He left to his smaller companions the task of making the lesser streams and creeks.

Then it rained for many days. All the watercourses overflowed their banks; the flood waters of the Tocantins joined those of the Araguaya. For two days the whole world was flooded. Many Apinayé fled to the Serra Negra, a mountain behind São Vicente, toward the Araguaya, which for that reason is called Ken-klimati (mountain of the meeting). Others took refuge in high jatoba' trees, still others clung to big bottle gourds, drifted hither and yon, and finally perished.

One married couple took three gigantic gourd bottles, put manioc cuttings, maize and other seeds inside, stopped the orifices thoroughly with wax, and tied the three vessels together. Then the two sat down in the middle and allowed themselves to drift on the water. The current drove their craft close to the Serra Negra, but it resisted the powerful whirlpool.

On the Serra Negra the water was already up to people's knees; quite suddenly at night it fell again. Those perched on the high jatoba' trees were now unable to get down and finally turned into nests of chope' bees and termites.

When the water had ebbed away, the couple with the three gourds looked for a dwelling site and started a farm there. The people of the Serra Negra, however, having no more cuttings, lived on palm sprouts and nuts. One day a boy there killed a dwarf parrot, which he took to his mother. When she prepared it, she found maize kernels in his crop. She asked the boy from what direction the bird had come, and when she had found out everybody went there to search. Finally they found the couple's farm and stayed there till harvest time in order to acquire more cuttings and seeds.

Apinayé (North Brazil)

THE BUNIA BIRD

TIME WAS WHEN the Indians had no cassava to eat; they all starved. Animals and birds also had nothing to eat; they likewise starved. It was the Maipuri alone who, going out regularly every morning and returning home of an evening, always appeared sleek and fat. The others, noticing his droppings—banana-skins, cane strips, etc., talked to one another after this manner: "Maipuri must have found a good place to get food. Let us watch him." So next morning they sent the bush-rat to dog his footsteps, and find out how he managed to keep in such good condition. The bush-rat did what he was told and followed Maipuri a long, long way into the bush, when he saw him pause under the shade of an immense tree and gather the fruit that had fallen. This tree was the Allepántepo and very wonderful, in that everything you could wish for grew upon its branches—plantains, cassava, yams, plums, pines, and all the other fruits that Caribs love. As soon as Maipuri had had his fill the bush-rat climbed the tree, and picked upon the corn to satisfy his hunger; when he could eat no more, he came down and brought with him a grain in order to show the others what he had succeeded in finding. The Indians thereupon followed the rat who led the way back to the tree, and by the time they reached it, many plantains, pines, and other things had fallen on the ground. After they had cleaned up everything, they tried to climb the tree to get more, but it was too big and smooth, so they all agreed to cut it down. They made a staging around the trunk, and began hacking with their stone axes, and they cut away there for ten days, but it would not fall—so big was Allepántepo. They cut away for another ten days and still it

245

would not fall. By this time their work had made them thirsty, so the Indians gave calabashes to all the animals except the Maipuri, to go fetch water; to the Maipuri they gave a sifter. When they all reached the waterside, they of course drank out of their vessels, except Maipuri out of whose sifter the water poured as fast as it was poured in: this was part of his punishment for being so greedy in keeping the secret of the bountiful tree all to himself. At the expiration of another ten days, cutting continuously, the tree at last fell. The Indians took away as their share all the cassava, cane, yams, plantains, potatoes, bananas, pumpkins, and watermelons, while the other creatures crept in among the branches to pick out all they wanted. By the time the Maipuri had got back to the tree from the waterside only the plums were left for him, and with these he has had to remain content even to the present day. What the Indians took they brought home with them and planted in their provision fields. But it was the Bunia bird who spoke to them and explained how each was to be propagated and cooked, and how some, like the bitter cassava juice, had to be boiled before drinking, while others could be eaten raw.

Guiana

THE MAN WHO ALWAYS HUNTED SCRUB-TURKEY

THERE WAS A MAN celebrated for his skill in hunting "maam"; he would regularly bring home four or five of these scrub-turkeys, and people warned him that if he continued in this way he would get into trouble with the maam's "mother," (i.e., Spirit), for killing so many of her brood. But he did not care, and went on destroying the birds in the same wasteful manner. On one occasion he stayed out later than usual, waiting to see on which particular trees the maams were going to roost. He could hear their peculiar call in all directions around; indeed, the birds were so plentiful about, that he was somewhat at a loss to know which particular one to follow. However, he proceeded to track one, but the farther he went, the farther off sounded the note, until at last he found himself deep in the forest. As night was beginning to fall, he had to hurry home, not daring to remain out in the dark for fear of the Yawahu (Spirit of the Bush) catching him. The same thing happened next day; he heard many birds calling, and, following one, again found himself deep in the forest, but this time he succeeded finally in coming up with the quarry. Locating the tree, he peered in among the branches to see where the bird was "hollo"-ing, but could see only a woman's leg. Recognizing this to be the Arch Spirit of the maams, he took careful aim, and shot an arrow right into the center of the foot. The leg fell down, and directly it touched ground, changed into an extraordinarily big scrub-turkey, which he immediately killed and carried home. There his friends knew it at once to be the maam's "mother" (Spirit), and advised him to cook and eat the whole of it himself, and not give away even the smallest particle of it. He did what was advised, and in subsequently hunting for maam he was invariably even more successful than before. And now that he had destroyed the maam-Spirit, he was not afraid of killing as many birds as he liked.

Guiana

246

PLATES 65-79

THE COAST AND THE

MOUNTAINS

PAMPAS, JUNGLES AND ISLANDS

FISH

BIRD

PUMA

MAN PUMA GOD FISH GOD BIRD GOD MAN

PERUVIAN DESIGN UNITS

MULTIPLE-HEADED GOD

CENTIPEDE GOD

BIRD-HEADED
HUMAN FIGURE

PUMA GOD

PUMA-HEADED
HUMAN FIGURE

SPOTTED CAT

FISH

BIRD DEMON

PERUVIAN TEXTILES

NAZCA, GIRDLE

NAZCA, PONCHO

PERUVIAN TEXTILES

TIAHUANACO

DETAIL OF A SHIRT

NAZCA

PONCHO

PERUVIAN TEXTILES

CHIMU
MANTLE

TIAHUANACO
FRAGMENT

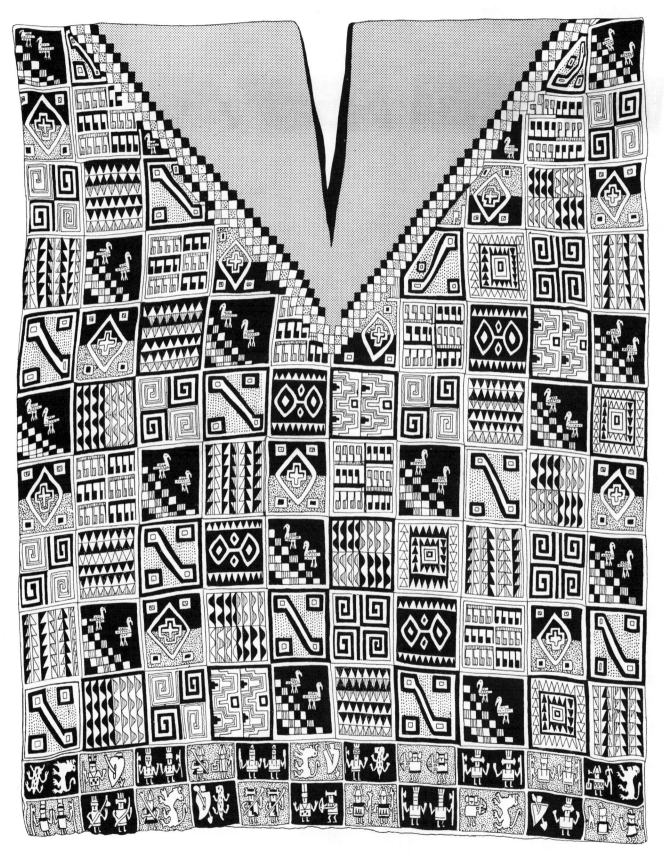

INCA, PONCHO (POST-SPANISH)

INCA, PONCHO

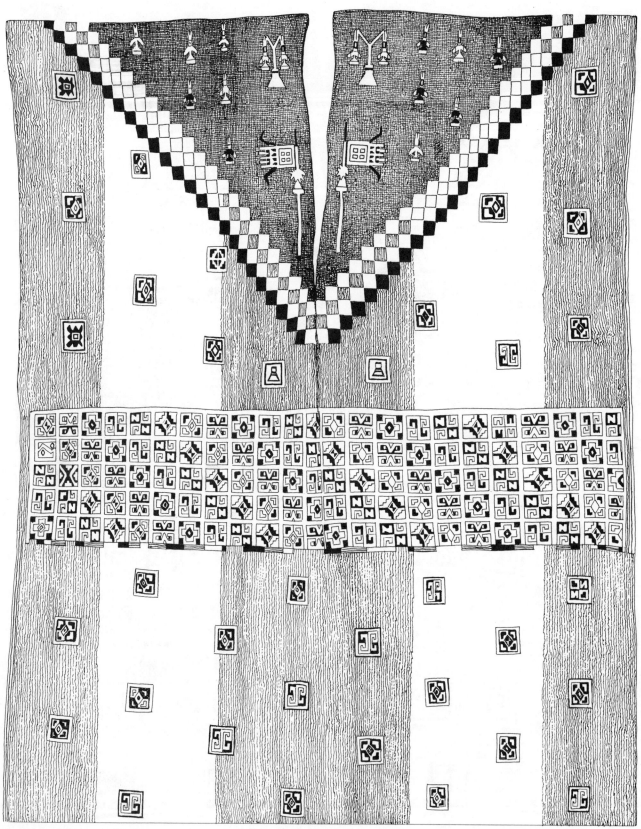

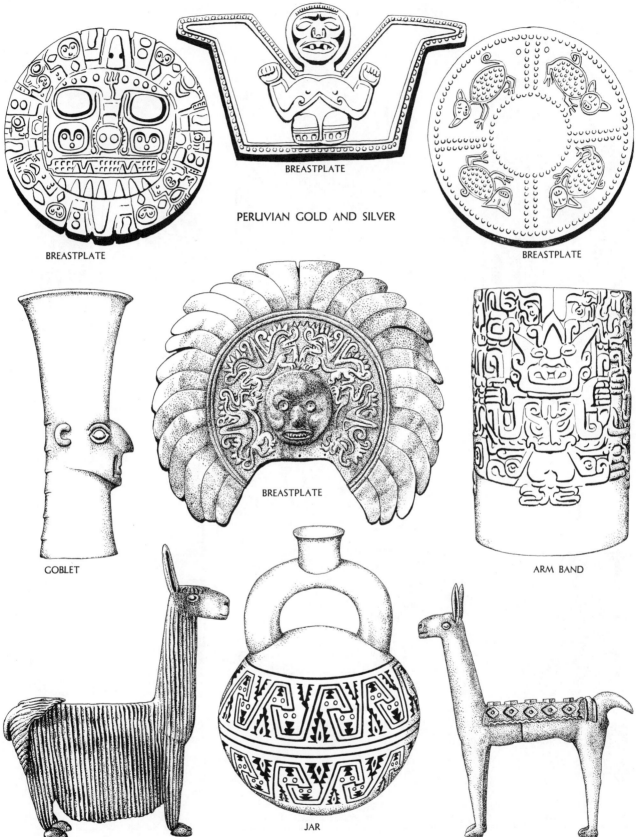

BREASTPLATE

PERUVIAN GOLD AND SILVER

BREASTPLATE

BREASTPLATE

GOBLET

BREASTPLATE

ARM BAND

JAR

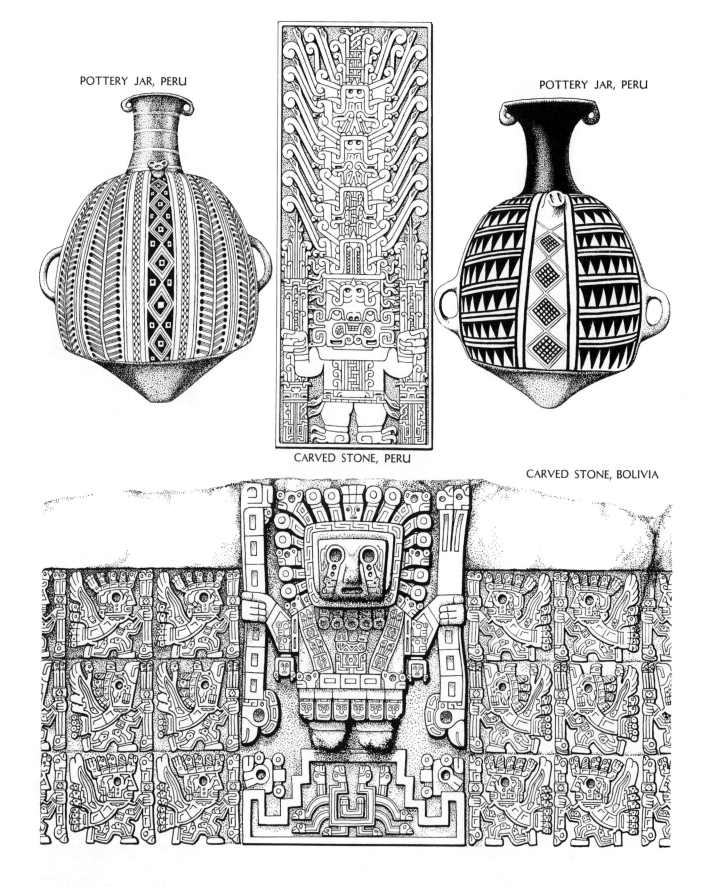

POTTERY JAR, PERU

POTTERY JAR, PERU

CARVED STONE, PERU

CARVED STONE, BOLIVIA

TIAHUANACO

NAZCA

PERUVIAN

NAZCA

NAZCA

POTTERY

NAZCA

NAZCA

TIAHUANACO

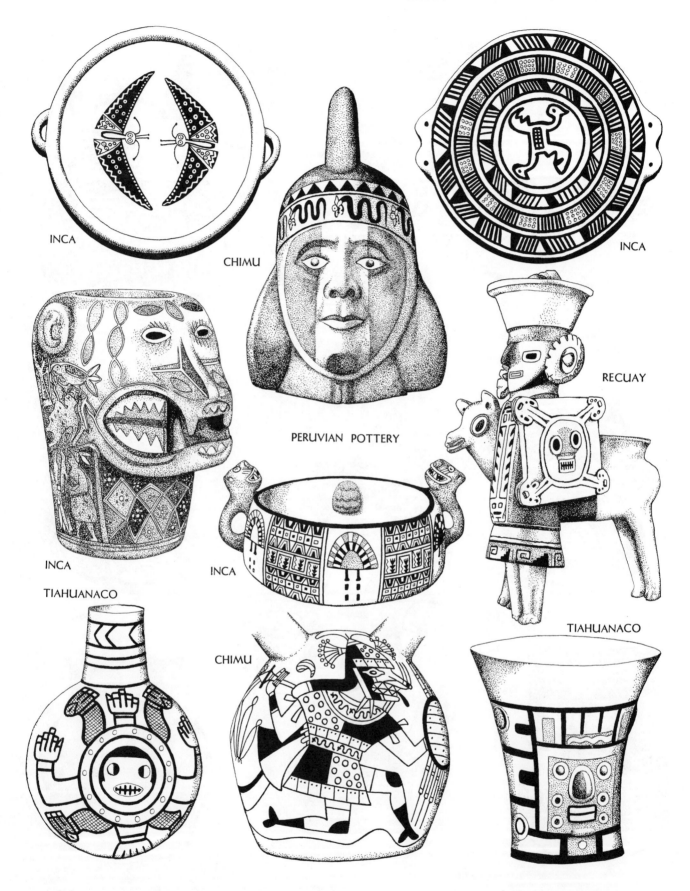

INCA

CHIMU

INCA

RECUAY

PERUVIAN POTTERY

INCA

INCA

TIAHUANACO

TIAHUANACO

CHIMU

ARGENTINA

ARGENTINA

PAINTING ON HIDE, PATAGONIA

POTTERY

PERU

CHILE

ARGENTINA

CHILE

CHILE

CHILE

BRAZIL (INCISED)

COLOMBIA

BRAZIL

POTTERY

COLOMBIA

COLOMBIA

BRAZIL

BRAZIL
(INCISED)

COLOMBIA

COLOMBIA

COLOMBIA

BRAZIL

POTTERY

BRAZIL

BRAZIL

BRAZIL

WOODEN DANCE CLUB, BRITISH GUIANA

WOODEN DANCE CLUB, BRITISH GUIANA

BEAD APRON, BRITISH GUIANA

BASKETRY

BRITISH GUIANA

BEAD APRON

BRITISH GUIANA

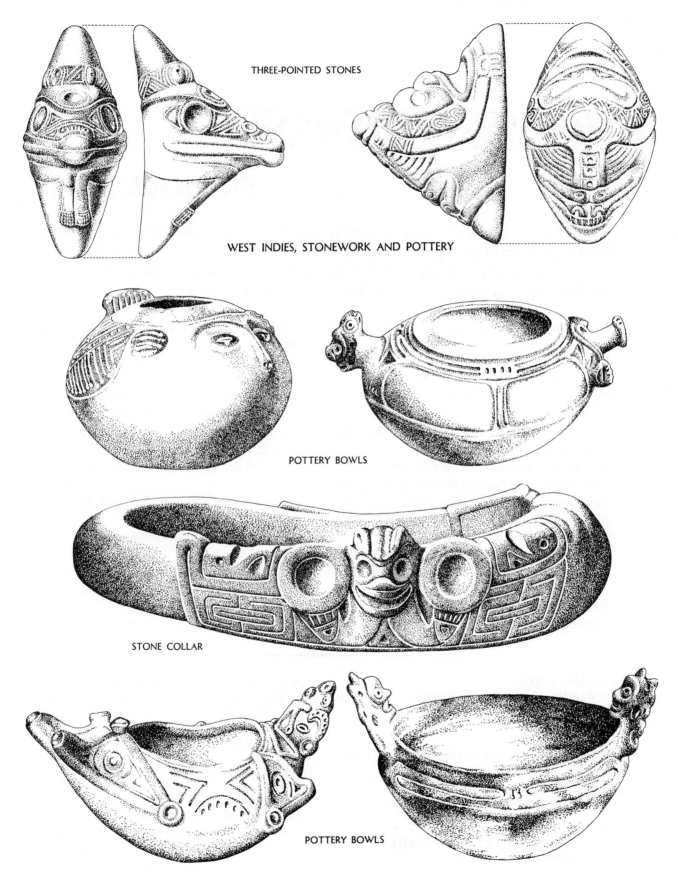

THREE-POINTED STONES

WEST INDIES, STONEWORK AND POTTERY

POTTERY BOWLS

STONE COLLAR

POTTERY BOWLS

BIBLIOGRAPHY

The list of authorities given below is selective, and suggests many works which will be of value more to the beginner than the specialist.

The following Institutions publish lists of books and monographs on the Indians of the Americas, and will be pleased to furnish such lists on application:

American Museum of Natural History, New York, N. Y.

British Museum, London

Brooklyn Museum, Brooklyn, N. Y.

Bureau of American Ethnology, Washington, D. C.

Carnegie Institution of Washington, Washington, D. C.

Denver Art Museum, Denver, Colorado

Field Museum of Natural History, Chicago, Ill.

Laboratory of Anthropology, Santa Fe, N. M.

Milwaukee Public Museum, Milwaukee, Wis.

Museum of the American Indian, Heye Foundation, New York, N. Y.

National Institute of Anthropology and History, Mexico City, D. F.

National Museum of Archaeology, Lima, Peru

National Museum of Canada, Ottawa, Ontario

National Museum of Mexico, Mexico City, D.F.

Ohio State Museum, Columbus, Ohio

Peabody Museum of Harvard University, Cambridge, Mass.

Phillips Academy, Andover, Mass.

Smithsonian Institution, Washington, D. C.

Superintendent of Documents, Washington, D. C.

United States National Museum, Washington, D. C.

University of California, Berkeley, Calif.

University of Chicago, Chicago, Ill.

University of Pennsylvania Museum, Philadelphia, Pa.

University of Washington, Seattle, Wash.

Yale University Publications in Anthropology, New Haven, Conn.

ADAIR, JOHN
The Navajo and Pueblo Silversmiths, Norman, Okla., 1945

ALEXANDER, H. B.
Pueblo Indian Painting, Nice, (France), 1932

AMSDEN, CHARLES AVERY
Navaho Weaving, L.A., 1949 (Dover, 1971)

American Folklore Society
Journal, Volumes XX, XXII, XXIII
Memoirs, Volumes V, XL

American Museum of Natural History
Anthropological Papers, Volumes X, XXI, XXXIV (Part 1)
(Handbooks are listed under the names of the authors)

BANCROFT, H. H.
The Conquest of Mexico, New York, 1883

BANDELIER, ADOLPH F.
Report of an Archaeological Tour in Mexico in 1881, Boston, 1884

BEDINGER, MARGERY
Navajo Indian Silverwork, Denver, 1936

BENNETT, WENDELL C.
"Weaving in the Land of the Incas," in *Natural History* (a magazine), New York, 1935
Archaeological regions of Colombia: A ceramic survey, New Haven, 1944

BINGHAM, HIRAM
Machu Picchu, A Citadel of the Incas, New Haven, 1930
Lost City of the Incas, New York, 1948

BIRKET-SMITH, KAJ.
The Eskimos, New York, 1936

BLOM, FRANS
The Conquest of Mexico, Boston, 1936
Tribes and Temples, New Orleans, La., 1926-27

BOAS, FRANZ
Primitive Art, Cambridge, Mass., 1927 (Dover)
The Decorative Art of the North Pacific Coast, New York, 1897 (American Museum of Natural History, Bulletin IX)

BRENNER, ANITA
Idols behind Altars, New York, 1932

BRINTON, DANIEL G.
The Maya Chronicles, Philadelphia, 1882
Ancient Nahuatl Poetry, Philadelphia, 1887
Rig Veda Americanus, Philadelphia, 1890

BUNZEL, RUTH
The Pueblo Potter, New York, 1929
Bureau of American Ethnology, Smithsonian Institution, Washington, D. C. (BAE)
Annual Report, Numbers 6, 8, 11, 13, 14, 15, 17, 19, 21, 25, 27, 30, 32, 34, 37, 38, 42, 43, 47
Bulletin, Numbers 28, 30, 39, 78, 86, 88, 98, 143

CAHILL, HOLGER
American Sources of Modern Art, New York, 1933

CASO, ALFONSO
"Monte Alban, Richest Archaeological Find in America," in *The National Geographic Magazine,* Washington, D. C., Jan. 1932
"Pre-Spanish Art," in *Twenty Centuries of Mexican Art,* New York, 1940
"Reading the Riddle of Ancient Jewels," in *Natural History,* New York, 1932

CATHERWOOD, FREDERICK
Views of Ancient Monuments in Central America, Chiapas, and Yucatan, (see Stephens, John L.)
Catholic University of America
"The Apinayé," by Curt Nimuendajú, Washington, D. C., 1939, *(Anthropological Series No. 8)*

CATLIN, GEORGE
Illustrations of the Manners, Customs, and Condition of the North American Indians, London, 1876 (Dover reprint)

CHAPMAN, KENNETH
Pueblo Indian Pottery, Nice, (France), 1933 and 1936
The Pottery of Santo Domingo Pueblo, Santa Fe, N. M., 1939

CODEX FLORENTINO
Illustrations for Sahagun's "Historia de las Casas de Nueva Espana," Madrid, 1905

CODEX NUTTALL (Codex Zouche)
Introduction by Zelia Nuttall, Cambridge, 1902

COLLIER, JOHN
Indians of the Americas, New York, 1947

COLLINS, HENRY B.
Prehistoric Art of the Alaskan Eskimo, Washington, 1929 (Smithsonian Institution, Miscel. Coll. Vol. 84)

COLTON, HAROLD S.
Hopi Kachina Dolls, Albuquerque, N. M., 1949

CORTES, HERNANDO
Letters of Cortes, Trans. and ed. by F. A. MacNutt, New York and London, 1908

CRAWFORD, M. D. C.
The Heritage of Cotton, New York, 1924

CURTIN, JEREMIAH
Myths of the Modocs, Boston, 1912

CUSHING, FRANK H.
Exploration of Ancient Remains on the Gulf Coast of Florida, Philadelphia, 1896

DE LANDA, FRIAR DIEGO
Yucatan Before and After the Conquest, Trans. William Gates, Baltimore, 1937

BIBLIOGRAPHY

DENSMORE, FRANCES
Chippewa Customs, Washington, 1929, (BAE, Bulletin 86)

DIAZ DEL CASTILLO, BERNAL
The True History of the Conquest of New Spain, trans., A. P. Maudslay, London, 1908-16
The Discovery and Conquest of Mexico, trans. A. P. Maudslay, London, 1928

DIXON, ROLAND B.
Basketry Designs of the Indians of Northern California, New York, 1902, (American Museum of Natural History, Bulletin 17)

DOUGLAS, FREDRIC, and
D'HARNONCOURT, RENÉ
Indian Art of the United States, New York, 1941

EMMONS, GEORGE T.
The Basketry of the Tlinkit, New York, 1903
The Chilkat blanket: with notes on the blanket designs by Frank Boas, New York, 1907

EWERS, JOHN C.
Plains Indian Painting, Palo Alto, Calif., 1939

FEWKES, JESSE WALTER
Tusayan Katcinas, (BAE, 15th Annual Report, Washington, D. C., 1893-4)
Archaeological expedition to Arizona, (BAE, 17th Annual Report, Washington, D. C., 1896)
Two Summers' work in Pueblo ruins, (BAE, 21st Annual Report, Washington, D. C., 1901)
The Aborigines of Porto Rico and Neighboring Islands, (BAE, 25th Annual Report, Washington, D. C., 1904)
A Prehistoric Island Culture Area of America, (BAE, 34th Annual Report, Washington, D. C., 1913)

FLETCHER, ALICE C. and
LA FLESCHE, FRANCIS
The Omaha Tribe, (BAE, 27th Annual Report, Washington, D. C., 1905-6)

GANN, THOMAS
Mounds in northern Honduras, (BAE, 19th Annual Report, Washington, D. C., 1897-8)
Glories of the Maya, London, 1938

GANN, THOMAS and THOMPSON, J. ERIC
The History of the Maya from the Earliest Time to the Present Day, New York, 1931

GODDARD, PLINY EARLE
Indians of the Southwest, New York, 1931
Indians of the Northwest Coast, New York, 1924

GORDON, G. B.
Examples of Maya Pottery in the Museum and Other Collections, ed. by J. A. Maison, Philadelphia, 1925 and 1928

GRINNELL, GEORGE B.
Blackfoot Lodge Tales, New York, Charles Scribner's Sons, 1892

GUEVARA, TOMAS
Folklore Araucano, Santiago (Chile), 1911

GUTHE, CARL E.
Pueblo Pottery Making, New Haven, 1925

HARTMAN, C. V.
Archaeological Researches in Costa Rica, Stockholm, 1901

HOWELL, EDGAR LEE
Ancient Life in the American Southwest, Indianapolis, 1930

HEWITT, J. N. B., ed.
Seneca fiction, legends, and myths, (BAE, 32nd Annual Report, Washington, D. C., 1910-11)

HEYE, GEORGE E.
Red Cloud's Folk: a history of the Oglala Sioux, Norman, Okla., 1937

HILL-TROUT, C.
British North America: The Far West, the Home of the Salish and the Déné, London, 1907

HODGE, FREDERICK W., ed.
Handbook of American Indians North of Mexico, (BAE, Bulletin 30, Washington, D. C., 1907-1910) (Dover reprint)

HOLMES, WILLIAM H.
Art in shell of the ancient Americans (BAE, 2nd Annual Report, Washington, D. C., 1880-1)
Ancient pottery of the Mississippi valley, and *Origin and development of form and ornament in ceramic art* (BAE, 4th Annual Report, Washington, D. C., 1883)
A study of the textile art in its relation to the development of form and ornament, and *Art of the province of Chiriqui, Colombia,* (BAE, 6th Annual Report, Washington, D. C., 1884-5)

JENNESS, DIAMOND
The Indians of Canada, Ottawa, 1934

JOYCE, THOMAS A.
Mexican Archaeology, London, 1914
Central American and West Indian Archaeology, London, 1916
Guide to the Maudslay Collection of Maya Sculptures (Casts and Originals) from Central America, London, 1923
Maya and Mexican Art, London, 1927

JUDD, NEIL MERTON
"Pyramids of the New World," in *National Geographic Magazine,* January, 1948

KELEMEN, PÁL
Medieval American Art, N.Y., 1943 (Dover)

KENNARD, EDWARD A.
Hopi Kachinas, New York, 1938

KIDDER, A. V.
An Introduction to the Study of Southwestern Archaeology, with a Preliminary Account of the Excavations at Pecos, New Haven, 1924

KINGSBOROUGH, EDWARD KING, LORD
Antiquities of Mexico, London, 1830-48

KROEBER, ALFRED L.
The Arapaho, New York, 1902
Handbook of the Indians of California, (BAE, Bulletin 78, Washington, D. C., 1925)

KURZ, FRIEDRICH
Journal of life on the Upper Missouri between 1846 and 1857. Ed. by J. N. B. Hewitt, (BAE, Bulletin 115, Washington, D. C., 1937)

LOTHROP, SAMUEL KIRKLAND
Tulum, an Archaeological Study of the East Coast of Yucatan, Washington, D. C., 1924
Pottery of Costa Rica and Nicaragua, New York, 1926

LOWIE, ROBERT H.
Crow Indian Art, New York, 1922

LUMHOLTZ, CARL
Unknown Mexico, New York, 1902
Decorative Art of the Huichol Indians, New York, 1904

MAC CAULEY, CLAY
The Seminole Indians, (BAE, 5th Annual Report, Washington, D. C., 1883-4)

MARKHAM, SIR CLEMENTS
The Incas of Peru, London, Smith, Elder and Co., 1910

MARKHAM, SIR CLEMENTS, (trans.)
History of the Incas, by Pedro Sarmiento de Gamboa, Cambridge: The Hakluyt Society, 1907
The First Part of the Royal Commentaries of the Incas, by Garcilaso de la Vega, London: The Hakluyt Society, 1871

MASON, J. ALDEN
Eskimo Pictorial Art, Philadelphia, 1927
"Preserving Ancient America's Finest Sculptures," in *National Geographic Magazine,* November, 1935

MATTHEWS, WASHINGTON
Navaho Silversmiths, (BAE, 2nd Annual Report, Washington, D. C., 1880-1)
Navaho Weavers, (BAE, 3rd Annual Report, Washington, D. C., 1881-2)
The Mountain Chant: a Navaho Ceremony, (BAE, 5th Annual Report, Washington, D. C., 1883-4)

MAUDSLAY, A. P.
Archaeology (Biologia Centrali-Americana), London, 1889-1902

MAC CURDY, GEORGE GRANT
A Study of Chiriquian Antiquities, New Haven, 1911

MEAD, CHARLES W.
Old Civilizations of Inca Land, New York, 1932

MEANS, PHILIP AINSWORTH
Ancient Civilizations of the Andes, New York, 1931
Peruvian Textiles: Examples of the Pre-Incaic Period, New York, 1930
A Study of Peruvian Textiles, Boston, 1932
"The Incas: Empire Builders of the Andes" in *Natural History,* February, 1928

MERA, H. P.
The "Rain Bird": A Study in Pueblo Design, Santa Fe, N. M., 1937 (Dover reprint)
Pueblo Indian Embroidery, Santa Fe, N. M., 1943
Navajo Textile Arts, Santa Fe, N. M., 1947

BIBLIOGRAPHY

MOONEY, JAMES
The Ghost Dance Religion, (BAE, 14th Annual Report, Part II, Washington, D. C., 1896)

MOOREHEAD, WARREN KING
Exploration of the Etowah Site in Georgia, New Haven, 1932

MORGAN, LEWIS H.
Houses and house life of the American Aborigines, Washington, D. C., 1881
The League of the Iroquois, ed., Herbert M. Lloyd, New York, 1922

MORLEY, S. G.
The Ancient Maya, Berkeley, Calif. and London, 1946

MORRIS, ANN AXTELL
Digging in Yucatan, Garden City, N. Y., 1933

MORRIS, E. H., CHARLOT, J., and MORRIS, A.
The Temple of the Warriors at Chichen-Itzá, Yucatan, Washington, D. C., 1931

NELSON, EDWARD WILLIAM
The Eskimo about Bering Strait, (BAE, 18th Annual Report, Washington, D. C., 1899)

ORCHARD, WILLIAM C.
Peruvian Gold and Gold Plating, in *Indian Notes,* Heye Foundation, New York, 1930
Beads and Beadwork of the American Indian, Heye Foundation, New York, 1929
The Technique of Porcupine-quill Decoration among the North American Indians, Heye Foundation, New York, 1916

OSBORNE, LILLY DE JONGH
Guatemala Textiles, New Orleans, La., 1935

PRESCOTT, WILLIAM H.
The Conquest of Mexico, ed., T. A. Joyce, New York, 1922
Conquest of Peru, New York, 1847

RADIN, PAUL
The Sources and Authenticity of the History of the Ancient Mexicans, Berkeley, Calif., 1920
The Story of the American Indian, New York, 1934

RECINOS, ADRIAN, (ed.)
Popol Vuh: Las Antiguas Historias Del Quiché, Mexico City, Fondo de Cultura Economica, 1947

REICHARD, GLADYS
Navaho Shepherd and Weaver, New York, 1936

RIES, MAURICE
"Stamping: A Mass-production Printing Method 2000 Years Old," in *Middle American Papers, Series IV,* New Orleans, La., 1932

ROBERTS, FRANK H., Jr.
"In the Empire of the Aztecs," *National Geographic Magazine,* June, 1937

ROEDIGER, VIRGINIA M.
Ceremonial Costumes of the Pueblo Indians, Berkeley, Calif., 1941

ROYS, R. L. (ed.)
The Book of Chilam Balam of Chumayel, (Carnegie Institution of Washington, Publication No. 438), Washington, D. C., 1933

SAHAGUN, BERNARDINO DE
A History of Ancient Mexico, Tr. by Fanny R. Bandelier, Nashville, Tenn., 1932

SAVILLE, MARSHALL H.
The Goldsmith's Art in Ancient Mexico, Heye Foundation, New York, 1920
Turquoise Mosaic Art in Ancient Mexico, Heye Foundation, New York, 1922
The Wood-Carver's Art in Ancient Mexico, Heye Foundation, New York, 1925

SELER, EDUARD
Ancient Mexican Feather Ornaments, (BAE, Bulletin 28, Washington, D. C., 1904)

SHETRONE, HENRY CLYDE
The Mound-Builders, New York, 1941

SLOAN, JOHN and LA FARGE, OLIVER
Introduction to American Indian Art, New York, 1931

SMITH, HARLIN I.
An Album of Prehistoric Art, Ottawa, Canada, 1923

SPECK, FRANK C.
Montagnais Art in Birchbark, New York, 1937
Decorative Art and Basketry of the Cherokee, Milwaukee, 1920

SPINDEN, HERBERT J.
A Study of Maya Art, Cambridge, Mass., 1913
"The Population of Ancient America," in *Geo-*

graphical Review, New York, 1928
Ancient Civilizations of Mexico and Central America, New York, 1928

STEPHENS, JOHN L. and
CATHERWOOD, FREDERICK
Incidents of Travel in Central America, Chiapas, and Yucatan, New York, 1841 (Dover)
Incidents of Travel in Yucatan, N.Y., 1843 (Dover)

STEVENSON, JAMES
Ceremonial of Hasjelti Dailjis and mythical sand painting of the Navaho Indians, (BAE, 8th Annual Report, Washington, D. C., 1886-7)

STEVENSON, MATILDA COXE
The Zuni Indians: their mythology, esoteric fraternities and ceremonies, (BAE, 23rd Annual Report, Washington, D. C., 1901-2)

STEWARD, JULIAN H., ed.
Handbook of South American Indians, (BAE, Bulletin 143, Washington, D. C., 1946-----).

STIRLING, MATTHEW W.
"Indians of Our Western Plains," in *National Geographic Magazine,* Washington, D. C., July, 1944
"Indians of the Southeastern United States," in *National Geographic Magazine,* Jan., 1946
"America's First Settlers, the Indians," in *National Geographic Magazine,* Nov., 1937
"Nomads of the Far North," in *National Geographic Magazine,* Oct., 1949
"Indians of Our North Pacific Coast," in *National Geographic Magazine,* Jan., 1945
"Indians of the Far West," in *National Geographic Magazine,* Feb., 1948
"Indian Tribes of Pueblo Land," in *National Geographic Magazine,* Nov., 1940

STRONG, WILLIAM DUNCAN
"Finding a Tomb of a Warrior-God," in *National Geographic Magazine,* April, 1947

SWANTON, JOHN R.
Aboriginal Culture of the Southeast, (BAE, 42nd Annual Report, Washington, D. C., 1924-5)
Myths and Tales of the Southeastern Indians, (BAE, Bulletin 88, Washington, D. C., 1929)
The Haida of Queen Charlotte Islands (American Museum of Natural History, *Memoirs,* Vol. V)

THOMPSON, EDWARD HERBERT
People of the Serpent, Boston and New York, 1932

THOMPSON, J. ERIC
Mexico Before Cortez, New York, 1933

TOTTEN, GEORGE OAKLEY
Maya Architecture, Washington, D. C., 1926

TOZZER, ALFRED M.
"The Domain of the Aztecs and their Relation to the Prehistoric Cultures of Mexico," in *Holmes Anniversary Volume,* Lancaster, Pa., 1918

UNDERHILL, RUTH M.
First Penthouse Dwellers of America, New York, 1938

VAILLANT, GEORGE C.
Indian Arts in North America, New York, 1939
Aztecs of Mexico: Origin, Rise and Fall of the Aztec Nation, Garden City, N. Y., 1944

VON HAGEN, VICTOR WOLFGANG
The Aztec and Maya Papermakers, New York, 1944

WARDLE, HELEN
Guatemalan Textiles, Philadelphia, Pa., 1934

WATSON, DON
"Ancient Cliff Dwellers of Mesa Verde," in *National Geographic Magazine,* Sept., 1948

WHEELRIGHT, MARY
Hail Chant and Water Chant, Santa Fe., N. M., 1946

WILLARD, T. A.
The City of the Sacred Well, London, 1925

WISSLER, CLARK
The American Indian, (Third Edition) New York, 1938
Indians of the United States, Garden City, N. Y., 1940
North American Indians of the Plains, New York, 1912

WOODWARD, ARTHUR
A Brief History of Navaho Silversmithing, Flagstaff, Ariz., 1938

INDEX TO STORIES

BY PAGE NUMBERS

INDEX TO STORIES

INDEX TO PLATES

(The Table of Plate Sources begins on the following page.)

SOURCES OF THE PLATES

The Indian art work from which the Plates in this book have been drawn may be found at the institutions and locations listed below.

In this listing, the following abbreviations are used:

AMNH — American Museum of Natural History, New York, N. Y.

MAI — Museum of the American Indian, Heye Foundation, New York, N. Y.

PH — Peabody Museum of Harvard University, Cambridge, Mass.

PY — Peabody Museum of Natural History, Yale University, New Haven, Conn.

O — Ohio State Museum, Columbus, Ohio

USNM — United States National Museum, Washington, D. C.

UP — The University Museum, University of Pennsylvania, Philadelphia, Pa.

MCM — Public Museum of the City of Milwaukee, Milwaukee, Wis.

Ot — National Museum of Canada, Ottawa, Ontario, Canada

NYSM — New York State Museum, Albany, N.Y.

SF — Laboratory of Anthropology, Santa Fe, N. M.

BM — The British Museum, London, England

BnM — The Brooklyn Museum, Brooklyn, N.Y.

NMM — National Museum of Mexico, Mexico City, D. F.

CW — Carnegie Institution of Washington, Washington, D. C.

Met — Metropolitan Museum of Art, New York, N. Y.

NMP — National Museum of Archaeology, Lima, Peru

PLATE 1 — AMNH, MAI
PLATE 2 — AMNH
PLATE 3 — AMNH
PLATE 4 — AMNH
PLATE 5 — AMNH
PLATE 6 — AMNH, MAI
PLATE 7 — AMNH
PLATE 8 — AMNH
PLATE 9 — AMNH, MAI, PH
PLATE 10 — AMNH, MAI
PLATE 11 — MAI, O, USNM

PLATE 12 — AMNH, MAI, O, USNM
PLATE 13 — MAI, USNM
PLATE 14 — MAI, UP
PLATE 15 — AMNH, MAI, UP
PLATE 16 — AMNH, MAI, MCM, PH
PLATE 17 — AMNH, MAI, Ot, USNM
PLATE 18 — MAI, NYSM
PLATE 19 — AMNH, MAI, Ot
PLATE 20 — AMNH, MAI
PLATE 21 — AMNH, MAI
PLATE 22 — AMNH, MAI, Ot
PLATE 23 — AMNH
PLATE 24 — AMNH
PLATE 25 — AMNH, USNM
PLATE 26 — AMNH, MAI
PLATE 27 — AMNH
PLATE 28 — AMNH, MAI
PLATE 29 — AMNH
PLATE 30 — MAI, PH
PLATE 31 — AMNH, USNM
PLATE 32 — AMNH, MAI
PLATE 33 — AMNH, MAI
PLATE 34 — Selections from many collections
PLATE 35 — AMNH, MAI, PH, SF
PLATE 36 — AMNH, MAI, SF
PLATE 37 — PH
PLATE 38 — AMNH, SF
PLATE 39 — MAI, SF, USNM
PLATE 40 — AMNH
PLATE 41 — MAI, PH, USNM
PLATE 42 — BnM, USNM
PLATE 43 — AMNH, MAI
PLATE 44 — AMNH, MAI, SF
PLATE 45 — AMNH, SF
PLATE 46 — AMNH, BM
PLATE 47 — AMNH, NMM
PLATE 48 — NMM
PLATE 49 — BM, NMM, PH
PLATE 50 — BM, CW, NMM
PLATE 51 — CW, PH, UP
PLATE 52 — Architectural details from Chichen-Itzá, Mitla, Uxmal, and Xochicalco
PLATE 53 — NMM, Date-symbols from Stela "D," Copan, Honduras

PLATE 54 – "Temple of the Sun," Palenque, Mexico

"Jaguar Temple," Chichen-Itzá, Mexico

PLATE 55 – Stela "H," Copan, Honduras

PLATE 56 – "Temple of Quetzalcóatl," NMM

PLATE 57 – Lintel 3, Yaxchilán, Mexico, BM

PLATE 58 – "Temple IV," Tikal, Guatemala (Original in Museum für Völkerkunde, Basle, Switzerland)

Yaxchilán, Mexico

PLATE 59 – Stela 10, Seibal, Guatemala

Stela 14, Piedras Negras, Guatemala

Lintel, Yaxchilán, Mexico

Stela 11, Yaxchilán, Mexico

Stela 13, Piedras Negras, Guatemala

PLATE 60 – AMNH, MAI

PLATE 61 – AMNH, MAI, PH, UP

PLATE 62 – MAI, PH

PLATE 63 – BnM, MAI, PH, USNM

PLATE 64 – MAI, PH

PLATE 65 – Selections from many collections

PLATE 66 – AMNH, Met

PLATE 67 – BnM, Met

PLATE 68 – BnM

PLATE 69 – AMNH

PLATE 70 – AMNH

PLATE 71 – AMNH, MAI, UP

PLATE 72 – AMNH, MAI; Raimondi monolith, NMP; Monolithic Gateway, Tiahuanaco, Bolivia

PLATE 73 – AMNH, MAI

PLATE 74 – AMNH, PH, PY

PLATE 75 – AMNH, BnM

PLATE 76 – AMNH, MAI, PY

PLATE 77 – AMNH, BnM, USNM

PLATE 78 – MAI, PH

PLATE 79 – AMNH, MAI, USNM